GILBERT'S MANUAL

FOR CHOIR-LOFT AND PULPIT

Gilbert's Manual

for Choir-Loft
and Pulpit

Compiled *by* HARRY GILBERT, *Organist and
Choir-Master of the Fifth Avenue Presbyterian Church, New York City*

✠

Foreword by
JOHN SUTHERLAND BONNELL, D.D.

New York: CHARLES SCRIBNER'S SONS · *1939*

DEDICATED TO

THE REVEREND LOCKHART AMERMAN, M. A.

*in friendship, and appreciation
of his invaluable aid in the
preparation of this book*

FOREWORD

IN this Manual for Pulpit and Choir-loft Mr. Harry Gilbert has produced a book that will be of very great value to ministers, organists, choir directors and all others who have responsibility for the service of praise in Christian churches.

Every minister and choir director has wished for an authoritative work which would make available to him at a moment's notice the anthems, duets, solos that might fittingly be used at special seasons of the Church Year, or which would illustrate the theme of the sermon. Mr. Gilbert's book will supply this long-felt need. By ample use of cross references, topical and textual listings, all the selections given are made readily accessible. This Manual will now make possible a dignified, integrated, worshipful order of service each Sunday of the year and other special days with the expenditure of a minimum of time and labor.

The author brings to his work a rich practical experience. For nineteen years he has been organist and choir director of The Fifth Avenue Presbyterian Church, New York City. Under his direction, in this choir, have been such well-known singers as Richard Crooks, Lawrence Tibbett, Nevada Vander Veer-Miller, and other celebrities.

Mr. Gilbert's expert knowledge of classical church music, his sensitive appreciation of reverence and dignity in worship and his wide acquaintance with the subjects and texts used by the best-known preachers of our time have peculiarly fitted him for the task which he has so well performed. I predict that his book will be eagerly received by all branches of the Protestant Church throughout the English-speaking world.

JOHN SUTHERLAND BONNELL

Minister's Study,
The Fifth Avenue Presbyterian Church,
New York, N. Y.
October, 1939.

CONTENTS

PART I

PART II

INTRODUCTION

IN a well-unified service of worship it is necessary to maintain an essential sympathy between music and sermon. Such sympathy comes primarily as the result of close co-operation between minister and choir-master. This Manual represents the fruits of co-operation, continued over a period of years. Topics, with texts and Scripture Lesson, have inevitably suggested appropriate musical selections. Records of such reference and association have been filed and edited. A final revision of the material thus accumulated has been the basis for the completion of this book.

The purpose of the Manual is to supply in small compass a handy consultant for organists, choir-masters, ministers, and all who have to do with the music of the church. It is, of course, not always the sermon which sets the tone of the service. The season of the Church Year and the occasion of the individual service will have much to do with determining the choice of music. Throughout Protestantism—and especially in the free, or non-liturgical churches—the sermon provides a unique focus for the thought of the worshipping congregation. Accordingly, the major listing in this Manual is presented with reference to topic and theme.

Since some of these themes and topics will naturally be used more often, some lists are accordingly much more complete than others. In no instance has an attempt been made to present an exhaustive list of all the selections that might possibly be appropriate. Under such general headings as CHRISTMAS, EASTER, or FAITH, for instance, the quantity of music would be almost unlimited.

Rather has it been intended to list under each topic music which is in itself peculiarly fitted to express the thought of the topic concerned. At the same time, by means of cross reference, alternative and related selections will be suggested. (For example, a person consulting the topic DOUBT will find thereunder certain suggestions, but will be referred to such related headings as THOMAS, DECISION.) Conversely, some selections will be found listed under several appropriate headings (e.g., van de Water's "Publican" which is appropriately listed under PUBLICAN, PHARISEE, BIGOTRY, HYPOCRISY, PRAYER, CONFESSION, etc.). By an increase of cross references it would have been possible to eliminate many of the smaller lists but it was felt that for the sake of convenience every possible topic should offer its own suggestions.

The nature of the topics themselves will best be discovered by an examination of the List of General Topics on pages xv–xxiv. Here the individual themes that appear alphabetically in the body of the book will be found listed under the broad categories to which they generally correspond. "Biblical Characters" are separated from "Christian Virtues," the "Church Year" is distinguished from "Theological Doctrines," and in the biblical section musical selections are listed with direct reference to the passages of Scripture which they quote, paraphrase, or parallel.

It may be as well to offer a working example of the Manual's use. Let us say that Dr. X, the minister, is called out of town during the week and leaves his sermon-topics behind him. There has been no opportunity this time for consultation with the choir-master and the latter must choose suitable music for sermons on "A Loving Father" and "The King's Image." Texts are respectively assigned to John 3:16 and Hebrews 1:3. Three sources of references are available. The Scripture passages may be consulted in the Biblical Passages, etc.; in the main alphabetical listing suggestions will appear under the key words LOVE, FATHER, KING, and IMAGE. And realizing the general reference of the two sermons—to God and to Christ—alternative and related topics may be found in the List of General Topics.

A word must be spoken of the type of music included in these pages. The first criterion of choice is, of course, religious value. It has been well said that the object of church music is neither to relieve the ennui of the congregation nor to display the proficiency of the choir. What is sensuous pleasure for some, however, may be the very soul of worship for others. Each of us is psychologically conditioned in music as in everything else, and it is always difficult for a single author to impose his individual reactions on the general public. A generation that is thrilled by Stainer may be spiritually allergic to Bach, and then within a decade the situation will reverse itself; but the reversal in turn will leave many to weep for what is gone. It is true that church music finds its ultimate focus in God—that it is not an æsthetic entertainment of the congregation. But unless the congregation can be moved to spiritual participation, God will be praised in the choir and ignored in the pew. With this in mind it has been intended in these pages to preserve the central tradition of church music which, while it avoids the austerities of purism, will be stimulating to the listener and worthy of the sanctuary.

It is not in the nature of such a book as this Manual to be conclusive. The words and music of selections will inevitably suggest other contexts besides those chosen here. Final decision and association will always remain the prerogative of the individual musician. But it is hoped that the use of these pages may at least facilitate selection and bring a measure of calm to those hectic mornings in the church office when the sermon-themes are late and the bulletin must go to press.

HARRY GILBERT

One or two notes should be added in regard to details. Generally speaking, hymn-texts and chorales have been omitted since it is not the purpose of this Manual to guide congregational music. Specimens of the better-known canticles are listed, but a full survey of the opportunities in this field can be made by referring to the publishers' catalogues. In wording topics the appropriate noun or gerund has been employed in preference to the verb. The editor wishes to acknowledge his indebtedness to the many publishers and composers who have co-operated with him.

LIST OF GENERAL TOPICS

THE GODHEAD

THE TRINITY

GOD
All in All
Alpha and Omega
Ascription to
Attributes of
Author
Builder
Care of
Cause of
Creator
Decrees of
Eternity
Faithfulness of
Fatherhood of
Fear of
Fellowship with
Forgiveness of
Glory of
Grace of
Guidance of
Hand
Help from
Holiness of
Image
Invitation
Jehovah
Judgment
Justice of
Kingdom
Kingship of
Knowledge of
Law
Likeness
Lord
Love for

Love of
Maker
Mercy
Mystery
Name
Nature
Omnipotence
Ordinances
Power
Praise to
Presence of
Protector
Providence of
Purposes
Rebuke
Refuge
Seeking, The
Sonship under
Source
Sovereignty
Statutes
Throne
Transformer
Vision
Voice
Will
Wisdom of
Word
Wrath

CHRIST
Advent of
Agony
Ascension of

Atonement of
Baptism
Beatitudes
Birth of
Blood
Bread of Life
Bridegroom
Burial of
Call of
Carpenter
Chastisement
Childhood of
Compassion
Confession
Cross
Crucifixion of
Death of
Deity of
Epiphany of
Everlasting
Example of
Fellowship with
Glorified
Gospel
Grave
Immanuel
Incarnation of
Invitation
Jesus
Kingship
Legends
Master
Mediator
Miracles

xv

CHRIST [*continued*]
Obedience
Parables
Passion
Pattern
Physician
Praise to
Presence of
Reign of
Resurrection of
Sacrifice
Salvation

Saviour
Sayings of
Second Coming of
Sepulchre
Shepherd
Son
Suffering
Teacher
Temptation
Transfiguration
Traveller
Triumphal Entry of

Triumphant
Types of
Victim
Vine
Way

HOLY SPIRIT
Breath
Light
Paraclete
Pentecost
Whitsuntide

MAN

RELIGIOUS EXPERIENCE
Accepted Time
Admonition
Adoration
Answering Christ's
    Call
Anticipation
Ascription
Asking
Aspiration
Awakening
Believing
Call
Challenge
Choice
Confession
Consecration
Contrition
Conversion
Conviction
Death
Decision
Dedication of Self
Dependence
Desire
Discovery
Dream

Entreaty
Evolution
Expansion
Finding
Following
Growth in Grace
Hearing
Intercession
Invitation
Joining Church
Knowing
Need of God
Penitence
Petition
Pilgrimage
Pleading
Praise
Prayer
Preparation
Promise
Prophecy
Quest
Quickening
Reasoning
Renunciation
Repentance
Resignation

Salvation
Search for God
Seeking
Struggle for Religious
    Freedom
Supplication
Surrender to God
Testimony
Triumph
Turning Back
Victory
Waiting on God
Walking with God
Watching
Witness
Worship

THE SINS OF MAN
Anger
Atheism
Bigotry
Bitterness
Complaining
Delay
Despising God
Fall
Falsity

THE CHRISTIAN'S HOME
[continued]

Infants
Marriage
Mother
Parting
Sleep
Son
Welcome
Widow
Worship
Youth

THE CHRISTIAN'S VIRTUES

Activity
Almsgiving
Boldness
Brotherhood
Bounty
Charity
Childlike Spirit
Compassion
Consecration
Conviction
Courage
Duty
Endurance
Faith
Faithfulness
Fasting
Fear of the Lord
Fidelity
Forbearance
Fraternity
Friendship
Goodness
Goodwill
Gratitude
Holiness
Hope
Hospitality
Humility

Independence
Innocency
Joy
Justice
Kindness
Love
Loyalty
Meekness
Mercy
Morality
Obedience
Patience
Penitence
Pity
Prudence
Purity
Renunciation
Resignation
Righteousness
Sacrifice
Service
Simplicity
Steadfastness
Stewardship
Temperance
Tenderness
Thanksgiving
Trust
Understanding
Unselfishness
Valor
Veneration
Virtue
Wisdom
Witness
Work
Zeal

THE CHRISTIAN'S REWARDS

Anointing
Assurance

Beauty
Benediction
Blessing
Boldness
Brotherhood
Bounty
Calm
Christianity
Comfort
Confidence
Consolation
Defence
Deliverance
Encouragement
Enrichment
Eternal Life
Faith
Fellowship
Foundation
Freedom
Friendship
Fulfilment
Gladness
Glory
Grace
Guidance
Healing
Heaven
Heirship
Help
Heritage
Holiness
Hope
Immortality
Inheritance
Joy
Justification
Keeping
Kindness
Leadership
Legacy

THE CHRISTIAN'S
REWARDS [*continued*]

Liberty
Life
Light
Love
Loveliness
Mental Health
Mercy
Nearness
Opportunity
Paradise
Pardon
Peace
Portion
Possessions

Power
Presence
Priesthood
Prosperity
Prudence
Purification
Quickening
Quiet
Redemption
Reformation
Rejoicing
Release
Rescue
Rest
Righteousness

Salvation
Sanctuary
Security
Shelter
Song
Strength
Support
Tongues
Triumph
Understanding
Unity
Valor
Victory
Vision
Wisdom

PEOPLE

IN GENERAL

All Saints
Apostles
Child
Communion of Saints
Disciples
Heroes
Martyrs
Peacemakers
Pilgrims
Pioneers
Poor, The
Prophets
Sages
Sailors
Saints
Schools
Seers
Soldiers

PEOPLE IN PARTICULAR

Abraham
Absalom

Adam
Andrew, St.
Augustus
Barak
Barnabas, St.
Bartholomew, St.
Belshazzar
Cæsar
Daniel
Dante
David
Deborah
Elijah
Elizabeth, St.
Eve
Francis, St.
Gabriel
Herod
Isaac
Isaiah
Jacob
James, St.
Jephtha

John the Baptist, St.
John the Divine, St.
Joseph
Joshua
Jubal
Judah
Judas
Lincoln
Luke, St.
Madonna, The
Magi, The
Mark, St.
Mary Magdalene, St.
Mary the Virgin, St.
Matthew, St.
Melchisedech
Michael, St.
Miriam
Moses
Nathaniel, St.
Nicholas, St.
Noah

PEOPLE IN PARTICULAR
[*continued*]
Patrick, St.
Paul, St.
Peter, St.
Pharaoh
Pharisee, The
Philip, St.
Prodigal Son
Publican, The

Refugee
Ruth
Samaritan
Samson
Samuel
Saul
Shut-ins
Simeon, St.
Simon, St.
Solomon

Sovereign
Stephen, St.
Thief, The
Thomas, St.
Uzziah
Virgin, The
Washington
Widow
Zacharias
Zadok

PLACES

Babylon
Bethel
Bethlehem
Calvary
Eden
Egypt
Emmaus
Flanders
Galilee

Gethsemane
Israel
Jerusalem
Jewry
Jordan
Judah
Nazareth
Olivet

Red Sea
Saba
Salem
Sennacherib
Sharon
Siloam
Zarephath
Zion

THE WORLD OF NATURE

Animals
Autumn
Beasts
Billows
Birds
Clouds
Creation
Darkness
Dawn
Day
Desert
Dew
Drought
Earth
Fields
Fire
Flowers
Forest

Fragrance
Garden
Harvest
Hills
Lake
Mountains
Nature
Nest
Plains
Rain
Rainbow
Reaping
River
Rock
Rose
Sea
Seasons
Seed

Sheep
Spring
Springs
Stars
Storm
Summer
Sun
Tempest
Trees
Universe
Valley
Vine
Water
Way
Wilderness
Winter
Woods

THE WORLD OF SUPER-NATURE

Adversary, The
Angels
Apollyon
Armageddon
Baal
Bible
Cherubim
Demons

Devil
Enemy, The
Fate
Gabriel
Heaven
Hell
Holy City

Host
Michael
Millennium
Paradise
Satan
Seraphim
Soul

SYMBOLS AND TYPES

Alpha
Altar
Ambassador
Anointing
Apple
Ark
Arm
Armageddon
Armor
Banner
Beggar
Blood
Branch
Bread of Life
Breath
Bride of Christ
Bridegroom
Bridge
Builder
Burden
Candle
Carpenter
Chains
Chariot
Cloister
Conqueror
Corner-stone
Courts
Covenant

Cross
Crown
Crucifix
Crusade
Cup
Dayspring
Depths
Desert
Door
Drink
Ear
Eye
Face
Fall
Fasting
Feast
Feeding
Fetters
Fire
Flesh
Fount
Fragrance
Gate
Hand
Harbor
Head
Heart
Heights
Heralds

Highway
Holy City
Hunger
Image
Incense
Jerusalem
Keys
King
Kingdom
Kneeling
Knocking
Lamb
Lamp
Lantern
Legend
Light
Lyre
Manger
Manna
Mansions
Meat
Melchisedech
Messenger
Milk and Honey
Music
Mystery
Nest
New Jerusalem
Ointment

SYMBOLS AND TYPES
[*continued*]

Omega
Paradise
Passover
Path
Pharisee
Physician
Pillars
Portal
Portion
Prison
Prodigal Son
Publican
Rainbow
Ransom
Reaping
River
Road
Rock
Rod
Rose
Sackcloth

Scent
Sceptre
Seed
Sepulchre
Serpent
Servant
Shackles
Shadow
Sharon
Shepherd
Shield
Ships
Signs
Source
Sower
Springs
Stable
Stone
Storm
Sun
Sword
Tabernacle
Table

Taste
Tears
Temple
Tents
Thirst
Thorns
Throne
Tongues
Traveller
Trumpet
Unction
Unveiling
Veil
Vine
Wall
Water
Way
Wayfarer
Wilderness
Wings
Word
Yoke
Zion

OCCASIONS

GENERAL DIVISIONS OF TIME

Autumn
Beginning
Close of Service
Dawn
End
Eternity
Eve
Evening
Future
Generation
Hour
Lord's Day
Midnight

Morning
Night
Opening of Service
Past
Sabbath
Seasons
Spring
Summer
Time
Today
Tomorrow
Winter

THE CHURCH YEAR

Advent

All Saints
All Souls
Annunciation
Ascension
Ash Wednesday
Christmas
Easter
Ember Days
Epiphany
Good Friday
Holy Saturday
Holy Thursday
Holy Week
Innocents' Day
Lent

THE CHURCH YEAR
[*continued*]

Maundy Thursday
Palm Sunday
Pentecost
Rogation Days
Trinity
Twelfth Night
Whitsunday

THE CIVIL YEAR

Armistice Day
Flag Day
Labor Day
Lincoln's Birthday
Memorial Day
Mother's Day
New Year's Day
Thanksgiving
Twelfth Night
Washington's Birthday

SPECIAL OCCASIONS

Anniversaries
Aviation
Baccalaureate Services
Bible Sunday
Blind, Services for
Brotherhood
Children's Services
Civic Observances
Colleges
Commencement
Convocations
Corner-stone Laying
Coronation
Deacons
Dedication
Drought
Elders
Evangelistic Services

Festivals
Foreign Missions
Fraternal Societies
Gold-Star Mother
Government
Greeting
Harvest
Hospitals
Huguenot
Induction
Installation
International
    Brotherhood
Jubilee
Labor Day Services
Masonic Rites
Medicine
Memorial Services
Mental Health
Military Occasions
Ministry
Missionary
Musical Services
Nation
Offerings
Ordination
Patriotism
Peace Services
People
Physician
Preaching Services
Psycho-Therapy
Reception of Members
Red Cross, The
Revival
Sailors
Schools
Separation
Shut-ins
Soldiers
Temperance

Thanksgiving
Tithing
Travellers
Unveiling
Watch-Night
Weddings
Workers
Youth

MUSICAL TYPES

Adaptations
Antiphons
Band
Bell
Boys' Voices
Carols
Children's Choir
Chimes
Congregation and Choir
Croon
Double Chorus
Echo Choir
Harp
Indian Music
Instrumental
    Accompaniment
Junior Choir
Lullabies
Novelties
Obbligatos
Orchestra
Organ
Pæans
Primitive Music
Processionals
Spirituals
Three Choirs
Three-part Anthems
Trios
Trumpet

THE CHURCH

ITS EXISTENCE

Anniversaries
Beloved of God
Cloister
Dedication
Expansion
Foreign Missions
Foundation
Gospel
Home Missions
House of God
Joining the Church
Law
Laying-on of Hands
Militant
Ministry
Missions
Organizations
Reception of Members
Sanctuary
Tabernacle
Temple
Triumphant
Unity
Witness
Youth

ITS THEOLOGICAL PRINCIPLES

Atonement
Bible
Communion of Saints
Decrees of God
Doctrine
Eternity
Evil
Faith
Fall

Grace
Immortality
Incarnation
Infinity
Intercession
Judgment
Justification
Last Things
Millennium
Priesthood of Believers
Redemption
Revelation
Salvation
Sanctification
Scripture
Sin
Sonship under God

ITS LITURGICAL EXPRESSION

Agnus Dei, The
Angelus
Archbishop
Ascription
Benedic Anima Mea, The
Benediction
Benedictus, The
Bible
Call to Worship
Canticles
Carols
Close of Service
Commandments
Compline
Creed, The
Deus Misereatur, The
Festivals

Gloria in Excelsis, The
Gloria Patri, The
Grace before Singing
Hallelujah
Hosanna, The
Introit
Invocation
Jubilate, The
Kneeling
Kyrie Eleison, The
Laying-on of Hands
Lord's Prayer, The
Magnificat, The
Miserere, The
Nunc Dimittis, The
Parables
Processionals
Psalms
Requiem
Sanctus, The
Sursum Corda, The
Te Deum, The
Tersanctus, The
Veneration
Vespers

ITS SACRAMENTS AND RITES

Baptism
Communion
Confirmation
Funeral
Last Supper
Lord's Supper
Marriage
Ordination
Weddings

KEY TO PUBLISHERS

Numerals immediately following name and address of publishers indicate agents.

*	Public Domain (Several Publishers).
1	Novello & Co., London. *See 9.*
2	Oliver Ditson Co., Boston. *See 12.*
3	G. Schirmer, New York.
4	J. Fischer & Bro., New York.
5	Arthur P. Schmidt Co., Boston.
6	Boston Music Co., Boston.
7	John Church Co., Cincinnati. *See 12.*
8	Carl Fischer, New York.
9	H. W. Gray Co., New York.
10	Associated Music Publishers, New York.
11	C. C. Birchard & Co., Boston.
12	Theodore Presser Co., Philadelphia.
13	Gamble Hinged Music Co., Chicago.
14	Curwen, Inc., Germantown, Philadelphia.
15	Oxford University Press, London. *See 8.*
16	Clayton F. Summy Co., Chicago.
17	G. Ricordi, New York.
18	Stainer & Bell, London. *See 25.*
19	White-Smith Co., Boston.
20	Augsburg Publishing House, Minneapolis.
21	Music Publishers Holding Corp., New York. (M. Witmark & Sons, Remick Music Corp., Harms, Inc., T. B. Harms Co.)
22	Chappell & Co., New York.
23	R. L. Huntzinger, Cincinnati.
24	Bosworth & Co., London and New York. *See 27.*
25	Galaxy Music Corp., New York.
26	Harold Flammer, New York.
27	Boosey-Hawkes-Belwin, New York.
28	Enoch & Sons, London. *See 27.*
29	R. D. Row, Boston.
30	C. W. Homeyer, Boston.
31	B. F. Wood, Boston.
32	Michael Keane, New York.
33	Fitz-Simons, Chicago.
34	E. B. Marks, New York.
35	E. C. Schirmer, Boston.
36	N. Simrock, Berlin.
37	Forster Music Publisher, Inc., Chicago.
38	Wm. B. Pond, Ridgefield Park, N. J.
39	Lorenz Publishing Co., Dayton, New York, Chicago.
40	Hall & McCreary Co., Chicago.
41	Whaley Royce & Co., Ltd., Toronto. *See 27.*
42	Sam Fox Publishing Co., Cleveland.
43	H. F. W. Deane & Sons, Ltd., London. *See 11.*
44	Banks & Son, York, England.
45	Schroeder & Guenther, New York.
46	Kürsteiner & Rice, New York.
47	Peates Music House, Utica, New York.
48	Hamilton S. Gordon, New York.
49	Harry L. Hunt, Publisher's Agent, Boston.
50	Hunleth Music Co., St. Louis.
51	Paxton & Co., Ltd., London. *See 34.*
52	Music Products Corp., Chicago.
53	Riker, Brown & Wellington, Chicago.
54	Enoch & Sons, London. *See 27.*
55	Faith Press Co., London. *See 26.*
56	D. L. Schroeder, Flushing, N. Y.

ABBREVIATIONS AND

EXPLANATIONS

A—Alto Solo, or one Alto part in Ensemble
(A)—Incidental Alto Solo
AA—Two Alto parts in Ensemble
A°—Alto Obbligato
a-c—a capella—unaccompanied
B—Baritone (or Bass) Solo, or one Baritone (or Bass) part in Ensemble
(B)—Incidental Baritone Solo
BB—Two Baritone (or Bass) parts in Ensemble
B°—Baritone Obbligato
Br—Brass
C—Cello
Cym—Cymbal
Dbl Ch—Double Chorus
Dr—Drum
Fl—Flute
H—High Voice
H-L—High and Low Voice Duet
Hrn—Horn
Hrp—Harp
Jr—Junior Choir
L—Low Voice
M—Medium Voice
O—Orchestra
Org—Organ
P—Piano

S—Soprano Solo, or one Soprano part in Ensemble
(S)—Incidental Soprano Solo
S-A—Soprano and Alto Duet
(S-A)—Incidental Soprano and Alto Duet
SATB—Mixed Voices
(S.A.T.B)—Incidental Solos for all Four Voices
S-A-T-B—Quartet
S°—Soprano Obbligato
Sr—Senior Choir
SS—Two Soprano parts in Ensemble
SSA—Women's Voices
Stgs—Strings
T—Tenor Solo, or one Tenor part in Ensemble
(T)—Incidental Tenor Solo
Tamb—Tambourine
T-B—Tenor and Bass Duet
T°—Tenor Obbligato
Tr—Trumpet
Trm—Trombone
TT—Two Tenor parts in Ensemble
TTBB—Men's Voices
Tym—Tympany
U—Unison
V—Violin
W.W—Wood Wind

Titles of Solos, Duets, and Trios printed in italics. Unless otherwise indicated, all other compositions are for Mixed Voices.

Numeral used between Title and Composer's name indicates number of voice-parts.

Numeral following name of Composer refers to Publisher, for which see Key on page xxv.

Parentheses indicate *incidental* Solos, Duets, Trios, etc.

A Hyphen separating key letters indicates Duets, Trios, etc.

PART I

GENERAL TOPICS

GENERAL TOPICS

ABANDONMENT [*v.* Forsakenness]

Go not Far from Me, O God	SSATBB	R. N. Dett	4
How Long Wilt Thou Forget Me?	M.	Tschaikowsky=Peery	12
Lord, We Pray, in Mercy Lead Us	(S)	Sibelius=Sammond	10
The Lost Sheep	(S.B)	M. B. Foster	3
The Ninety and Nine	H.M.L.	E. Campion	3
The Ninety and Nine	(A.B)	D. Protheroe	2

ABRAHAM

Hearken unto Me	(S)	F. Stevenson	2
Lord God of Abraham (Elijah)	B.	Mendelssohn	*
The God of Abraham Praise	(S)	H. R. Shelley	3

ABSALOM

O Absalom, My Son	a-c	F. M. Christiansen	20

ABSENT ONES

Be Still, Be Still	(A-B)	C. P. Scott	5

ACCEPTED TIME [*v.* Consecration, Decision, Opportunity]

And All the People Saw	J. Stainer	1
My God, Accept My Heart This Day	Kücken=Brackett	12

ACTIVITY [*v.* Work]

Awake, Awake, Put on Thy Strength		J. Stainer	1
Awake Up, My Glory	(B)	G. W. Chadwick	5
Blow Ye the Trumpet in Zion	(T)	R. H. Woodman	3
Make Us Strong	a-c	Nagler=Dickinson	9

ACTS [*v.* Biblical Passages, etc.]

ADAM [*v.* Creation, Oratorio by Haydn]

Adam Lay Ibounden	Ancient Carol	18

ADAPTATIONS

Adoration (Adoration)		F. Borowski	12
Angel's Song (Prize-Song)	(H)	Wagner=Hamma	8

ADAPTATIONS [*continued*]

ADMONITION [*continued*]

Go to Dark Gethsemane		T. T. Noble	9
Grieve Not the Holy Spirit	(H)	T. T. Noble	9
Grieve Not the Holy Spirit		J. Stainer	1
He Who Would Valiant Be	(M)	R. Broughton	3
Let All Mortal Flesh Keep Silence	(S.B)	G. Holst	18
Let Not the Wise Man Glory in His Wisdom	H.L.	J. G. MacDermid	37
Let This Mind Be in You	(S.B)	Mrs. H. H. A. Beach	7
Let This Mind Be in You		C. W. Cadman	26
Owe No Man Anything		F. McCollin	3
Repent Ye	H.L.	J. P. Scott	3
Rise Up, O Men of God	8 a-c	T. T. Noble	5
Rise Up, O Men of God	U.	Scull	9
Seek Him that Maketh the Seven Stars	(S)	J. H. Rogers	2
Seek Ye the Lord	(A.S-T)	F. W. Perry	2, 9
Today, If Ye Will Hear His Voice	H.L.	J. H. Rogers	5
Turn Back, O Man		G. Holst	17

ADORATION [*v.* Worship, Praise]

Father, Thy Children Bow in Adoration		A. Sullivan	2
Praise to the Lord	8	F. M. Christiansen	20

ADVENT

Arise, Shine, for Thy Light	H.M.L.	J. G. MacDermid	37
Behold, the Days Come	(T)	H. H. Woodward	1
Comfort Ye		G. H. Federlein	3
Comfort Ye (The Messiah)	T.	Handel	*
Dayspring of Eternity	8 a-c	J. S. Matthews	9
Hearken Unto Me	(S.A.T.B)	Mrs. H. H. A. Beach	5
Hearken Unto Me	(S.B)	A. Sullivan	3
Hosanna in the Highest	(S.B)	J. Stainer	1
Kingdom of Light	(H)	P. Lutkin	9
Let All Mortal Flesh Keep Silence	(S.B)	G. Holst	18
O Come, O Come, Emmanuel		T. F. H. Candlyn	9
O Come, Redeemer of Mankind	(S)	A. W. Marchant	1
O Sing as Thrushes		G. Holst	14
Patiently Have I Waited (Christmas Oratorio)		C. St.-Saens	3
Prepare Ye the Way	(T.B)	G. H. Federlein	3

ADVENT [*continued*]

Prepare Ye the way	(T.B)	L. Jewell	9
Rejoice Greatly		H. H. Woodward	1
Repent Ye		J. P. Scott	3
Springs in the Desert	(T)	A. B. Jennings	9
The Great Day of the Lord	Chime	G. C. Martin	1
Welcome, Dear Redeemer	(B)	C. Franck	3
What of the Night	(T)	R. G. Thompson	9

ADVERSARY [*v.* Satan]

AFFLICTION [*v.* Trials]

AGNUS DEI

Agnus Dei	(H.) v. Hrp.	G. Bizet	2
Lamb of God		B. S. Kallinikoff	6
Sheep and Lambs	H.L.	S. Homer	3

AGONY OF CHRIST [*v.* Gethsemane]

ALL IN ALL [*v.* God]

Our God Is All in All	M.	G. M. Abbott	1

ALL SAINTS

And I Saw Another Angel	(T.B)	C. V. Stanford	3
Beyond Life's Evening Star		H. A. Matthews	2
Forever Blest Are They	TTBB(S°)	Mendelssohn	*
Happy and Blest		Mendelssohn	*
Hark, Hark, My Soul	(A)	H. R. Shelley	3
I Beheld, and Lo	(S)	W. C. Gale	7
List the Cherubic Host (Holy City)	SSAA (S.B)	A. R. Gaul	*
O Happy Souls	S-A-B	C. St.-Saens	2
Souls of the Righteous	H.L.	T. T. Noble	3
Souls of the Righteous	8 or 4	T. T. Noble	3, 2
The Saints of God		T. T. Noble	5
These Are They (Holy City)	S.	A. R. Gaul	*
Who Are These?	(T)	R. Redhead	1

ALL SOULS' DAY [*v.* All Saints]

ALMSGIVING [*v.* Offerings, Stewardship, Man—Duty to Man]

ALPHA

| I Am Alpha and Omega | (H) | J. Stainer | 1 |

ALTAR

Approach, My Soul, the Mercy Seat	(M)	J. W. Thompson	5
I Will Go unto the Altar of God		C. Harris	1
I Will Go unto the Altar of God		H. Gadsby	1
See Now the Altar (The Palms)		J. Faure	*
Spirit of God		J. W. Thompson	8

AMBASSADOR [v. Herald]

| *Now Are We Ambassadors* (St. Paul) | (T-B.) | Mendelssohn | * |

AMERICA [v. Patriotism]

God Save America	M.	W. F. Harling	9
God Save America	SATB TTBB SSA	W. F. Harling	9
O Beautiful, My Country		M. Andrews	9

AMOS [v. Biblical Passages, etc.]

ANDREW, St.

Andrew (Come and See)	H.L.	Ward-Stephens	21
Andrew (Come and See)		Ward-Stephens	21
If Thou Shalt Confess with Thy Mouth		C. V. Stanford	1

ANGELS

All My Heart This Night Rejoices	8	F. M. Christiansen	20
And I Saw Another Angel	(T.B)	C. V. Stanford	1, 3
Angel Bright	(S)	F. M. Christiansen	20
Angels Are Singing	S-S	F. Abt	7
Christ, the Fair Glory of the Holy Angels		E. Bullock	3
Hark, Hark, My Soul	(A)	H. R. Shelley	3
Hymn to the Saviour	(S)	E. Kremser	3
Lead, Kindly Light	(B)	D. C. Jenkins	4
Like Angels that Softly (New Year)		J. Pache	9
List the Cherubic Host (Holy City)	(B.S°)	SSAA	A. R. Gaul	*
List the Cherubic Host	(B)		C. Harris	5
Now Let Every Tongue Adore Thee			Bach	*
The Angel	S-A		A. Rubinstein	7

ANGELS [*continued*]

The Angel Gabriel		H. Smart	1
There Was War in Heaven		W. A. C. Cruickshank	1
The Shepherds Had an Angel	(s) a-c	M. Besly	14
This Gospel Sang the Angels		F. White	18

ANGELUS

Angelus		E. Elgar	1
Angelus ("Maritana")	o.	M. V. Wallace	11

ANGER [*v.* Wrath]

Be Ye Kind, One to Another	(b. or t)	S. Liddle	14
Day of Anger, Day of Mourning (Dies Irae, REQUIEM)	TTBB	Mozart = James	9
Dear Lord, Who once upon the Lake	(s)	V. D. Thompson	3
O Israel Return		F. L. Sealy	9
The Lord Is the True God		J. Barnby	1
Why Do the Nations So Furiously Rage (Messiah)	B.	Handel	*
Why Do the Heathen Rage		R. H. Woodman	3

ANIMALS [*v.* Nature]

As Pants the Hart		H. Coleman	13
As Pants the Hart	(s)	S. Salter	9
Behold, the Days Come	(t)	H. H. Woodward	1
Fear Not, O Land		E. Elgar	1
Like As the Hart	H.M.L.	S. Liddle	18
Like As the Hart	(s)	S. Liddle	18
Like As the Hart	(T.B)	W. C. Steere	7
Like As the Hart	(s)	F. Allitsen	27
The Carol of the Beasts	(M°)	P. Lutkin	9
The Lost Sheep	(s.B)	M. B. Foster	3
The Ninety and Nine	H.M.L.	E. Campion	3
The Ninety and Nine	(A.B)	D. Protheroe	2

ANNIVERSARIES

Blow Ye the Trumpet in Zion	(t)	R. H. Woodman	3
Hearken unto Me	(S.A.T.B)	Mrs. H. H. A. Beach	5
I Have Considered the Days of Old		P. James	23
Now Rest Ye, Pilgrim Folk		F. W. Snow	9
O God, Our Help in Ages Past	(s) Chime	C. L. Williams	1

ANNIVERSARIES [continued]

O Light from Age to Age	a-c	L. Sowerby	9
O Sing unto the Lord	(T)	F. W. Snow	9

ANNUNCIATION (Feast of) [v. Advent, Mary, Magnificat]

And the Angel Gabriel		W. H. Monk	1
Ave Maria (Cavatina)	H.L. V.	J. Raff	5
The Angel Gabriel		H. Smart	1
The Annunciation	SSA (B)	H. Willan	9
The Annunciation	(A.T.B)	R. H. Woodman	3
The Annunciation (Carol)		Trad = Smith	18

ANOINTING

Zadok the Priest		Handel	1

ANSWERING CHRIST'S CALL [v. Consecration, Decision]

I Heard the Voice of Jesus Say	(B)	C. Huerter	6
I Heard the Voice of Jesus Say	H.L.	F. G. Rathbun	12
O Jesus, Thou Art Standing	(A)	D. Protheroe	13
Saviour Divine, I Hear Thy Gentle Calling	M.	M. Baines	12
Today If Ye Will Hear His Voice	H.L.	J. H. Rogers	5

ANTICIPATION [v. Heaven]

ANTIPHONAL CHOIR

A New Heaven and a New Earth (Holy City)	(B)	A. R. Gaul	*
Lo, a Great Multitude	(S)	H. Norris	2
Lord God of Israel		H. Norris	2
O Worship the King		J. H. Maunder	1
Remember, O Thou Man		C. S. Lang	9
Silent Night, Holy Night		Gruber = Wetzel	13
Whence Those Sounds Symphonious?		C. H. Kitson	18
When Wilt Thou Save the People?		F. W. Snow	9
While Shepherds Watched	SATB, TTBB, SSAA	H. Jüngst	9
While by My Sheep	SATB TTBB	H. Jüngst	3
Who Are These? (All Saints)	(T)	R. Redhead	1

ANXIETY [v. Abandonment, Bewilderment]
Man, His Need of God.

APOLLYON [v. Satan]

APOSTLES [*v.* Saints and Individual Names]

Jesus and His Twelve Apostles   H.L.   Ward-Stephens 22

Two Volumes of six songs each. All, with the exception of Thaddeus, arranged for SATB, and published separately in Octavo.

VOLUME I	VOLUME II
Andrew	John
Nathaniel	James
Matthew	Judas
Philip	Thomas
Thaddeus	Paul
Peter	Simon

And the Wall of the City   O. King   1
Knows't Thou Then, Poor Judas?   A. van Bruck   3
This Is the Record of John   SAATB (T) a-c   O. Gibbons   8
With Other Tongues Spake the
   Apostles   Palestrina 27

ARCHANGEL [*v.* Angels, Michael]

APPLE

Adam Lay Ibounden   Ancient Carol 18

ARCHBISHOP (**Enthronement**)

I Have Found David, My Servant   SSAATB   C. C. Palmer 15

ARK [*v.* Sanctuary]

Like Noah's Weary Dove   (A)   H. C. Banks   2
The Deluge (Short Oratorio)   C. St.-Saens   3

ARM (**a Symbol**)

The Arm of the Lord (The Passion)   F. J. Haydn   1
The Good Shepherd   A. B. Jennings   9

ARMAGEDDON [*v.* Last Things]

Let God Arise   T. W. Surette   9
Now Is Our Last Dread Enemy   Joseph = Dickinson   9

ARMOR

Put on Therefore, as God's Elect   (s)   E. S. Barnes   9

ARMISTICE DAY [v. Patriotism, War, Nation]

A Prayer for Our Country		W. R. Voris 9
Heroes' Hymn		G. Carle 6
He Maketh Wars to Cease	H.L.	J. P. Scott 26
In Flanders' Fields		F. LaForge 26

ART [v. Music]

Christmas in Art and Song. (Program of Songs with Lantern Slides)		Thomas = Bailey 11
Easter and the Forty Days, in Scripture, Art and Song. (With Lantern Slides)		E. Thomas 11
Praise	(S.B)	A. Rowley 15

ASCENSION DAY [v. Christ]

Alleluia! Sing to Jesus		Trad = Whitehead 5
Ascension		F. M. Christiansen 20
Golden Harps Are Sounding	a-c	I. J. Paderewski 20
King All-Glorious	(T.B)	J. Barnby *
Lift Up Your Heads, O Ye Gates		H. Norris 12
O Could I Speak	(T)	J. W. Thompson 13
Peace I Leave With You		J. V. Roberts 1
Thou Art Gone Up on High (Messiah)		G. F. Handel *
Unfold, Ye Portals Everlasting		C. Gounod *
Who Is This, So Weak and Helpless	(s)	H. E. Button 1

ASCRIPTION

Ascribe unto the Lord (Epiphany)		H. Blair 1
The Ascription	SSATB	R. H. Woodman 3

ASH WEDNESDAY

A Penitential Prayer		Trad = Riedel 9
Create in Me a Clean Heart	(A)	F. F. Harker 26
Thou Hast Turned My Heaviness (Widow of Zarephath)		Alan Gray 1
Turn Ye to Me		W. A. Barrett 1

ASKING [v. Man—Need of God]

I Do Not Ask, O Lord	H.L.	C. G. Spross 12
One Thing Have I Asked		V. D. Thompson 4

ATTRIBUTES [*v.* God—Attributes]

AUGUSTUS [*v.* Cæsar]

AUTHOR

Author of Life Divine		E. Rickett 26
Lord of All Power and Might		G. W. Chadwick 5
Praise	(s.b)	A. Rowley 15

AUTUMN [*v.* Seasons, Harvest]

AVIATION

Bless the Lord, O My Soul		H. W. Davies 1
Hymn for Aviators		W. H. Hall 9
Hymn for Aviators		A. Rowley 14
Thy Messengers Are Winged		M. Hardcastle 1
Wings of the Morning (Hymn)		D. M. Williams 9

AWAKENING [*v.* Quickening]

Awake, My Soul		M. P. Ingle 9
Awake, My Heart's Beloved		Reimann = Dickinson 9
Earth's Awakening	(b)	L. J. Downing 13
The Great Awakening	h.l.	A. W. Kramer 17
The Great Awakening	satb	A. W. Kramer 17

BAAL [*v.* Idolatry, Mendelssohn's Elijah]

BABYLON [*v.* Exile]

Babylon		Watson = Nevin 2
By Babylon's Wave		C. Gounod 3
*By the Waters of Babylon	(s)	Coleridge-Taylor 1
By the Waters of Babylon	h.l.	C. T. Howell 2
By the Waters of Babylon	(h)	C. T. Howell 2
By the Waters of Babylon	(a.t)	R. S. Stoughton 2
The Harp and the Willow		C. Loomis 13
The Vision of Belshazzar	ttbb	G. Bantock 51

BACCALAUREATE [*v.* Youth]

Baccalaureate Hymn	S. B. Hoppin 11
Gently, Lord, O Gently Lead Us	R. N. Dett 12

* Note: In place of the final verse of the Psalm ("Blessed shall he be that taketh thy children and throweth them against the stones") the Editor has adapted the verse preceding to the last twelve measures.

BACCALAUREATE [continued]

Let This Mind Be in You	(H)	C. W. Cadman	26
Let This Mind Be in You	(S.B)	Mrs. H. H. A. Beach	7
Lord, Make Me Strong	H.L.	V. Eville	27
Pilgrim's Song	SATB TTBB SSAA	Tschaikowsky	*
The Heavens Are Telling	(S-T-B)	F. J. Haydn	*
The Omnipotence	(S)	F. Schubert	*

BAND ACCOMPANIMENT [v. Instruments]

God Save Our President	W. F. Harling	9
Hail, Gladdening Light	G. C. Martin	1
Sunrise on Easter Morning	W. B. Olds	8

BANNER

Brightly Gleams Our Banner	T. T. Noble	3
In the Name of God We Will Set Up		
Our Banners	H. Willan	9
The Royal Banners Forward Go	Mendelssohn	3

BAPTISM

Accept My Heart	(M)	G. Borch	26
And They Brought Young Children	(S)	B. Lambord	9
Dearest Jesus, Gentle, Mild		Trad=Dickinson	9
Suffer Little Children	H.	C. Heinroth	9
Suffer Little Children	(T)	S. Salter	3
The Shepherd	M.	T. T. Noble	3

BARAK

The Song of Deborah	(A.T)	P. H. Goepp	3

BARNABAS, St.

They That in Much Tribulation		
(Lauda Sion)	Mendelssohn	*

BARTHOLOMEW, St. [v. Nathaniel]

Then Shall the Righteous (Elijah)	Mendelssohn	*
The Sun Shall Be No More	H. H. Woodward	1

BARUCH [v. Biblical Passages, etc.]

BEASTS [v. Animals, Nature]

BEATITUDES

Blessed Are the Merciful	H.L.	Ward-Stephens	3
Blessed Are the Peacemakers	H.L.	Ward-Stephens	3
Blessed Are the Poor in Spirit	A.	F. F. Harker	3
Blessed Are the Poor in Spirit	H.L.	Ward-Stephens	3
Blessed Are the Pure in Heart	a-c	Bourke⇒Holler	9
Blessed Are They Which Are Persecuted	H.L.	Ward-Stephens	3
Blessed Are They Which Hunger	H.L.	Ward-Stephens	3
Blest Are They Which Are Persecuted	(H)	W. Kienzl	6
The Beatitudes	(B)	A. B. Jennings	9
The Beatitudes	(S)	H. R. Shelley	3

BEAUTY [*v.* Nature]

For the Beauty of the Earth		H. Middleton	8
For the Beauty of the Earth		J. W. Work	4
How Beautiful Upon the Mountains	H.L.	F. F. Harker	3
How Beautiful Upon the Mountains	SATB SSA (S)	F. F. Harker	3
Lovely Appear	(S)	C. Gounod	3
My Eyes for Beauty Pine		H. Howells	15
Praise	(S.B)	A. Rowley	15

BEGGAR

The Lord of Heaven	M. (also TTBB)	C. Forsyth	9
The Living God	H.L.	G. O'Hara	23

BEGINNING [*v.* Creation]

I Am Alpha and Omega	(M)	A. Sullivan	1
In the Beginning Was the Word (Christmas)		E. C. Austin	9
In the Beginning Was the Word		E. S. Hosmer	2

BELIEVING [*v.* Faith]

Lord, I Believe	M.	J. C. H. Beaumont	9

BELLS [*v.* Chimes]

Built on a Rock	8 a-c	F. M. Christiansen	20
The Bells within the Steeples	a-c	M. Prætorius	9

BELSHAZZAR [*v.* Handwriting on the Wall]

BENEDIC ANIMA MEA
Bless the Lord, O My Soul		M. Kingston	1

BENEDICTION
Lord, Dismiss Us with Thy Blessing		J. C. Marks	1
The Lord Bless Thee	(s)	L. Sowerby	6
The Lord Bless You		P. Lutkin	16
Two Choral Benedictions		M. Andrews	17

BENEDICTUS
Blessed be the Lord God		W. S. Bennett	1

BETHEL
Bethel		D. Protheroe	31

BETHLEHEM [*v.* Christmas]
If I Had Lived in Bethlehem	H.	W. Barickman	13

BEWILDERMENT
At Evening Bring Us Home		S. Ledington	39
O Happy Day	(b) a-c	F. M. Christiansen	20
The Shepherd's Content	SAATB	J. S. Matthews	9
Through Life's Vapors Dimly Seeing		J. Raff	19

BIBLE (Bible Sunday)
Awake, My Heart's Beloved	(H)	Sachs=Dickinson	9
Come, Ye Children	(H)	Sullivan=Nevin	9
Glorious Things of Thee Are Spoken	(B)	W. P. Merrill	9
Great Peace Have They	(T)	J. H. Rogers	3
Hearken Unto Me, My People	(s.b)	A. Sullivan	3
Heavenly Truth		G. H. Knight	9
Ho, Every One That Thirsteth	(T)	G. MacFarlane	3
Ho, Every One That Thirsteth	(B)	G. C. Martin	1
Ho, Every One That Thirsteth	(s.b)	H. Vibbard	3
Is Not His Word Like A Fire!	B.	Mendelssohn	*
O Come, Every One That Thirsteth	S-A-T-B.	Mendelssohn	*
O Lord, Thy Word Endureth	(A-T)	E. Lemare	5
O Word of God Incarnate	(T)	C. P. Scott	2
Rise, Crowned with Light		V. Eville	2
Send Out Thy Light		C. Gounod	*
Teach Me, O Lord		T. Attwood	1
Teach Me Thy Way	(s)	L. Spohr	1

BIBLE [*continued*]

The Fining Pot Is For Silver	s-a-t-b.	A. R. Gaul	3
The Old, Old Story	(a-t)	E. S. Hosmer	2
Thy Word Is Like a Garden, Lord	(s.t) 8	C. Dickinson	9
Whatsoever Things Were Written			
Aforetime	ssa	C. H. Lloyd	1

BIBLICAL PASSAGES, PARAPHRASES AND PARALLELS [*v.* pages beginning at 161]

BIGOTRY

The Publican	h.m.l.	B. van de Water	2

BILLOW [*v.* Waves]

Lord Of Our Life	(s.b)	J. T. Field	1

BIRDS [*v.* Nature]

A White Dove Flew From Heaven	a-c	Brahms = Dickinson	9
Carol of the Birds	ssatbb	French = Clokey	11
Easter Sermon of the Birds		Father Finn	11
Like Noah's Weary Dove	(a)	H. C. Banks	2
Nightingale, Awake		A. Whitehead	5
O For the Wings of a Dove	(s)	Mendelssohn	*
The Birds. Christmas Carol	u.	J. M. Tatton	43
The Birds Praise the Advent of the			
Saviour	(s) 8	Millet = Schindler	2
The Song of the Birds	(h)	L. Millet	3

BIRTH OF CHRIST [*v.* Christmas]

I Sing the Birth		E. Elgar	1
The Lost Star	ssatbb a-c	B. Gross	13

BITTERNESS

Marah	F. M. Christiansen	20

BLESSING

Eventide		J. E. West	9
Holiest, Breathe an Evening Blessing	6 a-c	G. C. Martin	3

BLIND

Behold Two Blind Men Sitting by the		
Wayside	J. Stainer	1

BLIND [*continued*]

Blind and Alone	a-c	H. A. Matthews	3
The Blind Ploughman	H.L.	C. Clarke	22
The Blind Ploughman	SATB TTBB	C. Clarke	22
The People that Walked in Darkness	B.	Handel	*
They that Sit in Darkness	A.	H. W. Parker	1

BLOOD [*v.* Atonement, Good Friday]

A Few More Years Shall Roll		F. Butcher	9
Alas, and Did My Saviour Bleed		V. D. Thompson	2
A Legend	a-c	Tschaikowsky	*
I See His Blood Upon the Rose	SSSATB	A. Benjamin	15
I See His Blood Upon the Rose	H.	W. R. Voris	9
I See His Blood Upon the Rose	H.	E. R. Warren	9
My Blood Is Red (Short)		W. Davies	14
The Precious Blood	H.	R. W. Wilkes	3

BOLDNESS [*v.* Courage]

Let Us Come Boldly unto the Throne		C. H. Lloyd 1

BONDAGE

How Long, O Lord (Susanna)	TTBB	Handel=Dawe	2
[*v.* Israel in Egypt, Oratorio by Handel]			

BOUNTY

Because of Thy Great Bounty	H.	E. R. Warren	9
Enrich Us with Thy Bounty		Bach=Besly	27
O Bountiful Jesus		J. Stainer	1

BOYS' VOICES [*v.* Junior Choir]

O Clap Your Hands Together	U.	C. Thomas 5

BRANCH (a Symbol)

Behold, the Days Come	(H)	H. H. Woodward	1
I Am the Vine	(S.T)	P. James	23
O Israel, Return		W. R. Voris	9

BREAD OF LIFE [*v.* Communion]

Be Still, My Soul		C. H. Kitson	15
Bread of the World	(H)	L. Verrees	9
Bread of the World	(A)	H. B. Gaul	6
Very Bread, Good Shepherd, Tend Us		W. M. Hawkins	9

BREATH

Breathe on Me, Breath of God	(s°)	C. E. Wheeler	16
Breathe on Me, Breath of God		V. D. Thompson	9
Breathe on Me, Breath of God		W. R. Voris	9
Breath of God	H.L.	M. T. Salter	3
Holiest, Breathe an Evening Blessing	(s) 6 a-c	G. C. Martin	3
Holiest, Breathe an Evening Blessing		J. E. West	1
The Voice that Breathed o'er Eden (Hymn-Text)			

BRIDE OF CHRIST [*v.* Church Triumphant]

BRIDEGROOM (a Symbol)

At Midnight there Was a Cry		A. Ham	9
Wake, Awake	8 a-c	F. M. Christiansen	20
While the Bridegroom's Coming Tarried		J. H. Mee	1

BRIDGE

The Rainbow Bridge of Prayer	F. M. Christiansen	20

BROTHERHOOD [*v.* Man—Duty to Fellow Men, Brotherhood]

Because of Thy Great Bounty	H.	E. R. Warren	9
Beloved, if God so Loved Us		J. Barnby	1
Be Ye All of One Mind	(H)	A. E. Godfrey	1
Be Ye Kind, One to Another	(B. or T)	S. Liddle	14
Brethren	a-c	F. M. Christiansen	20
Dwell Ye in Love		B. F. Johnston	4
Grant, O Lord (Short)		C. Thomas	5
I Said; Let Me Walk in the Field		P. Lutkin	9
Let the Peace of God Rule	(H)	J. Stainer	1
Love	H.L.	M. van Dyke	27
Others	H.	E. R. Warren	9
Rise Up, O Men of God	a-c	T. T. Noble	5
Pilgrim's Song	SATB TTBB	Tschaikowsky = Williams	9
Pilgrim's Song	H.L.	Tschaikowsky	*
These Things Shall Be	(H)	R. Broughton	2
Turn Back, O Man		G. Holst	17
Worship		G. Shaw	1

BUILDER

Build Thee More Stately Mansions	(B)	M. Andrews	3
Build Thee More Stately Mansions		C. F. Mueller	26

BUILDER [continued]

I Have Surely Built Thee an House	(A.T.B)	W. Boyce	1
Temples Eternal		F. M. Christiansen	20
The Builder		C. W. Cadman	26
Praise	(S.B)	A. Rowley	15

BURDEN

Cast Thy Burden upon the Lord		Mendelssohn	*
O Cast Thy Burden upon the Lord	B.	J. H. Maunder	9
(Penitence, Pardon and Peace, Cantata)			

CÆSAR

When Cæsar Augustus (Carol)	SATBB	A. Whitehead	8

CALL [v. Invitation]

Saviour Divine, I Hear Thy Gentle Calling	(M)	W. Baines	12

CALL TO WORSHIP [v. Invocation, Introit]

O Come Let Us Worship.	(T)	Mendelssohn	*
The Shofar (or Trumpet) Is Sounded	(B)	Trad = Dickinson	9
The Lord Is in His Holy Temple		H. C. Banks	9
The Lord Is in His Holy Temple		G. A. Burdett	9

CALM

Dear Lord and Father of Mankind	(S.L)	A. B. Targett	9
Dear Lord, Who once upon the Lake	(S)	V. D. Thompson	3
Father, in Thy Mysterious Presence	(S)	J. S. & H. A. Matthews	2
I Do Not Ask	H.L.	R. R. Peery	37
I Do Not Ask		C. G. Spross	12
In Quietness and in Calmness	(T)	L. Jewell	9
O Calm of Soul	M.	W. R. Voris	9
Remain with Us, O Peace of God		Matthews	9
With Quiet Heart		F. Scherer	9

CALVARY

Calvary	H.M.	P. Rodney	3, 8
Calvary and Easter	8	W. Wild	8
Crown on Calvary	H.L.	D. Protheroe	13
Go to Dark Gethsemane		T. T. Noble	3
Lift High the Triumph Song		C. F. Mueller	3

CANDLE

No Candle Was there and no Fire   L. Lehmann 22
O Brightness of the Immortal Father's
    Face   a-c   W. R. Voris 9

CANTICLES [v. Agnus Dei] Listed Separately

Benedic Anima Mea
Benedictus
Deus Misereatur
Gloria in Excelsis
Gloria Patri
Jubilate
Kyrie Eleison
Magnificat
Miserere
Nunc Dimittis
Sanctus
Sursum Corda
Te Deum
Tersanctus

CAPTIVITY [v. Babylon]

CARE [v. Abandonment]

God Cares   H.L.   Ward-Stephens 21

CAROLS [v. Christmas, Easter, New Year]

CARPENTER

A Carpenter Cut the Manger Wood   8 a-c   F. M. Christiansen 20
O Son of the Carpenter   M.   G. B. Nevin 2

CAUSE

The Cause Is Thine, Lord Jesus Christ a-c   F. J. Haydn 8

CHAINS [v. Bondage, Prison]

CHALLENGE

Darest Thou Now, O Soul   (S.A)   D. M. Williams 9
We Who Have Challenged Fate   R. G. Cole 5

CHARIOT

Swing Low, Sweet Chariot	TTBB	H. B. Gaul	9
The Chariots of the Lord Are Strong		A. Whitehead	5

CHARITY [v. Almsgiving]

The Greatest of These Is Love	(S.A.T)	R. Bitgood	9
The Greatest of These Is Love	M.L.	R. Bitgood	9
The Red Cross Spirit	H.L.	H. W. Parker	9
The Red Cross Spirit	SATB TTBB SSAA	H. W. Parker	9

CHASTISEMENT [v. Tribulation, Rebuke]

Happy Is the Man Whom the Lord Correcteth (Job)		E. T. Chipp	1
Surely He Hath Borne Our Griefs (Messiah)		Handel	*

CHERUBIM

Seraphim Hymn	8 a-c	A. Gretchaninoff	9

CHILD

Christ Is Born in Every Child		E. S. Barnes	8
Father, Send a Child Again	a-c	B. Gross	13
Here, a Little Child I Stand	U.	E. M. Lee	15
What Child Is This?	8 a-c	Trad=Maryott	13
Who Is This?	(s)	H. E. Button	1

CHILDLIKE SPIRIT [v. Humility]

CHILDREN

And They Brought Young Children	(s)	B. Lambord	9
By Cool Siloam's Shady Rill		E. S. Barnes	2
Christ and the Children		F. Nagler	9
Christ and the Children	H.	L. Norden	9
Dearest Jesus	(s).	Trad=Dickinson	9
Heavenly Father, Send Thy Blessing		L. Jewell	12
I Think, When I Hear that Sweet Story	U.	H. Norris	3
O Jesus, Tender Shepherd	a-c	Trad=Brahms	1
O Sons and Daughters		C. C. Harwood	15
Suffer Little Children	H.	C. Heinroth	9
Suffer Little Children		B. Lambord	9

*   *   *   *   *   *   *

Sacred Songs for Little Singers		H. Tolhurst	51

CHILDREN'S CHOIR [v. Junior Choir]

CHIMES

Bell Carol		A. Whitehead	6
Eternal Father		G. Holst	14
Legend of the Bells	SSAATBB (S)	R. V. Rhodes	13
List to the Lark	(S)	C. Dickinson	9
O Bells, Send forth the Triumph		E. S. Kelley	2
O God, Our Help in Ages Past	(S)	C. L. Williams	1
Ring Out the Sweet Message		A. E. Adams	22
Ring Out, Wild Bells		P. L. Fletcher	1
Ring Out, Wild Bells	H.L.	C. Gounod	*
Ring Out, Wild Bells		C. Gounod	*
The Great Day of the Lord		G. C. Martin	1

CHOICE [v. Decision]

Choose Ye, this Day	(S.A)	C. Nordman	39

CHRIST

ADVENT [v. Advent]

AGONY OF [v. Gethsemane]

ASCENSION [v. Ascension]

ATONEMENT [v. Purification]

Behold the Lamb of God (Messiah)		Handel	*
Christ Went up into the Hills to Pray	H.L.	R. Hageman	8
Christ Went up into the Hills to Pray		R. Hageman	8
Christ Went up into the Hills to Pray	H.L.	E. R. Warren	9
Christ Went up into the Hills to Pray	SATB SSAA	E. R. Warren	9
Come unto Me	(A)	W. C. Gale	12
Come unto Me	TTBB (A) a-c	C. B. Hawley	26
Faith in His Love		E. H. Lemare	5
Far from Their Home		H. H. Woodward	1
God's Peace Is Peace Eternal	(S)	E. Grieg	3
Greater Love Hath No Man	(S.B)	J. Ireland	18
Kol Nidrei		Trad = Roberts	8
Let All Mortal Flesh Keep Silence	(S.B)	G. Holst	18
None Other Lamb	(S) 6	H. Sanders	2
O Bountiful Jesu		J. Stainer	1
O Lord, Most Holy	a-c	A. Bruckner	9
Surely He Hath Borne Our Griefs (Messiah)		G. F. Handel	*

CHRIST [*continued*]

The Following Love	(T)	J. S. Matthews	9
There Is No Sorrow, Lord, too Light	(S)	A. E. Godfrey	1
The Shofar (Trumpet) Is Sounded		Trad=Dickinson	9

BIRTH OF [*v.* Christmas]

BURIAL OF [*v.* Holy Saturday]

CALL OF [*v.* Invitation]

CHILDHOOD OF

A Legend	a-c	Tschaikowsky	*
The Little Christ Is Coming Down		O. Speaks	3

CONFESSING CHRIST

Let this Mind Be in You	(S.B)	Mrs. H. H. A. Beach	7
O Jesus Thou Art Standing	(A)	D. Protheroe	13
The King of Love	(A.S-B)	H. R. Shelley	3

CRUCIFIXION [*v.* Good Friday]

DEATH OF [*v.* Good Friday, Atonement]

DEITY OF

Lo, My Shepherd Is Divine		F. J. Haydn	1
Rise, Crowned with Light		V. Eville	2

EPIPHANY OF [*v.* Epiphany]

EVERLASTING

Fling Wide the Gates (Crucifixion)		J. Stainer	3
Gloria	H.M.L.	A. Buzzi-Peccia	26
Gloria	(H)	A. Buzzi-Peccia	26
Open the Gates of the Temple	H.L.	Mrs. J. F. Knapp	38
Who Is This?	(S)	H. E. Button	1

EXAMPLE OF

Behold the Master Passeth By	(A)	F. Stevenson	2
O Wondrous Type		F. M. Christiansen	20
Worship	O.	G. Shaw	1

FELLOWSHIP WITH [*v.* God, Fellowship with]

My Master and My Friend	TTBB	F. H. Brackett	6
O Saviour, Friend (Largo)	(S)	Handel	14

CHRIST [*continued*]
GLORIFIED [*v.* Ascension]

INCARNATION [*v.* Advent, Christmas, Incarnation]
Hosanna   F. M. Christiansen 20

KINGSHIP OF [*v.* King]

MASTER [*v.* Master]

MEDIATOR

In the Hour of Trial		Rubinstein = Milligan	5
I Will Pray the Father	(T)	F. W. Holloway	5
Lead, Kindly Light	(B)	C. Jenkins	4
My Master and My Friend	TTBB	F. H. Brackett	6
My Redeemer Lives	H.L.	H. Gilbert	4
Save Us, O Lord		E. C. Bairstow	1

PASSION [*v.* Lent, Good Friday]

PRAISE TO [*v.* Praise]

PRESENCE OF [*v.* Presence]

RESURRECTION [*v.* Easter]

SAYINGS OF [*v.* Beatitudes, Invitation, Parables]

Christ's Message	H.L.	C. Warford	5
Follow Me	(T)	H. R. Shelley	39
Hear the Words that Jesus Spake	H.L.	Ward-Stephens	5
I Am the Bread of Life		J. S. Matthews	2
I Am the Vine	(S.T)	P. James	23
I Am the Water of Life		J. P. Dunn	4
I Heard the Voice of Jesus Say	(S)	W. C. Gale	7
In My Father's House Are Many Mansions	H.M.L.	J. G. MacDermid	37
In My Father's House Are Many Mansions	H.L.	R. G. Cole	5
Sayings of Jesus (Five Sayings)	(T)	H. W. Davies	1
Sayings of Jesus (Three Sayings)	a-c	H. W. Davies	1
Sayings of Our Lord (Solo, or Semi-Chorus of Men)		H. W. Davies	1
The Words on the Cross (Motet)		G. B. Nevin	2
What Christ Said	(B)	P. Lutkin	9

CHRIST [*continued*]
SECOND COMING

Prepare Ye the Way	(T.B)	G. H. Federlein	3
Prepare Ye the Way	(T.B)	L. Jewell	9

SYMBOLS AND TYPES OF [*v.* Table of Contents]

TRIUMPHAL ENTRY [*v.* Palm Sunday]

TRIUMPHANT

Christ Conquereth		J. W. Clokey	4
O Could I Speak	(T)	J. W. Thompson	13

CHRISTIAN [*v.* Man]
CONSECRATION OF SELF

From Every Earthly Pleasure	(H)	S. R. Gaines	3
How Fair the Church of Christ Shall Stand		F. M. Christiansen	20
Saviour, Thy Dying Love	8 a-c	W. R. Voris	9
Take My Life and Let It Be	(S)	Trad = Sanders	5
Thee Will I Love		Tschaikowsky	3
The King of Love	(A.S-B)	H. R. Shelley	3
There's a Wideness in God's Mercy	(H)	J. S. Matthews	9

DISCIPLINES

Put on therefore as God's Elect	(S)	E. S. Barnes	9
Turn Back, O Man		G. Holst	17

ENCOURAGEMENT

In the Year that King Uzziah Died		D. M. Williams	9
Let Not Your Heart Be Troubled	(T.B)	E. Faning	1
Rise Up, O Men of God		T. T. Noble	5

FELLOWSHIP

Let the Peace of God Rule	(H)	J. Stainer	1
Put On Therefore as God's Elect	(S)	E. S. Barnes	9
Worship		G. Shaw	1

GROWTH IN GRACE [*v.* Growth]

New Every Morning Is the Love	B. L. Selby	1

CHRISTIAN [*continued*]

PRIVILEGES

Grant Me, O God		W. R. Davis	9
O Lord of Life	(T)	F. L. Sealy	9

CHRISTIANITY

Eternal Ruler of the Ceaseless Round .	M. Genet	9
Eternal Ruler of the Ceaseless Round	F. L. Sealy	9

CHRISTMAS

Before the Paling of the Stars	H.L.	A. W. Kramer	4
Before the Paling of the Stars		A. W. Kramer	4
Come, Mary, Take Courage	M.	C. Thorp	25
Christmas Bells	(S.A.T.B)	F. Stevenson	2
Christmas, Fantasy on Carols	(S.A.B)	G. Holst	1
Christmas Eve	H.L.	R. Hageman	25
Christmas Eve	SATB	Hageman = James	25
Christmas Eve	TTBB	Hageman = Greenfield	25
Christmas Eve	SSA	Hageman = Gilbert	25
Gold, Frankincense and Myrrh	(S.A.T.B)	H. Gilbert	9
Holy Night, Peaceful Night	(H)	C. B. Hawley	7
How Far Is it to Bethlehem?	SSA	R. Donovan	9
I Beheld a Great Multitude		Rheinberger = Whitehead	14
Mary Kept All these Things to Herself	(S.A.T.B)	E. S. Barnes	2
O Holy Night	(H)	A. Adam	*
O Holy Night	(H) TTBB	A. Adam	*
Rejoice in God	a-c	Whitford	5
Sing, Christmas Bells	(S)	H. A. Matthews	2
The Birth of Christ	(S.T.B)	W. Richter	26
The Great Eternal Christmas	(A.B) v.c.Hrp.	H. Gilbert	9
The Lame Shepherd	(T)	W. R. Voris	9
The Lonely Shepherds	(B) a-c	C. Black	9
Whence Those Sounds Symphonious? (Echo Choir SSAA)		C. H. Kitson	18

v. Publishers' Announcements and Catalogues

CHRISTMAS CAROLS OF THE NATIONS

American Indian

Stars Lead Us Ever on		2
'Twas in the Moon of Wintertime	(T)	25

CHRISTMAS CAROLS [*continued*]

Austria
A Babe Lies in a Cradle	(H.L.) v.c.Hrp	9
Shepherds' Christmas Song		9

Czecho-Slovakia
Four Slovak Christmas Carols		9
Still Grows the Evening over Bethle- hem		9

Corsica
In a Stable Mean and Lowly	(S.L) v.c.Hrp	9

England
The Cherry-tree Carol	(s)	3
The First Nowell	8 a-c	9

France
A Joyous Christmas Song	a-c	9
Angels O'er the Fields	8 a-c	9
Bring a Torch, Jeanette, Isabella		9
Come, Marie, Elisabette		9

Germany
The Inn at Bethlehem		9

Greece
Shepherds on the Hill	(S.T.B) Fl.v.c.Hrp	9

Holland
Sleep, my Jesus, Sleep	(L) v.c.Hrp.	9

Ireland
O Shepherds, Leave Your Watching		2

Italy
Is this the Way to Bethlehem?	a-c	9
Whence Come Ye?	v.c.Hrp	9

Jugoslavia
Croatian Christmas Song	a-c	9

Lithuania
What a Wonder		9

CHRISTMAS CAROLS [*continued*]
Mexico
The Shepherds and the Inn   2
Norway
The Babe in the Manger   (s) v.c.Hrp   9
The Christmas Bells of Norway   26
Poland
Sleep, Baby Jesus   a-c   25
The Quest of the Shepherds   4
Roumania
Jesus Christ Is Born   3
Russia
Carol of the Russian children   3
Holy Angels Singing   a-c   9
Spain
⎧ Andalusian Christmas Carol   Dbl. Ch.   9
⎪ Basque Christmas Carol   9
⎨ Catalonian Christmas Carol   9
⎩ Galician Christmas Carol   9
   (All four with Castanets, Cymbals, Tambourine)
O Bethlehem   (A.T-S) v.c.Hrp   9
Sweden
Christmas Snows of Sweden   25
Swedish Yule Carol   25
Switzerland
Little Child in Manger Bare   (M)   9
The Angels at the Manger   9

I CHRONICLES [*v.* Biblical Passages, etc.]

II CHRONICLES [*v.* Biblical Passages, etc.]

CHURCH

ANNIVERSARY [*v.* Anniversaries]

BELOVED OF GOD
A Day in Thy Courts   W. Macfarlane 3
Arise, O Lord, into Thy Resting-Place   (s)   G. F. Cobb   1

CHURCH [*continued*]

Blessed Are They that Dwell in Thy House	SSAA	J. Brahms	9
Blessed Are They that Dwell in Thy House	(T)	C. Dickinson	9
Great Peace Have They	(T)	J. H. Rogers	3
How Lovely Are Thy Dwellings	H.L.	S. Liddle	27
How Lovely Are Thy Dwellings		E. Delamarter	33
Lord of the Worlds Above	(S.A.B)	Mrs. H. H. A. Beach	2
O How Amiable Are Thy Dwellings		Mana-Zucca	28
The Lord Is in His Holy Temple		J. W. Elliott	1

DEDICATION

Except the Lord Build the House		A. C. Edwards	9
Except the Lord Build the House	Br.	E. Faning	1
I Have Surely Built Thee	(A.T.Boy)	W. Boyce	1
In the Name of Our God We Will Set up Our Banners	(T)	H. Willan	9
I Was Glad when They Said	(B)	J. L. Galbraith	5
Lord God of Israel	(T)	C. S. Norris	2
The Builder		C. W. Cadman	26

MILITANT

Fight the Good Fight		C. H. Doersam	9
In the Name of Our God We Will Set Up Our Banners	(T)	H. Willan	9
Lead on, O King Eternal	(M)	J. Pache	9
Lord of Our Life	(S.B)	J. T. Field	1
Make Us Strong	8 a-c	Nagler=Dickinson	9
Send Out Thy Light		C. Gounod	*
The Son of God Goes Forth		A. Sullivan	1

SECURITY OF

Approach, My Soul, the Mercy Seat		J. W. Thompson	5
Blow Ye the Trumpet in Zion	(T)	R. H. Woodman	3
Far Down the Ages		A. C. Edwards	9
Glorious Things of Thee	(B)	W. P. Merrill	9
Lord, Thou Hast Been Our Dwelling-Place		L. B. Phillips	27
O God, Our Help	(S) Chime	C. L. Williams	1
O Lord, Thou Art Our God	(L)	C. Dickinson	9
Pray for the Peace of Jerusalem		E. H. Thorne	1

CHURCH [*continued*]
TRIUMPHANT

Glorious Things of Thee Are Spoken	(B)	W. P. Merrill	9
O God Who Set the Seers Aflame		H. L. Baumgartner	9
Rise, Crowned with Light		V. Eville	2
The Hymn Triumphant	(S.B)	C. W. Cadman	12
The Lord Hath Done Great Things		J. E. West	1
The Saints of God	a-c	T. T. Noble	5
The Soul Triumphant	(B) o.	T. T. Noble	9

UNITY

Be Ye All of One Mind	(H)	A. E. Godfrey	1
Dwell Ye in Love		R. D. Shure	4
Grieve Not the Holy Spirit	(H°)	T. T. Noble	9
Grieve Not the Holy Spirit		J. Stainer	1
I Am the Vine	(S.T)	P. James	23
Let the Peace of God Rule	(H)	J. Stainer	1
Lord of Our Life	(S.B)	J. T. Field	1
Make Us Strong	8 a-c	Nagler = Dickinson	9

APPROPRIATE HYMNS

Onward, Christian Soldiers
The Church's One Foundation

WITNESSING [*v.* Missions, Witnessing]

CIVIC OBSERVANCES [*v.* Anniversaries, Memorial, Patriotism]

CLOISTER

The Cloister	M.	W. A. Thayer	3

CLOSE OF SERVICE [*v.* Benediction]

God that Madest	8 a-c	F. L. Lawrence	9
Lord, Dismiss Us	TTBB	H. W. Parker	3
Nunc Dimittis	U.	D. M. Williams	9
Remain with Us, O Peace of God		H. A. Matthews	9
The Lord Bless Thee	(S)	L. Sowerby	6
The Lord Bless You		P. Lutkin	16

CLOUD

Clouds and Darkness	H.L.	A. Dvorak	36
From Clouds a Light of Light Arises		W. H. Hall	9
When Sorrow's Heavy Cloud	TTBB	G. B. Nevin	3

COLLEGES [*v.* Baccalaureate, Schools, Youth]

COLOSSIANS [*v.* Biblical Passages, etc.]

COME [*v.* Invitation, Supplication, Answering Christ's Call]

Come, Dearest Lord		Bach=Holler	9
He Is Blessed	8 a-c	Söderman=Christiansen	20
O Come to My Heart, Lord Jesus	H.L.	P. Ambrose	2
O Come to My Heart, Lord Jesus	SATB (B)	P. Ambrose	2

COMFORT

Abide with Me	(S.A.T.B)	A. Depew	6
Abide with Me	(A)	S. Liddle	27
All Ye that Cried unto the Lord (Hymn of Praise)		Mendelssohn	*
And God Shall Wipe Away All Tears	(A)	A. W. Coombs	3
Beneath the Shadow		C. Dickinson	9
Beside Still Waters	(H)	B. Hamblen	41
Be Still, Be Still	(A-B)	C. P. Scott	5
Blessed Are the Poor in Spirit	H.L.	F. F. Harker	3
Come unto Me		W. C. Gale	7
Come unto Me	(A)	C. B. Hawley	26
Come unto Me	(S. or B)	C. Huerter	2
Evening and Morning		M. Spicker	3
Eye Hath Not Seen		M. B. Foster	1
Eye Hath Not Seen	A.	A. R. Gaul	*
He Shall Feed His Flock	A.	Handel	*
He Watching over Israel (Elijah)		Mendelssohn	*
Hymn to the Saviour	(s) Hrp	E. Kremser	3
I Heard a Great Voice	(A)	E. F. Johnston	4
In My Father's House Are Many Mansions	H.M.L.	J. G. MacDermid	37
Out of Heaven		F. H. Cowen	3
The Comforter		D. Protheroe	13
They Shall Run and not Be Weary	H.L.	J. G. MacDermid	37

COMMANDMENT

A New Commandment (Olivet to Calvary)	B.	J. H. Maunder	*
Beloved, if God so Loved Us		J. Barnby	1
Follow Me	(T)	H. R. Shelley	39

COMMANDMENT [*continued*]

I Am the Vine	(s.t)	P. James 23
If Ye Love Me, Keep My Commandments		G. George 9
If Ye Love Me, Keep My Commandments	(h)	F. F. Harker 26
If Ye Walk in My Statutes		J. Chippingdale 1
Love (*First Commandment*)	h.l.	B. Clifford 16
This Is My Commandment	h.l.	P. J. Clark 13
The New City	(t)	F. L. Carver 5

COMMENCEMENT [*v.* Baccalaureate]

Farewell, Dear School We Love		H. McCarthy 17
Let Our Theme of Praise Ascending	TTBB	Mendelssohn 6

COMMUNION OF SAINTS [*v.* Saints, Church Unity]

COMMUNION (The Sacrament) [*v.* Victim]

At Thy Table, Lord	(s)	A. Floyd 25
Before the Sacrament	h.	T. M. Spelman 25
Be Still, My Soul		C. H. Kitson 15
Bread of the World	(a)	H. B. Gaul 6
Bread of the World		F. W. Wadely 15
Deck Thyself, My Soul		Crüger = Whitehead 5
God So Loved the World	(s)	W. R. Voris 9
Greater Love Hath No Man	(s.t.b)	J. Ireland 18
I Am the Bread of Life		J. S. Matthews 2
I Am the Living Bread	STB	L. Urteaga 9
Jesus, Thou Joy of Loving Hearts	(s)	E. H. Davies 1
Let All Mortal Flesh Keep Silence	(b.s)	E. Holst 18
O Bread of Life	(b°)	F. M. Christiansen 20
O Living Bread, Who Once Did Die		P. W. Whitlock 5

COMPASSION [*v.* Mercy]

O Lord of Love Compassionate		Brahms = Dickinson 9
Put on, as God's Elect		E. S. Barnes 9

COMPLAINING

Murmur Not, O My Soul	a.	Bach 15

COMPLINE [*v.* Evening]

Before the Ending of the Day	(b)	C. Huerter 3

COMPLINE [*continued*]

Compline Hymn (Te lucis ante terminum)		N. Ponsonby	43
O Lord, Support Us All the Day Long	(A.T)	H. McAmis	3
Save Us, O Lord		E. C. Bairstow	1

CONDEMNATION [*v.* Judgment]

His Sceptre Is the Rod of Righteousness (Occasional Oratorio)	B.	Handel	1

CONFESSION [*v.* Faith, Sin]

Father, Once More within Thy Holy Place		H. A. Matthews	3
If Thou Shalt Confess		C. V. Stanford	1
O Jesus, Thou Art Standing	(A)	D. Protheroe	13
The Publican	H.M.L.	B. van de Water	2

CONFIDENCE [*v.* Assurance]

Art Thou Weary?	(B)	G. W. Chadwick	5
Art Thou Weary?	(S.A.T) V.	T. del Riego	2
A Song in the Night	(S.B)	R. H. Woodman	3
Be Still, Be Still	(A-B)	C. P. Scott	5
How Beautiful upon the Mountains	(S)	F. F. Harker	3
I Know that My Redeemer Liveth	S.	Handel	*
I Know that My Redeemer Liveth	SATB	Handel=Christiansen	20
My Redeemer Lives	H.L.	H. Gilbert	4
Open the Gates of the Temple	H.L.	Mrs. J. F. Knapp	38

CONFIRMATION [*v.* Joining the Church]

I Will Lift up Mine Eyes	H.L.	J. G. MacDermid	37
I Will Lift up Mine Eyes		J. H. Brewer	12
I Will Lift up Mine Eyes		F. F. Harker	26
I Will Lift up Mine Eyes	(A)	L. Sowerby	2
My God, Accept My Heart	(S)	Kücken=Brackett	12
O Love that Wilt Not Let Me Go	8	M. Andrews	9
O Man of God		S. Bett	8
Wherewithal Shall a Young Man	(T)	H. Hiles	1
Take Us to Thy Care	8	Handel=Ganschow	40

CONGREGATION AND CHOIR

Abide with Me		H. Coleman	18
As Pants the Hart		H. Coleman	18

CONGREGATION AND CHOIR [*continued*]

Blest Are the Pure in Heart		J. A. Sowerbutts 18
Conquering Kings Their Titles Take		J. H. Maunder 6
Faith of Our Fathers		J. S. Matthews 9
Lo, a Great Multitude	(s)	C. S. Norris 2
O Worship the King		J. H. Maunder 2
The Head that Once		J. A. Sowerbutts 18
The King of Love		H. Coleman 18

— — — — — — — — — —

Anthems for Congregations		E. N. Anderson 12
Forty-Five Short Congregational Anthems		O. A. Mansfield 51

CONQUEROR

Christ Conquereth		J. W. Clokey 4
Conquering Kings Their Titles Take		J. H. Maunder 6
Conqueror	H.L.	S. Salter 8
The Conqueror (Easter)		L. Baumgartner 2

CONSECRATION

A Song of Consecration		D. W. Kennedy 9
Faith and Consecration		A. H. Prentiss 3
From Every Earthly Pleasure	(T)	S. R. Gaines 3
Just as I Am	(S.A)	J. Herbeck 2
Master, No Offering Costly and Sweet. Hymn-Text (E. P. Parker)		
My God, Accept My Heart		Kücken = Brackett 12
My Master and My Friend	TTBB a-c	F. H. Brackett 6
When I Survey the Wondrous Cross	(A.B)	M. Andrews 2
They that Wait upon the Lord		F. W. Snow 9

CONSOLATION [*v.* Comfort]

Come, Ye Disconsolate	M.	M. Andrews 3

CONTRITION [*v.* Penitence]

O God, Have Mercy upon Me (St. Paul)	B.	Mendelssohn *

CONVERSION

Behold, the Master Passeth By	(A)	F. Stevenson 2
Blind and Alone	a-c	H. A. Matthews 3
Dear to the Heart of God	H.	F. W. Vanderpool 12

CONVERSION [*continued*]

If with All Your Hearts	T.	Mendelssohn	*
Let Not Your Heart Be Troubled		E. Faning	1
The Heart Worships	H.L.	G. Holst	18

CONVICTION [*v.* Confidence]

CONVOCATION [*v.* Festival]

I CORINTHIANS [*v.* Biblical Passages, etc.]

II CORINTHIANS [*v.* Biblical Passages, etc.]

CORNER-STONE [*v.* Church—Corner-Stone]

CORONATION (of a Sovereign)

Coronation Offertorium (O Hearken Thou)		E. Elgar	1
Let My Prayer		E. C. Bairstow	15
The King Shall Rejoice		Handel	1
Zadok the Priest		Handel	1

CORRECTION [*v.* Chastisement]

Behold, Happy Is the Man Whom the Lord Correcteth (Job)		E. T. Chipp	1
When Thou with Rebukes		E. Bullock	18

COURAGE [*v.* Boldness]

Awake, My Soul		M. P. Ingle	9
Darest Thou Now, O Soul?		D. M. Williams	9
He Who Would Valiant Be	(B)	R. Broughton	3
Let Not Your Heart Be Troubled		E. Faning	1
The Chariots of the Lord		A. Whitehead	5
We Who Have Challenged Fate		R. G. Cole	5

COURTS

A Day in Thy Courts		G. A. MacFarren 1

COVENANT

Let Not the Wise Man Glory	H.L.	J. G. MacDermid	37
Lord God of Israel	(T)	C. S. Norris	2
The Secret of the Lord		J. E. West	1

CREATION

Creation Hymn		Rachmaninoff = Bornschein	4
God that Madest Earth and Heaven	(s)	H. A. Matthews	2
God that Madest Earth and Heaven		Trad = Lutkin	9
The Creation	SSAATTBB TTBB a-c	W. Richter	26
The Lord by Wisdom Hath Founded the Earth		G. Mead	25

CREATOR [v. God, Creation]

We Praise Thee, O Creator God	(H)	D. Protheroe	6

See Haydn's Oratorio "The Creation"

CREED [v. Faith]

Credo	M.	M. Andrews	9
Credo		D. S. Barrows	9
Credo		D. M. Williams	9
I Believe in One God		A. Gretchaninoff	9
My Creed	H.	E. Garrett	13
My Creed	SATB	E. Garrett	13
Nicene Creed		A. Gretchaninoff	9
Nicene Creed (Monotone)		G. E. Stubbs	9
The Cross		Tschaikowsky = Dickinson	9

CRISIS

Hear Our Prayer, O God	Tschaikowsky = Row	29

CROON

Croon Carol	S.	A. Whitehead	8
Croon of the Christ-Child		B. Posamanick	25

CROSS [v. Good Friday]

Come, Healing Cross		W. Berwald	9
Crucifix; Before the Cross	H.L.	F. LaForge	26
John ("Behold Thy Son")	H.L.	Ward-Stephens	21
John ("Behold Thy Son")	SATB	Ward-Stephens	21
The Cross	(B)	J. Ecker	2
The Cross	H.L.	H. Ware	3
The Veneration of the Cross		Rachmaninoff	9
When I Survey the Wondrous Cross	(A.B)	M. Andrews	2

[v. Stabat Mater   G. Rossini]
[v. Stabat Mater   A. Dvorak]

CROWN

Awake, My Soul	8 a-c	M. P. Ingle	9
Crown Him With Many Crowns	(S.B.)	J. W. Thompson	13
Crown on Calvary	H.L.	D. Protheroe	13
Lead On, O King Eternal		R. H. Terry	4
Rise, Crowned with Light		V. Eville	2

OF THORNS

A Legend	a-c	Tschaikowsky	9

CRUCIFIX

Crucifix; Before the Cross	H.L.	F. LaForge	26
The Crucifix	H-L	J. B. Faure	3

CRUCIFIXION [*v.* Good Friday]

CRUSADE [*v.* Church—Militant]

The Chariots of the Lord Are Strong	A. Whitehead	5

CRY [*v.* Advent, Voice]

Hear My Cry, O God	A. Kopyloff	2

CUP (a Symbol) [*v.* Communion]

DANGER [*v.* Trust]

In God We Trust	Mana-Zucca	28
Lighten Our Darkness (Short)	J. Booth	1

DANIEL [*v.* Biblical Passages, etc.]

The Vision of Belshazzar	TTBB	G. Bantock	51

DANTE

O Our Father Who Art in Heaven (The Lord's Prayer according to Dante)	N. Lockwood	25

DARKNESS

Clouds and Darkness		A. Dvorak	36
They that Sit in Darkness (Wanderer's Psalm)	A.	H. W. Parker	9
He Sent a Thick Darkness (Israel in Egypt)		Handel	*
Lighten Our Darkness (Short)		J. Booth	1

DARKNESS [*continued*]

Light in Darkness	(s)	D. C. Jenkins	1
The People that Walked in Darkness	(b)	Handel	*
Thou Wilt Keep Him in Perfect Peace		S. S. Wesley	1

DAVID

Hosanna to the Son of David		M. Mauro-Cottone	25
I Have Found David, My Servant	SSAATB	C. C. Palmer	8

DAWN [*v.* Morning]

Before Dawn		H. K. Andrews	15
Dawn in the Garden (Easter)	Jr and Sr	W. A. Goldsworthy	4
The Dawn Is Slowly Breaking	SSATTBB	V. d'Indy	2
Twilight and Dawn		O. Speaks	3
What of the Night	(t)	R. G. Thompson	9

DAY

A Day in Thy Courts		G. A. McFarren	1
Day Is Dying in the West	(m)	M. T. Salter	3
Eternal Day	s-a	H. W. Wareing	5
God Sends the Night		G. Rathbone	1
In That Day		F. W. Holloway	39
The Day of the Lord	u.	A. S. Warrell	15
The Great Day of the Lord	Chime	G. C. Martin	1

DAYSPRING

Dayspring of Eternity		J. S. Matthews	9
Dayspring of Eternity	(s.m)	R. Wichman	9

DEACONS [*v.* Stephen, Elders, Almsgiving, Charity]

DEATH

As Sinks beneath the Ocean		F. M. Christiansen	20
Behold, Ye Despisers		H. W. Parker	9
Blest Are the Departed	TTBB a-c	H. W. Parker	3
Come, Soothing Death	SSAA a-c	Bach=Davis	3
Come, Soothing Death	SATB	Bach=Christiansen	20
Come, Thou Last Summer Ray		F. M. Christiansen	20
Crossing the Bar	H.L.	C. Willeby	12
Death, I Do Not Fear Thee	TTBB	Bach	3
Death Is only an Old Door	M.	W. Harris	27

DEATH [*continued*]

From Thy Love, as a Father (Redemption)		C. Gounod	*
I Know no Life Divided	(B)	E. S. Barnes	2
In the Hour When Death	TTBB	H. M. Dow	3
I Sought the Lord	(A)	F. Stevenson	2
The Heart of the Night		H. Bath	1
There Is No Death	H.L.	G. O'Hara	22
There Is No Death	SATB TTBB	G. O'Hara	22
There Is a Reaper	S-S	C. Pinsuti	7
They Have Taken away My Lord	(S)	A. L. Scarmolin	39
Whispers of Heavenly Death	(M)	D. M. Williams	9

DEBORAH

The Song of Deborah	(A.T)	P. H. Goepp	3

DEBT

O Forgive Our Debts		F. Thome	26
Owe No Man Anything		F. McCollin	3

DECISION [*v.* Courage]

Choose Ye This Day	(S.A)	C. Nordman	39
He Who Would Valiant Be	(B)	R. Broughton	6
Like as the Hart	H.M.L.	F. Allitsen	27
Like as the Hart	H.L.	S. Liddle	27
Like as the Hart	(S)	S. Liddle	18
Love Not the World		A. Sullivan	1
If with All Your Hearts	T.	Mendelssohn	*
Silent and Alone	(A.T)	C. W. Henrich	2
The Ways	H.	D. H. Jones	1
Tomorrow Comes the Song	H.L.	P. Ambrose	5
What Christ Said	(B)	P. Lutkin	9

DECREES

How Dark, O Lord, Are Thy Decrees	O.	Handel	11

DEDICATION

A Life in God		F. M. Christiansen	20
Dedication Ode	(S.A.T.B.) O.	G. W. Chadwick	5

OF A CHURCH [*v.* Church—Dedication]

DEDICATION [*continued*]

OF CHIMES

O Bells, Send Forth the Triumph of Your Song		E. S. Kelley 2

OF SELF [*v.* Consecration]

DEFENCE

Give Ear to My Words		J. H. Rogers 2
Ninety-first Psalm	H.L.	J. H. MacDermid 37

DELAY

Lord, What Am I	(S-T) a-c	E. Margetson 9
While the Bridegroom's Coming Tarried		J. H. Mee 1

DELIVERANCE [*v.* Atonement, Salvation]

A Psalm of Deliverance	(S.A)	H. Gaul 17
Haste Thee, Lord, to Deliver Me	(S)	P. W. Smale 18
Ho! Everyone that Thirsteth	(B)	G. C. Martin 1
Ho! Everyone that Thirsteth	(T)	W. C. Macfarlane 3
Peace and Light	(T)	G. W. Chadwick 5

DEMONS [*v.* Satan]

DEPARTED [*v.* Funeral, Man—Hope of Immortality]

DEPENDENCE

Abide with Me	(S.A.T.B)	A. Depew 6
Abide with Me	(L.)	G. H. Federlein 39
Abide with Me	H.L.	S. Liddle 27
Abide with Me	(S.A)	S. Liddle 27
I Could not Do without Thee		E. A. Barrell 12
My Defence Is of God		B. Huhn 3

DEPTHS

Out of the Deep	H.L.	R. L. Bedell 3
Out of the Depths	L.	J. H. Rogers 5
Out of the Depths (De Profundis)	AATBB	L. Saminsky 11

DESERT [*v.* Wilderness]

Springs in the Desert	(T)	A. B. Jennings 9
The Ninety and Nine	H.L.	E. Campion 2

DESERT [continued]

The Ninety and Nine	(A.B)	D. Protheroe	2

DESIRE

Jesu, Joy of Man's Desiring		Bach	*
Lord, Thou Knowest All My Desire		S. Bett	8
More Love to Thee, O Christ	(s)	O. Speaks	3
Prayer, the Soul's Desire		F. N. Barbour	5

DESPISED

He Was Despised (Messiah)	A.	Handel	*
He Was Despised	(S.A.T)	E. S. Hosmer	2

DESPISING GOD

Behold, Ye Despisers	(B)	H. W. Parker	9
Invictus	H.L. (also TTBB)	B. Huhn	5
I Was a Foe to God	L.	G. W. Chadwick	9
The Fool Hath Said "There Is No God"		G. O'Hara	8

DESPONDENCY [v. Discouragement, Courage, Faith]

Be Not Dismayed, Thou Little Flock		M. Prætorius	8
He That Is Down	(s)	E. T. Sweeting	18
Like as the Hart	H.M.L.	F. Allitsen	27
Like as the Hart	(s)	F. Allitsen	27
Like as the Hart	M.L.	S. Liddle	27
Like as the Hart	(T.B)	W. C. Steere	7
My Hope Is in the Everlasting	T.	J. Stainer	1

DEUS MISEREATUR, THE

Deus Misereatur		Mrs. H. H. A. Beach	3

[v. Publishers' Catalogues]

DEUTERONOMY [v. Biblical Passages, etc.]

DEVIL [v. Satan]

DEW

A Prayer for Dew and Rain		Trad = Gaul	2
God of the Dew, God of the Sun	(S.A.T)	C. Whitmer	27
Soft Are the Dews of God	(Dbl Ch.)	C. Dickinson	9

DILIGENCE [*v.* Activity]

DISCIPLES [*v.* Apostles]

One of My Disciples	a-c	M. Haydn 3

DISCORD

As Discords 'neath a Master's Hand	(4 or 8)	M. Andrews 9
God's Peace Is Peace Eternal	(s)	E. Grieg 3

DISCOURAGEMENT [*v.* Despondency, Depths]

Beside Still Waters	(H)	B. Hamblen 41
Come, Ye Disconsolate	(S.A)	E. K. Macrum 9
Should E'er His Face Seem Turned from Thee (Church Cantata No. 186)		Bach *
Thy Servant Is Downcast		J. Brahms 8
Why Art Thou so Full of Heaviness	(H)	P. D. deCoster 9

DISCOVERY

If with All Your Hearts	T.	Mendelssohn *
The King's Highway	(s)	D. M. Williams 9

DISMISSAL [*v.* Close of Service, Nunc Dimittis]

DIVINITY [*v.* Christ, Deity of]

DOCTRINE

A New Commandment (Olivet to Calvary)		J. H. Maunder 1
Christ's Message	H.L.	C. Warford 5
How Fair the Church of Christ Shall Stand		F. M. Christiansen 20
My Doctrine Shall Drop as the Rain		P. Armes 1
There Is No Condemnation		H. S. Irons 1

DOOR [*v.* Gate, Portal]

Arise, Shine, for Thy Light Is Come	H.L.	J. G. MacDermid 37
Behold, I Stand at the Door (Long Anthem)	(M)	C. Whitmer 9
Behold, I Stand at the Door	(B.S)	Bach *
O Jesus, Thou Art Standing	(A)	D. Protheroe 13
The Lord Opened the Doors of Heaven		F. F. Harker 3
Unfold Ye Portals (Redemption)		C. Gounod *

DOUBLE CHORUS [*v.* Junior and Senior Choir]

All Glory, Laud and Honor		Bach = Aschenbrenner	8
Console My People		N. Hawkes	9
Holy Art Thou (Largo)	(s) o.	Handel = Whitehead	2
My God, O Why Hast Thou Forsaken Me?		Mendelssohn	*
O Eternal Truth (Commencement)		H. B. Gaul	4
O Praise the Lord of Heaven		R. V. Williams	18
O Saviour of the World		F. A. G. Ouseley	1
Praise the Lord		C. St.-Saens	3
Remember, O Thou Man		C. S. Lang	1
Sing to the Lord (Psalm 98)		Mendelssohn	1
Sing We Merrily (Festival)	a-c	M. Shaw	1
Soft Are the Dews of God		C. Dickinson	9
The Reproaches	a-c	H. Willan	9

DOUBT [*v.* Thomas, Decision]

Doubt Not Thy Father's Care	s-a	E. Elgar	9
If I but Lift Mine Eyes	h.l.	C. B. Lent	5
I Was a Foe to God	l.	G. W. Chadwick	9
The Fool Hath Said "There Is No God"		G. O'Hara	8
The Voice	h.l.	B. Leibert	3
Three Men Trudging		Provençal = Gaul	2

DOWN

He that Is Down	(s)	E. T. Sweeting	18

DREAM [*v.* Vision]

Sweet Dreams Form a Shade	ssa	E. S. Barnes	9

DRIFTING

Tomorrow Comes the Song	h.l.	P. Ambrose	5

DRINK

Ho! Everyone that Thirsteth	(t)	W. C. Macfarlane	3
Ho! Everyone that Thirsteth	(b)	G. C. Martin	1, 2
Ho! Everyone that Thirsteth	(s.b)	H. L. Vibbard	3
Whosoever Drinketh of this Water		P. Ambrose	5

DROUGHT [*v.* Mendelssohn's "Elijah"]

A Prayer for Dew and Rain	Trad = Gaul	21
If Ye Walk in My Statutes	J. Clippingdale	1

DUTY [*v.* Debt, Obligations]

EAR

Eye Hath not Seen		M̂. B. Foster	1
Eye Hath not Seen	A.	A. R. Gaul	*
Give Ear unto My Prayer		J. Arcadelt	1

EARTH [*v.* World]

Darkness Obscured the Earth	a-c	M. Haydn	3
The Lord by Wisdom Hath Founded the Earth		G. Mead	25

EASTER

Alleluia! Christ Is Risen	a-c SATB TTBB SSA	A. Kopyloff	2
Alleluia! O Day of Glory	Dbl Ch.	L. F. Heckenlively	9
An Easter Antiphon	Dbl Ch.	T. F. H. Candlyn	9
Beyond the Starry Skies	(S.B) v.c.Hrp.	H. Gilbert	9
Calvary and Easter	SSATTBB a-c	W. Wild	8
Christ Conquereth		J. W. Clokey	4
Christ Is Risen Today	SSA	K. K. Davis	25
Christ the Lord Hath Risen	Dbl Ch. o.	C. S. Lang	1
Christ Triumphant	(T) o.	P. A. Yon	4
Easter Bells	8 a-c	F. M. Christiansen	20
Hail, Thou Glorious Easter Day		Nagler = Dickinson	9
(o. or v.c.Hrp. or 2 Tr 2 Trm & Tym)			
Hearken Unto Me	(S.B) Hrp	C. F. Manney	2
Hymn Exultant	(M)	J. W. Clokey	9
Joy Dawned again on Easter Day	Jr and Sr	R. Bitgood	9
Spring Bursts Today	6 a-c	V. D. Thompson	9
Star of the Coming Day	(A.T) v.c.Hrp	H. Gilbert	9
The Day New-Born		H. A. Matthews	2
The Lights of Easter	(T) a-c	Norwegian = Gaul	25
The Strife Is O'er		F. W. Snow	29
There Is No Death	H.M.L.	G. O'Hara	22
There Is No Death	SATB	G. O'Hara	22
The World Itself Keeps Easter Day	SSAA (S)	K. K. Davis	25

[*v.* Publishers' Announcements and Catalogues]

EASTER CAROLS OF THE NATIONS

Alsace

Victory		Trad = Gaul	2

America

Easter Carol		S. Jessop	9
Six Carols	U.	E. S. Barnes	3

Brittany

The Three Lilies		Trad = Gaul	25

Czecho-Slovakia

Our Risen Lord		Trad = Gaul	21

England

All in the Morning		R. V. Williams	18

France

We Come with Voices Swelling		Trad = Voris	9

Germany

A Joyous Easter Song	SATB TTBB	Trad = Dickinson	9
Ancient German Easter Carol		Trad = Gaul	2

Holland

Today Did Christ Arise		Trad = Whitehead	2

Norway

The Lights of Easter	(T)	Trad = Gaul	25

Poland

When the Dawn Was Breaking	(S.A) v.c.Hrp	Trad = Dickinson	9

Russia

Alleluia ! Christ Is Risen		A. Kopyloff = Gaul	2

Spain

Spanish Easter Procession		Trad = Gaul	2

Negro

Jedus Is Risen		Trad = Gaul	2

ECCLESIASTES [*v.* Biblical Passages, etc.]

ECCLESIASTICUS [*v.* Biblical Passages, etc.]

ECHO CHOIR [v. Antiphonal Choir]

Hark! What Mean those Holy Voices?	(A)	C. W. Henrich	2
Lord God of Israel	(T)	C. S. Norris	2
The Lame Shepherd	(T)	W. R. Voris	9
Whence those Sounds Symphonious?		C. H. Kitson	18
While Shepherds Watched	SATB TTBB SSAA	Jüngst=Dickinson	9

EDEN [v. Heaven]

Eastward in Eden	(A)	C. W. Cadman	26
Hearken unto Me	(S)	F. Stevenson	2

EGYPT

Israel in Egypt, Oratorio		Handel	1
The Song of Miriam, Cantata	(S)	Schubert	1

ELDERS

All They from Saba Shall Come	(T)	L. Sowerby	9
And When They Had Ordained Them Elders		E. H. Thorne	1
Blow Ye the Trumpet	(T)	R. H. Woodman	3
Now There Lightens upon Us		L. Sowerby	9

ELEGY [v. Memorial, Funeral]

ELIJAH

Elijah, Oratorio	Mendelssohn	*

ELIZABETH, St. [v. Benedictus, John the Baptist]

Come Marie, Elizabette	SATB, U., 2	C. Dickinson	9

EMBER DAYS

A Day in Thy Courts		G. A. MacFarren	1
Awake, Awake, Put on Thy Strength		J. Stainer	1
Ho! Every One that Thirsteth	(T)	W. C. Macfarlane	3
Ho! Every One that Thirsteth	(B)	G. C. Martin	1
How Beautiful upon the Mountains	(S)	F. F. Harker	3
O Come, Every One That Thirsteth (Elijah)		Mendelssohn	*

EMMAUS

The Walk to Emmaus		H. W. Davies	1
The Walk to Emmaus	(H.B)	G. B. Nevin	5

ENCOURAGEMENT

He Who Would Valiant Be	(B)	R. Broughton	3
Master of Men		J. S. and H. A. Matthews	2

END

Before the Ending of the Day	(B)	C. Huerter	3
I Am Alpha and Omega	(M)	A. Sullivan	1
Lord, Make Me to Know Mine End		C. Lucas	17
The Year Will Be Soon Ended	a-c	J. A. Schulz	8

ENDURANCE [v. Church—Militant]

Blessed Are They Which Are Persecuted	H.L.	Ward-Stephens	3
He Who Would Valiant Be	(B)	R. Broughton	3
O Lord, Thy Word Endureth	(A-T)	E. H. Lemare	5

ENEMY [v. Foe]

Be Merciful unto Me	(B)	E. A. Sydenham	1
Hear My Prayer, O Lord		W. Berwald	9
Hear My Prayer, O Lord	(A.T)	L. B. Phillips	2
Let God Arise and Let His Enemies Be Scattered		T. W. Surette	9
Now Is Our Last Dread Enemy		Joseph = Dickinson	9

ENRICHMENT

Enrich Us with Thy Bounty	Bach = Besly	27

ENTREATY [v. Supplication]

Entreaty	M.	R. R. Peery	37
Intreat Me Not to Leave Thee	A.	W. Watts	3

EPHESIANS [v. Biblical Passages, etc.]

EPIPHANY [v. Benedictus]

For Behold, Darkness Shall Cover the Earth	B.	Handel	*
Now There Lightens upon Us		L. Sowerby	9
When to the Temple Mary Went		A. B. Jennings	9

ETERNAL LIFE [v. Immortality, Heaven, Eternity]

Eternal Day	S-A	H. W. Wareing	5
Eternal Father	Chimes	G. Holst	14
Eternal God, Whose Power Upholds	U.	R. H. Woodman	9
Eternal Love	H.L.	W. H. Pfarre	41
Eternal Ruler of the Ceaseless Round	(A)	F. L. Sealy	9
God, the Eternal Ruler		T. T. Noble	5
Hymn to the Eternal		Schubert	8
I Know a Home Eternal	(B)	F. M. Christiansen	20
Lead On, O King Eternal		G. Edmundson	4
O Perfect and Eternal One	H.L.	M. Browning	27
The Eternal Shepherd	(A.B)	A. H. Ryder	2

ETERNITY

Dayspring of Eternity	8 a-c	J. S. Matthews	9
Dayspring of Eternity	(M°)	R. Wichman	9
Great Is Thy Love	(A)	Bohm = Arnold	26
Immanuel's Land		F. F. Bullard	6
Jesus, the Very Thought of Thee	(S)	H. Housely	5

EVANGELISTIC SERVICES [v. Invitation]

The Ninety and Nine	H.M.L.	E. Campion	3
The Ninety and Nine	(A.B)	D. Protheroe	2

EVE [v. Adam]

EVE

Christmas Eve	SAATB (A)	H. Howorth	13
Easter Eve	H.	C. Gounod	*

EVENING

Before the Ending of the Day	(B)	C. Huerter	3
Darkening Night the Land Doth Cover	a-c (S)	E. Margetson	25
Evening Hymn to the Trinity	a-c	M. Andrews	9
Nightfall		F. L. Lawrence	9
Now the Day Is Over	(A)	A. B. Targett	9
Now the Shades of Evening	S-A-T	Mendelssohn = Cornell	3
O Most Blessed Jesu	a-c	H. C. Banks	9
The Shadows of the Evening Hour	TTBB (B)	Barri = Salter	3
Thou Who Dwellest Supreme	(A)	T. C. Whitmer	9

EVIL

O Ye that Love the Lord		H. W. Wareing	1
Remember Now Thy Creator		A. R. Gaul	1
Remember Now Thy Creator		J. P. Scott	26

EVOLUTION

Eternal Ruler of the Ceaseless Round		M. Genet	9
Eternal Ruler of the Ceaseless Round	(A)	F. L. Sealy	9
Eternal Mysteries	a-c	T. T. Noble	5

EXAMPLE [v. Christ—Example]

EXILE

Behold the Days Come	(T)	H. H. Woodward	1
By the Waters of Babylon	(H)	S. Coleridge-Taylor	1
[v. Babylon]			
Far from Their Home		H. H. Woodward	1
The Flight into Egypt	SSA	M. Bruch	3
The Harp and the Wilderness		C. Loomis	13

EXODUS [v. Biblical Passages, etc.]

[v. Egypt]

EXPANSION [v. Growth]

EYE

Battle-Hymn of the Repubiic		W. Steffe	*
Eye Hath not Seen		M. B. Foster	1
Eye Hath not Seen (Holy City)	(A)	A. R. Gaul	3
I Will Lift Up Mine Eyes		J. H. Barnby	1
I Will Lift Up Mine Eyes		F. LaForge	12
I Will Lift Up Mine Eyes		J. H. Mortimer	1
I Will Lift Up Mine Eyes	(A)	L. Sowerby	2
Lift Thine Eyes	S-S-A	Mendelssohn	*
Lord, Let Thy Spirit	(B)	W. Y. Webbe	9
My Eyes for Beauty Pine		H. Howells	15
The Eyes of the Lord		H. B. Gaul	6

EZEKIEL [v. Biblical Passages, etc.]

FACE

Behold, Two Blind Men		J. Stainer	1
Here, O My Lord, I See Thee Face to Face		P. W. Whitlock	15
In Heaven Above	8 a-c	F. M. Christiansen	20
Now the Shades of Evening	S-A-T	Mendelssohn	3
Now to the Lord a Noble Song	(S.A)	G. Borch	6
O Wondrous Type	8 a-c	F. M. Christiansen	20
Rock of Ages	SATB (H) TTBB	D. Buck	2
Turn Thy Face from My Sins	(H)	T. Atwood	3

FAITH

A Prayer of Faith	M.	Lawson = Rogers	3
Be Still, Be Still	(A-B)	C. P. Scott	5
Come, Faithful Lord	(T)	Handel = Trench	9
Faith	L.	H. Enders	16
Faith in His Love		E. H. Lemare	5
Faith Is the Way	H.L.	Ward-Stephens	21
Faith of Our Fathers		M. H. Carroll	2
Faith of Our Fathers		J. S. Matthews	9
From Thy Love as a Father (Redemption)		C. Gounod	*
I Do Not Ask, O Lord	H.L.	C. G. Spross	12
I Do Not Ask, O Lord	M.	R. R. Peery	37
In Faith I Calmly Rest	(M)	Bach = Dickinson	9
In Heavenly Love Abiding	(S)	H. W. Parker	1
Lord, I Believe	M.	J. C. H. Beaumont	9
My Faith Looks up to Thee	(S.A.B) V.	P. A. Schnecker	2
O Thou in All Thy Might	(T)	C. P. Scott	2
The King of Love	(A.S-B)	H. R. Shelley	3
The Lord Is My Shepherd		J. W. Clokey	4
The Lord Is My Shepherd	(S)	S. B. Gaines	2
The Lord Is My Shepherd	O.	Schubert	1
Thomas (Be Not Faithless, But Believing)	H.L.	Ward-Stephens	21
Thomas (Be Not Faithless, But Believing)		Ward-Stephens	21

FAITHFULNESS [*v.* Fidelity]

FALL

Adam Lay Ibounden		Ancient Carol	18
There Is No Condemnation		H. S. Irons	1
[*v.* Creation, Oratorio]		Haydn	

FALSITY

Seek Not after False Prophets	H.L.	H. Grunn	3

FAMILY [*v.* Generation]

Blow Ye the Trumpet	(T)	R. H. Woodman	3

FAR

How Far Is it to Bethlehem?	SSA	R. Donovan	9
How Far Is it to Bethlehem?		G. Shaw	9

FAREWELL

Mary's Farewell to Her Friends at Bethlehem	a-c	A. Whitehead	1
Shepherd's Farewell to the Holy Family		H. Berlioz	35
The Lord Bless You and Keep You	SATB TTBB SSA	P. Lutkin	16

FASTING [*v.* Lent]

Lord, Who throughout the Forty Days		A. Fickenscher	11
Turn Ye to Me		W. A. Barrett	1

FATE

We Who Have Challenged Fate		R. G. Cole	5

FATHER [*v.* God]

Be Near Me, Father	H.L.	W. M. Felton	12
Dear Lord and Father	(T)	J. L. Galbraith	2
Dear Lord and Father	(S.A.B)	A. B. Targett	9
Faith of Our Fathers		M. H. Carroll	2
Father, in Thy Mysterious Presence	(S)	J. S. and H. A. Matthews	2
Father Most Holy	(B) 8	F. M. Christiansen	20
Father of Liberty	U.	C. J. Roberts	8
Father of Love (Still wie die Nacht)		Bohm = Lester	13
Father of Mercies	(B)	S. P. Waddington	1
Father, Send a Child Again	a-c	B. Gross	13
Father, Take My Hand	S-A-B	C. E. Scott	8
Father, Thy Children Bow	a-c	A. Sullivam	2

FATHER [*continued*]

Father, We Are Pilgrims	(B)	N. W. Gade 39
Father, within Thy House We Kneel	(S)	S. D. Nevin 12
Like as a Father (Ruth)	L.	F. H. Cowen 3

FEAR

A Ballad of Christ on the Waters	a-c	E. S. Barnes 3
Could We but Know the Land		H. A. MacKinnon 9
Fear Not, O Israel	(S.A.T.B)	M. Spicker 3
Fear Not Ye, O Israel	H.L.	D. Buck 3
Fear Not Ye, O Israel		Buck = Deis 3
Fierce Was the Wild Billow	4 or 8	T. T. Noble 3
Hold Thou Me Up		S. B. Gaines 9
If the Lord Had Not Helped Me	(B)	E. C. Bairstow 1
I Sought the Lord	(A)	F. Stevenson 2
Let Not Your Heart Be Troubled		E. Faning 1
Lost in the Night	a-c	F. M. Christiansen 20
O Lord, Support Us All the Day Long	(A.T)	H. McAmis 3
O Love that Casts out Fear		W. Berwald 3
O Love that Casts out Fear		N. Coke-Jephcott 9
Prayer	M.	D. Guion 3
The Lord Is My Light	H.M.L.	F. Allitsen 27
The Ninety-first Psalm	H.M.L.	J. G. MacDermid 37
The Presence in the Silence		T. T. Noble 5

FEAR OF THE LORD

And All the People Saw		J. Stainer 1
Blessed Is He that Feareth the Lord		H. A. MacKinnon 9
Dwell Ye in Love		R. D. Shure 4
I Sought the Lord	(A)	F. Stevenson 2
The Ninety-first Psalm	H.M.L.	J. G. MacDermid 37

FEAST [*v.* Communion, Festival]

On the Feast of the Holy Kings		F. Erickson 9
O Sacred Feast		H. Willan 9

FEEDING

He Shall Feed His Flock	A.	Handel *

FELLOWSHIP [*v.* Brotherhood]

Master of Men		J. S. and H. A. Matthews 2
O for a Closer Walk with God	(H)	M. B. Foster 3

FESTIVAL

Behold, a King Shall Reign		H. C. Banks	9
Blow Ye the Trumpet	(T)	R. H. Woodman	3
Fantasia (Angel-voices Ever Singing)	(S.A.T)	E. S. Barnes	3
Festival Prelude		Bach = Stoessel	11
Hearken unto Me	(S.A.T.B)	Mrs. H. H. A. Beach	5
Hear, O Thou Shepherd of Israel		G. H. Federlein	9
Hear, O Thou Shepherd of Israel		H. B. Gaul	9
If the Lord Had Not Helped Me	(B)	E. C. Bairstow	1
I Have Surely Built Thee an House		W. Boyce	1
Let All Mortal Flesh Keep Silence			
Before Him	(S) 3 Trs, Bells, Cym. Tym.	Trad = Butcher	2
Lord, Thou Hast Been Our Refuge		E. C. Bairstow	1

FETTERS [v. Chains, Fetters]

Glory		C. W. Cadman	25

FIDELITY [v. Faith, Man—Duty to God]

Be Thou Faithful unto Death (St. Paul)	T.	Mendelssohn	*
Could Ye not Watch (The Atonement)	B.	S. Coleridge-Taylor	1
Could Ye not Watch (Crucifixion)	(B)	A. R. Gaul	*
Faith of Our Fathers		M. H. Carroll	2
Forever with the Lord	H.L.	C. Gounod	*
Still, Still with Thee	(S.A.T.B)	A. Foote	5
Still, Still with Thee	(S.T)	S. Salter	2

FIELDS [v. Forest, Nature, Woods]

Christ of the Fields and Flowers	(S)	H. B. Gaul	25
I Said, "Let Me Walk in the Field"		P. Lutkin	9
Out in the Fields		D. Protheroe	33
The Meadows of the Lord	H.	C. W. Cadman	12

FINDING [v. Seeking]

Art Thou Weary?	(S.A) v.	T. del Riego	2
If with All Your Hearts	T.	Mendelssohn	*
Jesus, the Very Thought of Thee	(H)	H. Houseley	5
O that I Knew Where I Might Find Him		W. S. Bennett	1

FIRE

O Lord, Send the Fire		N. Cain	40

FIRST-BORN
He Sent a Thick Darkness (Israel in Egypt)   Handel 1

FLAG-DAY [v Patriotism]

FLANDERS
In Flanders' Fields   SSATTBB   F. LaForge 3

FLESH
Behold All Flesh Is as the Grass
(Requiem)   J. Brahms 3
Let All Mortal Flesh Keep Silence   (S.B)   G. Holst 18

FLIGHT [v. Exile]
The Flight into Egypt   SSA (S) O.   M. Bruch 3
The Flight into Egypt (Oratorio)   H. Berlioz 3

FLOOD
Like Noah's Weary Dove   (A)   H. C. Banks 2
The Deluge, Cantata   C. St.-Saens 3

FLOWERS [v. Nature, Garden]
Angels Breathe on Flowers (Children's
Day)   J. Naylor 2
A Spotless Rose (Christmas Carol)   a-c   A. Rowley 18
Beauty in Humility   8 a-c   F. M. Christiansen 20
Christ of the Fields and Flowers   H. B. Gaul 25
Consider the Lilies   S-A   H. Topliff 7
Consider the Lilies   H.L.   R. Lee 13
Every Flower that Blossoms   8   H. R. Shelley 3
Gloria   H.L.   A. Buzzi-Peccia 26
Jesu, Fair Flower of Mary   TTBB   D. S. Smith 3.
Lo, How a Rose   M. Prætorius *
O Lovely Flowers (Song of Thanksgiving)   J. H. Maunder *
Praise   (S.B)   A. Rowley 15
The Flowering Manger   SSA   P. C. Buck 43
The Flower of Love   (M)   F. M. Christiansen 20
The Gardener God   M.   W. Barickman 13
We Thank Thee for the Flowers   F. H. Wood 18

FOLLOWING [v. Guidance]
Art Thou Weary?   (B)   G. W. Chadwick 5

FOLLOWING [*continued*]

Behold the Master Passeth By	(A)	F. Stevenson	2
Be Ye Therefore Followers of God	(T)	J. H. Rogers	3
Follow Me	(T)	H. R. Shelley	39
He Who Would Valiant Be	(B)	R. Broughton	3
The Following Love		J. S. Matthews	9
This Is the Sight that Gladdens	8	F. M. Christiansen	20

FORBEARANCE [*v.* Patience]

FOREIGN MISSIONS [*v.* Missions]

Declare His Glory	(A)	G. H. Federlein	3
Lost in the Night	a-c	F. M. Christiansen	20
Springs in the Desert	(T)	A. B. Jennings	9
The Lost Sheep	(S.B)	M. B. Foster	3
The Ninety and Nine	H.M.L	E. Campion	3
The Ninety and Nine	(A.B)	D. Protheroe	2

FOREST [*v.* Fields, Nature, Woods]

Down in Yon Forest	SSAA (S)	R. V. Williams	18
I Heard a Forest Praying	H.L.	P. de Rosa	22

FORGETTING

Forget, O Man, Thy Sorrow (Christmas Eve)		N. W. Gade	1
How Long Wilt Thou Forget Me?	M.	W. Oetting	9
How Long Wilt Thou Forget Me?	M.	Tschaikowsky=Peery	12
How Long Wilt Thou Forget Me?		A. D. Schmutz	13

FORGIVENESS

Dear Lord and Father	(T)	J. L. Galbraith	2
Dear Lord and Father	a-c	F. McCollin	25
Dear Lord and Father	(S.A.B)	A. B. Targett	9
Father, Forgive Them (Seven Last Words)		T. Dubois	3
Ho! Every One that Thirsteth	(T)	W. C. Macfarlane	3
Ho! Every One that Thirsteth	(B)	G. C. Martin	1
Ho! Every One that Thirsteth	(S.B)	H. L. Vibbard	3
O Forgive Our Debts		F. Thomé	26
O God Have Mercy (St. Paul)	B.	Mendelssohn	*
O Hear Thou from Heaven	(B)	Noble=Milligan	3
O Israel, Return		F. L. Sealy	9

FORGIVENESS [*continued*]

Praise the Lord		D. Protheroe	13
Put On, as God's Elect		E. S. Barnes	9
The Ninety and Nine	H.L.	E. Campion	3
The Ninety and Nine	(A.B)	D. Protheroe	2
The Lord Is Long-Suffering (Judith)		C. H. H. Parry	3
The Lost Sheep	(S.B)	M. B. Foster	3
The Prayer Perfect	SATB TTBB	O. Speaks	3
The Prayer Perfect	H.M.L.	C. J. Stenson	42
The Prayer Perfect	SATB TTBB SSAA SSA	C. J. Stenson	42
Turn Thee to Me		F. F. Harker	3

FORSAKENNESS [*v.* Abandonment]

Calvary	H.L.	P. Rodney	*
Go Not Far From Me, O God		R. N. Dett	4
Go Not Far From Me, O God		Zingarelli = Holler	9
How Long Wilt Thou Forget Me?	L. V.	Tschaikowsky	12
How Long Wilt Thou Forget Me?	M.	J. H. Rogers	3

FORWARD

Forward Be Our Watchword	(With Jr Choir)	W. L. Frost	14
Forward Be Our Watchword	(With Jr Choir)	L. Parker	14
Forward to God		G. O'Hara	22

FOUNDATION

Behold, I Lay in Zion a Stone	(B)	R. H. Prutting	26
The Lord by Wisdom Hath Founded the Earth		G. Mead	25

FOUNT

O Fount of Love Eternal	Wagner = Black	9

FRAGRANCE [*v.* Flowers]

Matins		M. Righter	21
The Woods and Every Sweet-smelling Tree	(S.T)	J. E. West	1
Whence Is that Goodly Fragrance?	U.	French = Baker	11
Whence Is that Goodly Fragrance?		French = Kitson	11

FRANCIS, St.

All Creatures of Our God and King	E. T. Chapman	11
Canticle of the Sun	Mrs. H. H. A. Beach	5

FRANCIS, St. [*continued*]

Canticle of the Sun		M. Shaw	14
Christmas in Greccio	a-c	C. Thomas	5

FRATERNAL SOCIETIES

God Is Love	TTBB	H. M. Dow	3
In the Hour When Death	TTBB	H. M. Dow	3
Light! Glorious Light	TTBB	H. M. Dow	3
O Ye Who Seek for Wisdom Here	TTBB	Wagner = Holden	2
To Him Who Rules	TTBB	H. M. Dow	3

FRATERNITY [*v.* Brotherhood]

These Things Shall Be	(H.M)	R. Broughton	2
They Shall Beat Their Swords	(A.T)	M. Andrews	25
Turn Back, O Man		G. Holst	17

FREEDOM [*v.* Bondage, Fetters, Nation, Release]

Flanders Requiem	H.L.	F. LaForge	26
Flanders Requiem		F. LaForge	26
Glad Tidings to Zion		F. M. Christiansen	20
Hymn of Thanksgiving		E. Kremser	*
Lord, I Pray Thee Set Me Free	TTBB	Kalliwoda	1
O Lord God of Hosts		H. B. Gaul	3
On, O Thou Soul (Marche Slav)	TTBB	Tschaikowsky = Page	11
The Pilgrim Fathers (Religious Freedom)	8 a-c	E. J. Stringham	9
These Things Shall Be		M. H. Carroll	2

FRIENDSHIP

Greater Love Hath No Man		J. Ireland	18
My Master and My Friend	TTBB a-c	F. H. Brackett	6
O Jesus, I Have Promised		D. Protheroe	13
O Saviour, Friend (Largo)	(s)	Handel	14

FULFILMENT [*v.* Church Triumphant, Immortality]

Asleep in Jesus	a-c	O. Bull	20
Fulfilment	L.	A. F. Kellog	12

FUNERAL

Blest Are the Departed	8	L. Spohr	1
Blest Are the Departed	TTBB	L. Spohr	1

FUNERAL [continued]

Blot Out Our Transgressions	(4 Trms)	Beethoven	1
Crossing the Bar	a-c	J. Barnby	3
Crossing the Bar	H.L.	C. Willeby	12
For a Soldier's Burial	(B)	L. Boulanger	17
Forever Blest Are They	TTBB (S°)	Mendelssohn	*
Invocation (Military)		Grieg = Harling	9
Now the Day Is Over	TTBB	Barnby = Lewis	2
O Blest Are They	8 a-c	Tschaikowsky = Cain	13
Requiem for a Little Child	SSAA	V. Harris	9
When Our Heads Are Bowed with Woe		G. W. Chadwick	5

FUTURE

God Holds the Future		R. S. Ambrose	5
Past and Future		H. Oakeley	9
These Things Shall Be	(H.M)	R. Broughton	2
They Shall Beat Their Swords	(A.T)	M. Andrews	25
Turn Back, O Man		G. Holst	17

GABRIEL [v. Angel, Annunciation]

And the Angel Gabriel	W. H. Monk	1
The Angel Gabriel	H. Smart	1
The Annunciation (Carol)	Trad = Smith	18

GALATIANS [v. Biblical Passages, etc.]

GALILEE

Galilee	(H)	C. W. Cadman	22

GARDEN

Christ Hath a Garden		E. Thiman	1
Christ Jesus in the Garden		Woyrsch = Dickinson	9
Dawn in the Garden	Jr and Sr	W. A. Goldsworthy	4
Our Jesus Hath a Garden		Trad = Whitehead	9
Our Jesus Hath a Garden	SSA v. or Fl.	Trad = Whitehead	9
Our Master Hath a Garden	(S)	H. E. Crimp	1
Our Master Hath a Garden		Trad = Clokey	11
The Gardener God	M.	W. Barickman	13
The Soul of the Garden	H.	W. Sektberg	17
Thy Word Is Like a Garden	(S.T.B)	C. Dickinson	9

GATE [v. Door, Portal]

A New Heaven and a New Earth (Holy City)	(B)	A. R. Gaul	3
Fling Wide the Gates (Crucifixion)		J. Stainer	*
Open the Gates of the Temple	H.L.	Mrs. J. F. Knapp	38
Open Wide, Ye Gates	8 a-c	W. Howorth	13
The Soul at Heaven's Gate	M. v.c.Hrp	C. Dickinson	9

GENERATION [v. Anniversaries]

Blow Ye the Trumpet	(T)	R. H. Woodman	3
Lord, Thou Hast Been Our Dwelling-Place	H.L.	L. B. Phillips	27
One Generation Passeth Away (Motet)	a-c	E. Walker	15
One Generation Shall Praise Thy Name to Another	TTBB (T)	J. N. Ashton	4

GENESIS [v. Biblical Passages, etc.]

GETHSEMANE

Christ Jesus in the Garden		Woyrsch = Dickinson	9
Could Ye Not Watch with Me? (The Atonement)	(B)	S. Coleridge-Taylor	1
Could Ye Not Watch with Me? (Crucifixion)	(B)	A. R. Gaul	1
Go to Dark Gethsemane		T. T. Noble	9
In Quiet Night		Trad = Brahms	8

GIFT [v. Offering]

Father, Once More within Thy Holy Place	8 a-c	H. A. Matthews	3
Giving to God		C. F. Manney	2
The Eternal Gift	H.L.	H. I. Harris	11
The Gift Supreme	H.M.L.	C. Smith	42

GLADNESS [v. Joy]

A Glad Prayer	H.M.L.	E. J. Stenson	42
A Glad Prayer	SATB TTBB	E. J. Stenson	42
Let Us with a Gladsome Mind		E. P. Chapman	55

GLORIA IN EXCELSIS, The

From Glory unto Glory		E. R. Warren	26

GLORIA IN EXCELSIS [*continued*]

Gloria in Excelsis		G. Borch	26
Gloria in Excelsis	TTBB	B. Tours	3
Whence those Sounds Symphonious?		C. H. Kitson	18
(Antiphonal Cho. ssAA)			

GLORIA PATRI, The

Gloria Patri	J. Barnby	9

[*v.* Publishers' Catalogues]

GLORY [*v.* Ascension, Gloria in Excelsis]

Angels from the Realms of Glory		H. C. Banks	9
Angels from the Realms of Glory	TTBB	H. C. Banks	9
Battle Hymn of the Republic		W. Steffe	*
Christ the Fair Glory		E. Bullock	8
Earth Is Full of the Glory of God		P. Lutkin	9
Gloria	H.L.	A. Buzzi-Peccia	26
Gloria	(H)	A. Buzzi-Peccia	26
Glory		C. W. Cadman	25
Holy, Holy, Holy	(M)	D. R. Emery	9
King of Glory	8 a-c	F. M. Christiansen	20
Sanctus (St. Cecilia Mass)	(T)	C. Gounod	*
The Glory of His Presence	H.	E. R. Warren	9

GOD

ATTRIBUTES OF

How Great, O God, Is Thy Goodness	(s)	R. F. Donovan	6
Lord of All Being	(B)	M. Andrews	9
My God, How Wonderful Thou Art		F. M. Christiansen	20
O Lord, Most Holy		A. Bruckner	9
Praise	(s.b)	A. Rowley	15
The Lord Is the True God		O. A. Mansfield	6
We Praise Thee, O Creator God	(H)	D. Protheroe	6

CREATOR [*v.* Creator]

FAITHFULNESS OF

Come, Faithful Lord (Largo)	(T)	Handel=Trench	9
He Faileth Not	(H)	H. W. Parker	9

GOD [*continued*]

Know then the Lord, Thy God, Is a Faithful God		Haydn 1
My Hope Is in the Everlasting	T.	J. Stainer 1
Trust in God at All Times	(H)	G. H. Knight 6

FATHERHOOD OF [*v.* Father]

FELLOWSHIP WITH

At Thy Feet	(M)	Bach = Liddle 18
Father, Teach Us to Know		C. Ellis 52
I Know No Life Divided	(S.B)	E. S. Barnes 2
I See Him Everywhere	H.L.	F. T. Maley 3
To Whom then Will Ye Liken God?		H. W. Parker 9
To Whom then Will Ye Liken God?	TTBB	H. W. Parker 9

FORGIVENESS OF [*v.* Forgiveness]

GLORY OF [*v.* Glory]

GRACE OF [*v.* Grace]

GUIDANCE OF [*v.* Guidance]

Search Me, O God	(A)	J. H. Rogers 3
Show Me Thy Way, O Lord		V. D. Thompson 9

HELP FROM [*v.* Help, Helplessness]

O God, Our Help	(s) Chime	C. L. Williams 1
Thou Hast Turned My Heaviness (Widow of Zarephath)		A. Gray 1

HOLINESS OF

Hear, O My People		de Vittoria = Strickling 40
Holy, Holy, Holy	(M)	D. R. Emery 9
I Saw the Lord		J. Stainer 1
O Holy Father		L. Jewell 9

INFINITY OF [*v.* Glory]

JUSTICE OF [*v.* Judgment]

KINGSHIP OF [*v.* King]

KNOWLEDGE OF [*v.* Understanding]

GOD [*continued*]

LONGING FOR [*v*. Man—Need of God]

Be Near Me, Father	H.L.	W. M. Felton 12
My Soul Is Athirst for God	(L)	F. J. Madsen 9
O for a Closer Walk with God	(H)	M. B. Foster *

LOVE FOR [*v*. Aspiration, Man—Need of God]

Dwell Ye in Love	(T)	R. D. Shure 4
O Lord of Life		F. L. Sealy 9

LOVE OF

And All the People Saw		J. Stainer 1
Behold What Manner of Love	H.L.	J. G. MacDermid 37
Behold What Manner of Love	(T)	C. A. Scholin 3
But the Lord Is Mindful of His Own	A.	Mendelssohn *
Come, O Thou Traveller Unknown		H. B. Gaul 6
Come, O Thou Traveller Unknown	(a-c 4 or 8)	T. T. Noble 3
God Is Love	(B)	H. R. Shelley 3
God So Loved the World		J. Stainer *
In Heavenly Love Abiding	(S)	H. W. Parker 1
Love Divine	S-T	J. Stainer *
The King of Love	(A.S-B)	H. R. Shelley 3

OMNIPOTENCE

Eternal God, Whose Power Upholds	U.	R. H. Woodman 9

PRAISE TO [*v*. Praise]

Awake up My Glory	(B)	G. W. Chadwick 5
The God of Abraham Praise	(S)	H. R. Shelley 3

PRESENCE OF [*v*. Presence]

Be Still, Be Still	(A-B)	C. P. Scott 5

PROTECTOR

Thou, O Lord, Art My Protector	H.	C. St.-Saens 3
Whoso Dwelleth under the Defence		G. C. Martin 1

PROVIDENCE OF [*v*. Thanksgiving]

Now Thank We All Our God		Bach = Holler 9

GOD [*continued*]
THE SEEKING

The Lost Sheep	(s.b)	M. B. Foster	3
The Ninety and Nine	h.m.l.	E. Campion	3
The Ninety and Nine	(a.b)	D. Protheroe	2

WILL OF [*v.* Will]

Whosoever Shall Do the Will of My Father (The Passion)		J. V. Roberts 1

WISDOM OF [*v.* Wisdom]

GODLESSNESS [*v.* Atheism]

Silent and Alone	(a.t)	C. W. Henrich	2

GOLD-STAR MOTHER

Gold-Star Mother of Mine	h.l.	G. O'Hara	17

GOOD FRIDAY [*v.* Holy Week, Passion]

A Ballad of Trees and the Master		C. W. Chadwick	2
At the Cry of the First Bird	m.	D. Guion	3
Darkness Obscured the Earth	a-c	M. Haydn	3
Greater Love Hath No Man		J. Ireland	18
Greater Love Hath No Man (Man of Nazareth)	h.	J. H. Rogers	3
Legend (Into the Woods)	(b) 6	W. Goodell	16
Near the Cross Was Mary Weeping		D. W. Kennedy	9
O Sacred Head now Wounded	(s)	F. Liszt	3
O Was there Ever Loneliness? (Olivet to Calvary)		J. H. Maunder	1
There Is a Green Hill Far Away	h.l.	C. Gounod	*
The Reproaches on Good Friday (Impropria)		Victoria = Schindler	2
The Sunlit Hill		C. A. Scholin	50

— — — — — —

LARGER WORKS

Olivet to Calvary	J. H. Maunder	1
The Passion Service for Good Friday	F. F. Harker	3
The Crucifixion	J. Stainer	1
The Seven Last Words	T. Dubois	3
The Story of the Cross	M. B. Foster	1

GRATITUDE [continued]

Psalm of Thanksgiving	(s)	F. Allitsen	6
Hymn of Thanksgiving		E. Kremser	*

GRAVE [v. Holy Saturday]

At the Sepulchre	(B)	G. B. Nevin	2
At the Sepulchre	TTBB	G. B. Nevin	2
Christ Lay in Death's Dark Prison		Bach=McKinney	4
Mary Magdalene at the Sepulchre		Schuetz=Dickinson	9

GREETING

How Beautiful upon the Mountains	H.L.	F. F. Harker	3
How Beautiful upon the Mountains	(s)	F. F. Harker	3
O Welcome in Our Midst (Hymn)		M. Shaw	14
We Wish You a Merry Christmas (Children)		C. H. Roth	48

GRIEVING GOD [v. Atheism, Despising God]

Surely He Hath Borne Our Griefs (Messiah)		Handel	*

GROWTH [v. Guidance, Pilgrimage]

From Glory unto Glory		E. R. Warren	26
New Every Morning Is the Love		B. L. Selby	1
O For a Closer Walk with God	(H)	M. B. Foster	1
O Master, Let Me Walk with Thee	(A.A-B)	G. C. Stebbins	2

GUARD

My Soul, Be on Thy Guard	H.	H. Nearing	9

GUEST

Come, O Thou Traveller		H. B. Gaul	6
Come, O Thou Traveller	8 or 4 a-c	T. T. Noble	*
Gaelic Rune of Hospitality	8	M. W. Hill	40

GUIDANCE [v. Bewilderment, Man—Need of God]

A Prayer (Ave Maria)	(s)	Schubert=Voris	9
Father of Mercies	(B)	S. P. Wadlington	1
Father, Take My Hand	TTBB	C. P. Scott	5
Gracious Lord of All Our Being		Bach	1
Guide Me, O Thou Great Jehovah	(A)	W. Berwald	9
Hold Thou My Hand	H.L.	C. S. Briggs	2

GUIDANCE [*continued*]

NATIONAL GUIDANCE

HABAKKUK [*v.* Biblical Passages, etc.]

HAGGAI [*v.* Biblical Passages, etc.]

HALLELUJAH

HAND

HAND [continued]

Hold Thou My Hand	H.L.	C. S. Briggs	2
Hold Thou My Hand	V.	C. S. Briggs	2
In His Hands (Come, let us Sing)	S-M	Mendelssohn	1
I Will Wash My Hands in Innocency		E. C. Bairstow	15
I Will Wash My Hands in Innocency	(S)	J. H. Rogers	3
Light	H.L.	F. Stevenson	2
My Hand in Thine		G. Borch	6
Shepherd, Take Me by the Hand	H.L.	Ward-Stephens	21
Shepherd, Take Me by the Hand		Ward-Stephens	21
Soft Were Your Hands, Dear Jesus	H.L.	G. O'Hara	3

HANDWRITING ON THE WALL

The Vision of Belshazzar	TTBB	G. Bantock	51

HARBOR

What Joy to Reach the Harbor	8	F. M. Christiansen	20

HARP [v. Instruments, Babylon]

And the Heavenly Hosts (Creation)		F. J. Haydn	3
List the Cherubic Host (Holy City)	(S.B)	A. R. Gaul	*
Lord of Spirits	a-c	F. M. Christiansen	20
O'er Waiting Harp-Strings of the Mind		J. G. MacDermid	49
Praise Ye the Lord (Long)		W. R. Voris	9
The Harp and the Willow		C. Loomis	13

HARVEST [v. Thanksgiving Day, Nature]

Fear Not, O Land		E. Elgar	1
O God, Who Is Like unto Thee?		M. B. Foster	1
Rejoice in the Lord		H. E. Darke	15
The Eyes of All Wait on Thee		M. B. Foster	1
The Parable of the Harvest		F. J. Sawyer	1
The Wilderness	(A.T.B)	J. Goss	1
Ye Shall Dwell in the Land	(S.B)	J. Stainer	1

HATE [v. Comminatory Psalms, such as Psalm 137]

This Is the Land where Hate Should Die		W. A. Fisher	2

HEAD

Christ Is the Head of the Church (Hymn)		G. E. Stubbs	9

HEAD [continued]

God Be in My Head		C. H. Kitson 18
Lift Up Your Heads, O Ye Gates	a-c	B. Klein 8
O Sacred Head now Wounded (Chorale)		Bach 9
O Sacred Head now Wounded	(s)	F. Liszt 3

HEALING [v. Physician]

Come, Healing Cross		W. Berwald 9
Come, Walk with Love	H.L.	S. Liddle 27
Heal Me, O My Saviour	L.	G. Godfrey 27
He Sent His Word and Healed Them		W. B. Olds 13
He that Dwelleth	H.L.	L. Meslin 27
Holy Spirit	H.L.	W. H. Pfarre 41
Light of God		Humperdinck = Shattuck 9
O Lord of Life	H.L.	Schubert = Rogers 25
Perfect Man		W. H. Pfarre 27
Prayer	SATTBB a-c	W. R. Davis 25
The Healing Christ	H.L.	W. H. Pfarre 41

HYMN-TEXTS

Jesus, Lord of Life and Glory	J. J. Cummins
Thou to Whom the Sick and Dying	G. Thring

HEARING

Hark, Hark, My Soul	(A)	H. R. Shelley 3
Hearken unto Me	(S.A.T.B)	Mrs. H. H. A. Beach 5
Hearken unto Me	(S)	F. Stevenson 2
Hearken unto Me	(S.B)	A. Sullivan 3
Hear Ye, Israel (Elijah)	S.	Mendelssohn *
Hear My Prayer	(A)	L. Saminsky 8
Hear My Prayer, O Lord		W. Berwald 9
Hear My Prayer, O Lord	(A.T)	L. B. Phillips 2
Lord God of Abraham (Elijah)	B.	Mendelssohn *
Today if Ye Will Hear His Voice	H.L.	J. H. Rogers 5

HEART [v. Sursum Corda]

Dear to the Heart of God		F. W. Vanderpool 12
If with All Your Hearts	T.	Mendelssohn *
Let Not Your Heart Be Troubled		E. Faning 1
The Heart Worships	H.L.	G. Holst 18
The Living God	H.L.	G. O'Hara 21

HEAVEN [v. Church—Triumphant, Man—Hope for Immortality]

ANTICIPATED

Behold the Days Come	(T)	H. H. Woodward	1
Dayspring of Eternity	(M°)	R. Wichman	9
Father of Mercies	(B)	S. P. Waddington	1
Here Life Is Quickly Gone (Hora Novissima)	S-A-T-B	H. W. Parker	1
Hymn to the Saviour	(s) Hrp	E. Kremser	3
Out of Heaven	(s)	F. H. Cowen	3
The City of God	(A)	W. H. Jones	8
The Vision of Christ	8 a-c	F. M. Christiansen	20
Who Is This?	(s)	H. E. Button	1

KEYS TO

Thou Art Peter	Palestrina	24
Thou Art Peter	Mendelssohn	1

LONGING FOR

Blessed Are the Poor in Spirit	(A)	F. F. Harker	3
Blessed City, Heavenly Salem		E. C. Bairstow	44
Far from My Heavenly Home	(S-M)	W. G. Hammond	7
God's Peace Is Peace Eternal	(s)	E. Grieg	3
I Know a Home Eternal	(B)	F. M. Christiansen	20
Lord of Our Life	(S.B)	J. T. Field	1
Sing Alleluia Forth	(S.T.B)	D. Buck	2
When to the Temple Mary Went	v.Hrp.	A. B. Jennings	9
Whoso Dwelleth under the Defense	(H)	G. C. Martin	1

HEBREWS [v. Biblical Passages, etc.]

HEIGHTS [v. Heaven, Glory, Aspiration, Growth]

Be Thou Exalted	S-T, A-B	B. Huhn	3
Save Me, O God	H.	A. Randegger	3
The Humble Shall Be Exalted	H.L.	J. E. Roberts	5
To God on High Enthroned (Mors et Vita)		C. Gounod	*
Unfold, Ye Portals Everlasting (Redemption)		C. Gounod	*
Whoso Dwelleth under the Defense	(H)	G. C. Martin	1

HEIRSHIP [v. Inheritance, Beatitudes]

HELL
God of Righteousness   H.L.   H. Gilbert 23
The Pains of Hell   E. G. Monk 1

*   *   *   *   *   *

The Last Judgment, Oratorio   L. Spohr 1

HELP [*v.* God—Help from, Hills]
If the Lord Had not Helped Me   (B)   E. C. Bairstow 1
Prayer for Daily Help (Short)   G. A. Burdett 3

HELPLESSNESS [*v.* Abandonment, Bewilderment, Guidance, Need]

HERALD [*v.* Ministry, Messenger]
Good Tidings to Zion   F. M. Christiansen 20
How Beautiful upon the Mountains   H.L.   F. F. Harker 3
How Beautiful upon the Mountains   (S)   F. F. Harker 3
How Lovely Are the Messengers   Mendelssohn *
Lovely Appear   (S)   C. Gounod *

HERITAGE [*v.* Inheritance]
Lord, Thou Hast Been Our Dwelling-
Place   L. B. Phillips 27
O God, Our Help   (S) Chime   C. L. Williams 1

HEROD
In the Days of Herod   (T.B)   S. Salter 3

HEROES [*v.* Saints, Martyrs]
Homage to Washington   F. Bornschein 11
Let Us Now Praise Famous Men   (S.T.B)   H. B. Gaul 17
Let Us Now Praise Famous Men   S. H. Nicholson 55
Let Us Now Praise Famous Men   U.   V. Williams 14
Lincoln   J. W. Clokey 11
To the Wayfarer   C. Forsyth 2

HESITANCY [*v.* Decision, Delay]
Christ's Knocking at My Sad Heart   P. A. Otis 16
O Jesus, Thou Art Standing   (A)   D. Protheroe 13
The Night Is Far Spent   (T)   H. V. Milligan 5

HIDING PLACE [*v.* Refuge]

HIGHWAY [*v.* Road]

| Springs in the Desert | (T) | A. B. Jennings | 9 |
| The King's Highway | (S) | D. M. Williams | 9 |

HILLS [*v.* Aspiration, Nature]

I Will Lift up Mine Eyes		J. H. Barnby	1
I Will Lift up Mine Eyes		J. H. Brewer	12
I Will Lift up Mine Eyes		F. F. Harker	26
I Will Lift up Mine Eyes		L. Sowerby	2
I Will Lift up Mine Eyes	(T)	L. Jewell	5
Christ Went up into the Hills	H.L.	R. Hageman	8
Christ Went up into the Hills	(H)	R. Hageman	8
Christ Went up into the Hills	H.L.	E. R. Warren	9
Christ Went up into the Hills	(S)	E. R. Warren	9
Hills		F. LaForge	17
O Silent Hills		R. D. Shure	4
There Is a Green Hill Far Away	H.M.L.	C. Gounod	*
There Is a Green Hill Far Away		C. Gounod	*
The Sunlit Hill		C. A. Scholin	50

HOLINESS [*v.* God—Holiness of]

| *The Beauty of Holiness* | H.L. | M. Van Dyke | 27 |
| Worship the Lord in the Beauty of Holiness | | T. Smith | 2 |

HOLY CITY [*v.* Heaven, New Jerusalem]

| Awake, Awake, Put on Thy Strength | | J. Stainer | 1 |
| The City of God | (A) | W. H. Jones | 5 |

— — — — — — — — —

| The Holy City, Oratorio | | A. R. Gaul | * |

HOLY GHOST [*v.* Holy Spirit]

HOLY SATURDAY

At the Sepulchre	(B)	G. B. Nevin	2
At the Sepulchre	TTBB	G. B. Nevin	2
Christ Lay in Death's Dark Prison		Bach=McKinney	4
Mary Magdalene at the Sepulchre		Schuetz=Dickinson	9

HOLY SPIRIT

| Come, Holy Spirit | | N. Coke-Jephcott | 9 |

HOLY SPIRIT [*continued*]

Come, Holy Spirit	(s)	C. St.-Saens 2
Fear Thou Not, for I Am with Thee		J. Booth 1
Grieve Not the Holy Spirit	(t)	T. T. Noble 9
Holy Spirit	h.l.	W. H. Pfarre 41
King All-Glorious	(t.b)	J. H. Barnby 1
Spirit of God		J. W. Thompson 8
Spirit of God		P. Weaver 25

HOLY THURSDAY [*v.* Communion, Confirmation, Passion]

Master, No Offering Costly and Sweet
Hymn-Text by E. P. Parker

HOLY WEEK [*v.* Good Friday, Passion]

TWELVE PASSION MOTETS	a-c	M. Haydn 3

All My Friends Forsake Me
Are Ye Come with Swords?
Could Ye then Not Watch!
Darkness Was over All
Now Are Mine Eyes Grown Dim
One of My Disciples
On Yon Dark Mount of Olives
Our Shepherd Is Departed
Sad Is My Soul
See How the Righteous One Dieth
Then the Veil Was Rent
Yonder Behold Him

The Angel of the Lord	8	von Woess = Williams 9

(Appropriate for Easter Monday)

HOME

Behold the Days Come	(t)	H. H. Woodward 1
Bless This House	h.l.	M. Brahe 27
Goin' Home		Dvorak = Fisher 2
Homeland, Dear Homeland		S. B. Gaines 11
Longing for Home	(m) a-c	F. M. Christiansen 20
Man Goeth Forth to His Work		A. Carnall 1
Peace Be to This House	8	R. L. Baldwin 3
Return, O Wanderer, to Thy Home	(s)	W. Berwald 2
The Eternal God Is Thy Home		Wolf = Davies 1

HOME [*continued*]

The Home-Light		J. C. Macy 2
Thy Home Is with the Humble, Lord		
Hymn-Text by F. W. Faber		

HOME MISSIONS [*v.* Social Service]

A Prayer for Our Country		W. R. Voris 9
Behold, Thou Shalt Call a Nation	(A.B.)	F. Stevenson 2
Beloved, if God So Loved Us		J. H. Barnby 1
Be Ye Kind One to Another	(B)	S. Liddle 14
Faith of Our Fathers		M. H. Carroll 2
Though I Speak with Tongues	(S.T)	E. Rohde 2
Thy Home Is with the Humble, Lord		
Hymn-Text by F. W. Faber		

HOPE

Gracious Lord of All Our Being		Bach 1
Hope Thou in God	TTBB	F. C. Mayer 3
My Hope Is in the Everlasting	T.	J. Stainer 1
Now the God of Hope	(B)	G. B. Nevin 6
To Us a Child of Hope Is Born	(S)	W. Berwald 3
Whoso Dwelleth	(H)	G. C. Martin 1

HOSANNA, The

Hosanna		T. Facer 14
Hosanna	H.L.	J. Granier *
Hosanna	SATB	J. Granier *
Hosanna in the Highest		F. M. Christiansen 20
Hosanna to the Son		Gibbons=Bantock 14
Hosanna to the Son		Prætorius=Buszin 50
Hosanna in the Highest		A. Sullivan 1
Hosanna to the Son of David		M. Mauro-Cottone 25

HOSPITAL [*v.* Physician]

HOSPITALITY [*v.* Greeting, Guest]

Gaelic Rune of Hospitality	8 a-c	M. W. Hill 40
Two Kings	8 Trs and Trms	J. W. Clokey 4

HOST [*v.* Heaven]

List the Cherubic Host	SSAA (S.B)	A. R. Gaul *

HOST [*continued*]
List the Cherubic Host   (B)   C. Harris   5

HOUR
In the Hour when Death (Masonic)   TTBB   H. M. Dow   3
In the Hour of Trial   W. Stickles 21
In the Hour of Trial   H-L   Rubinstein = Milligan   5

HOUSE OF GOD [*v.* Sanctuary, Tabernacle, Temple]

HUGUENOT [*v.* Reformation]
Jesus Lives   Trad = Gaul 25
Supplication (Huguenot Hymn of 16th
    Century)   A. Fuleihan   3

HUMILITY [*v.* Beatitudes]
A Little Child Came He   H.L.   C. Warford   5
Beauty in Holiness   a-c   F. M. Christiansen 20
But Who Am I and What Is My
    People?   H. W. Richards   1
In Humble Faith and Holy Love   H. M. Garrett   1
The Humble Shall Be Exalted   H.L.   J. E. Roberts   5
The Publican   H.L.   B. van de Water   2
Thy Home Is with the Humble, Lord
    Hymn-Text by F. W. Faber

HUMILIATION
Gallia   (S)   C. Gounod   *
Hear, O My People   de Vittoria = Strickling 40
Song in the Valley of Humiliation   E. Bullock 15

HUNGER [*v.* Thirst]
O For a Closer Walk with God   (S)   M. B. Foster   *
Like as the Hart   H.M.L.   F. Allitsen 27
Like as the Hart   (S)   F. Allitsen 27
Like as the Hart   H.L.   S. Liddle 27
Like as the Hart   S. Liddle 27
Like as the Hart   (T.B)   W. C. Steere   7
They Shall Hunger No More   S-A   A. R. Gaul   *

HYPOCRISY

Behold, Ye Despisers	(B)	H. W. Parker 9
The Publican	H.L.	B. van de Water 2

IDOLATRY

If with All Your Hearts (Elijah)	T.	Mendelssohn *

IMAGE [v. Likeness]

As We Have Borne the Image	SSATBB	J. H. Barnby 1
Behold What Manner of Love	H.L.	J. G. MacDermid 37
Behold What Manner of Love	(T)	C. A. Scholin 3
O God, Who Is Like unto Thee?		M. B. Foster 1
Source of Calm Repose	8 a-c	F. M. Christiansen 20

IMMANUEL [v. Christ]

Behold, a Virgin Shall Conceive (Messiah) (Recit.)		Handel *
Immanuel's Land	(A)	F. F. Bullard 6

IMMORTALITY [v. Church—Triumphant, Heaven]

Follow Me	(T)	H. R. Shelley 39
Forever with the Lord	H.L.	C. Gounod *
Forever with the Lord	SATB	C. Gounod *
Hark, Hark, My Soul	(A)	H. R. Shelley 3
I Am the Resurrection		C. Demarest 9
Immortality	M.	R. Kingsley 8
Immortality	H.L.	E. R. Park 5
Immortal Love	H.	Handel = Milligan 9
In My Father's House	H.M.L.	J. G. MacDermid 37
In My Father's House	H.M.L.	Ward-Stephens 22
The Righteous Live Forevermore		C. E. Miller 18

IMPORTUNITY [v. Petition]

INCARNATION [v. Christmas]

God Was Made Manifest in the Flesh		G. M. Garrett 1
He Sent His Word	H.L.	J. G. MacDermid 37
In the Beginning Was the Word		M. Andrews 9
Let All Mortal Flesh Keep Silence	(S.B)	G. Holst 18

INCENSE

Incense and a Pure Offering	(SATB)	Brock=Macrum 17
In Every Place Incense		J. E. West 1

INDECISION [*v.* Hesitancy]

INDEPENDENCE

Invictus	H.L.	B. Huhn 5
Invictus	TTBB	B. Huhn 5

INDIAN

Stars Lead Us Ever On	Trad=Gaul 2
The Sun-Worshippers	Zuni=Loomis 11
'Twas in the Moon of Winter Time	Indian=Yon 25

INDUCTION [*v.* Installation]

We Sent unto Thee	A. Hollins 1

INFANTS [*v.* Children]

INFINITY [*v.* Glory]

Eternal Ruler of the Ceaseless Round	(A)	F. L. Sealy 9
Infinite Mind	H.L.	W. H. Pfarre 41
To the Infinite	L.	Schubert 9

INGRATITUDE [*v.* Thanksgiving]

Behold, Ye Despisers	(B)	H. W. Parker 9
Thou Who Art Love Divine	SATB	G. W. Chadwick 5

INHERITANCE [*v.* Heritage, Beatitudes]

Come, Ye Blessed	H.L.	J. P. Scott 3
Come, Ye Blessed	(T)	J. P. Scott 3
The Lord Is the Portion of Mine Inheritance		C. B. Rootham 18

INNOCENCY

I Will Wash My Hands in Innocency		E. C. Bairstow 15
I Will Wash My Hands in Innocency	(S)	J. H. Rogers 3

INNOCENTS' DAY

My Hope Is in the Everlasting	T.	J. Stainer 1
These Were Redeemed (Introit)		G. A. Macfarren 1

INSTALLATION [*v.* Chimes, Organ, Minister]

How Beautiful upon the Mountains	H.L.	F. F. Harker	3
How Beautiful upon the Mountains	(s)	F. F. Harker	3
Lovely Appear	(s)	C. Gounod	*
They Shall Be Named the Priests of God		E. H. Thorne	1
We Sent unto Thee		A. Hollins	1
Zadok the Priest		Handel	1

INSTRUMENTS (Accompanying)

A Babe Lies in a Cradle	v.c.Hrp	Trad = Dickinson	9
Agnus Dei (Lamb of God)	(s)v.Hrp	G. Bizet	2
Andalusian Christmas Carol	Dbl. Ch.	Trad = Erickson	9
	(Castanets, Cym., Tamb.)		
Angelus (Maritana)	o.	M. V. Wallace	11
Art Thou Weary?	(s.a) v.	T. del Riego	2
A Song of Penitence	Hrp	Beethoven	9
Ave Maria	(s) v.Hrp	Bach = Gounod	2
Ave Maria (Cavatina)	H.L. V.	J. Raff	5
Basque Christmas Carol	(Castanets, Cym., Tamb.)	Trad = Erickson	9
Catalonian Christmas Carol	(Castanets, Cym., Tamb.)	Trad = Erickson	9
Christ the Lord Hath Risen	Dbl. Ch. o.	C. S. Lang	1
Christ Triumphant	(T) o.	P. A. Yon	4
Galician Christmas Carol	(Castanets, Cym., Tamb.)	Trad = Erickson	9
Hail, Gladdening Light	o. or Br.	G. C. Martin	1
Hail, Thou Glorious Easter Day		Nagler = Dickinson	9
	o. v.c.Hrp. 2 Tr. 2 Trms. Tym.		
Hearken unto Me	(s.B) Hrp	C. F. Manney	2
Heavenly Truth	c.Hrp	G. H. Knight	9
He Is Ours	(H) v.	H. Haaf	17
Hold Thou My Hand	H.L. V.	C. S. Briggs	2
Holy Art Thou (Largo)	(s) o.	Handel = Whitehead	2
Hymn to the Madonna	(s) Hrp	E. Kremser	3
Let All Mortal Flesh Keep Silence	(s.B) o.	G. Holst	18
Let All Mortal Flesh Keep Silence	(s)	Trad = Butcher	2
	3 Tr. Bells, Cym., Tym.		
My Faith Looks up to Thee	(s.a.B) v.	P. A. Schnecker	2
My Soul Doth Magnify (Christmas Oratorio)	s-T-B Hrp	C. St.-Saens	2
O Bethlehem	(a.s-T) v.c.Hrp	Trad = Dickinson	9
O Lord Most Holy	(T) v.c.Hrp	C. Franck	6
Our Jesus Hath a Garden	ssa v. or Fl.	Dutch = Whitehead	9

INSTRUMENTS [continued]

Pilgrims' Chorus	o.	R. Wagner	*
Remember Now, O Virgin Mary	ssa (s) p. and Org.	J. Massenet	3
Rex Gloriæ (Cantata, 8 min.)	v.p.Org.	S. R. Gaines	11
See Now the Altar (The Palms)	o.	J. Faure	*
Send Forth Thy Spirit	8. o.	F. J. Schuetky	11
Shepherds on the Hill	v.Fl.c.Hrp	Trad = Dickinson	9
Sleep, My Jesus	v.c.Hrp	Trad = Dickinson	9
Song of Praise (Adagio Pathetique)	(A) o.	Godard = Howorth	13
Star of the Coming Day	(A.T) v.c.Hrp	H. Gilbert	9
The Babe in the Manger	(s) v.c.Hrp.	Trad = Dickinson	9
The Flight into Egypt	ssa (s) o.	M. Bruch	3
The Great Eternal Christmas	(A.B) v.c.Hrp	H. Gilbert	9
The Red Cross Spirit Speaks	h. o.	H. W. Parker	9
	Also satb ttbb ssaa		
The Soul Triumphant	o.	T. T. Noble	9
Two Kings	2 Tr, 2 Trm.	J. W. Clokey	4
Whence Come Ye	v.c.Hrp	Trad = Dickinson	9
When to the Temple Mary Went	v.Hrp	A. B. Jennings	9

INTERCESSION [v. Mediator, Petition]

Intercession	ttbb	C. B. Rutenber	2
Intercessory Hymn		E. German	1
I Will Pray the Father	(t)	F. W. Holloway	5
Lord God of Abraham (Elijah)	(b)	Mendelssohn	*

INTERNATIONAL BROTHERHOOD [v. Brotherly Love]

A Prayer for the Nations	J. H. Rogers	12
Lord of the Nations (Lascia ch'io piango)	Handel	8

INTROIT [v. Call to Worship, Opening of Service]

Come, Let Us Sing		Mendelssohn	1
I Was Glad When They Said	(b)	J. L. Galbraith	5
God Is in His Holy Temple	(ttbb)	C. F. Mueller	3
v. "Introits for Sundays and Holy Days"		G. C. Martin	9

INVISIBILITY

O Love Invisible		H. A. Matthews	2

INVITATION

Come unto Him (Messiah)	s.	Handel	*

INVITATION [*continued*]

Come unto Me	H.L.	Beethoven=Aslanoff	3
Come unto Me	(S)	W. Coenen	2
Come unto Me	(A)	W. C. Gale	7
Come unto Me		C. B. Hawley	26
Come unto Me	(S or B)	C. Huerter	2
Come unto Me	H.M.L.	S. Liddle	18
Come unto Me	(B)	S. Liddle	18
Come unto Me	(H)	Tschaikowsky=O'Hare	26
Come, Ye Disconsolate	(S-A)	E. K. Macrum	9
Come, Ye Sin-Defiled and Weary		J. Stainer	1
Jesus Is Calling	H.L.	A. P. Risher	5
The Light of Life	(H)	V. Eville	27

INVOCATION [*v.* Opening of Service]

Invocation	M.L.	W. G. Hammond	3
Invocation	SAATB	A. Tregina	3
Invocation	ATTB a-c	C. Wood	8
Six Invocations		R. K. Biggs	26

ISAAC

Lord God of Abraham (Elijah)	B.	Mendelssohn	*

ISAIAH [*v.* Biblical Passages, etc.]

In the Year that King Uzziah Died	D. M. Williams	9

ISRAEL

Fear Not, O Israel	SSAATB (S.A.T.B)	M. Spicker	3
Hear, O Thou Shepherd of Israel		G. H. Federlein	9
Hear, O Thou Shepherd of Israel	(S.B)	H. B. Gaul	9
Hear Ye, Israel (Elijah)	S.	Mendelssohn	*
Lord God of Israel		H. N. Norris	2
O Israel, Return unto the Lord		F. L. Sealy	9

JACOB

And Jacob Was Left Alone		J. Stainer	1
God Is Our Refuge and Strength	8	C. F. Mueller	3
He that Is God of Jacob		L. Saminsky	6
Jacob's Well and Living Water		J. M. Fox	1
Jacob Lamented		Morales=Schindler	2
There Shall a Star from Jacob (Christus)		Mendelssohn	1

JAIRUS
v. The Daughter of Jairus, Cantata   J. Stainer   *

JAMES, St.
James (What Is Life?)	H.L.	Ward-Stephens	21
James (What Is Life?)	SATB	Ward-Stephens	21

JEHOVAH [*v.* God]
Great Is Jehovah	(s) o.	Schubert	*
Guide Me, O Thou Great Jehovah	(A)	W. Berwald	9

JEPHTHA
v. Jephtha, Oratorio   Handel   1

JEREMIAH [*v.* Biblical Passages, etc.]

JERUSALEM [*v.* Holy City, Zion]
A New Heaven and a New Earth	(B)	A. R. Gaul	*
If Thou Hads't Known, O Jerusalem		Ward-Stephens	21
Jerusalem	H.L.	H. Parker	*
Jerusalem	(L)	Parker=Protheroe	13
Jerusalem	TTBB (T)	H. Parker	*
Jerusalem, O Turn Thee (Gallia)	(s)	C. Gounod	*
Jerusalem the Golden		S. Thompson	13
The City of God		W. H. Jones	5

JESUS [*v.* Christ]

JEWRY [*v.* Israel]
In Jewry Is God Known	o.	J. C. Whitfield	14
In Jewry Is God Known		F. A. G. Ouseley	1

JOB [*v.* Biblical Passages, etc.]

JOEL [*v.* Biblical Passages, etc.]

JOHN, St. [*v.* Apostles, Biblical Passages, etc.]
John (Behold Thy Son)	H.L.	Ward-Stephens	21
John (Behold Thy Son)	SATB	Ward-Stephens	21

JOHN THE BAPTIST, St.

Among those that Are Born of Women		C. T. Powell	1
A Voice by Jordan's Shore			
Hymn-Text by S. Longfellow			
O Thou that Tellest (Messiah)	(A)	Mendelssohn	1
Prepare Ye the Way	(T.B)	G. H. Federlein	3
Prepare Ye the Way	(T.B)	L. Jewell	9
Saint John the Baptist		E. Bullock	15
This Is the Record of John	SAATB(T) a-c	O. Gibbons	1

JOINING THE CHURCH [v. Confirmation]

Accept My Heart	(M)	G. Borch	26
Learn to Say "Yes"	(S)	S. B. Gaines	19
My God, Accept My Heart this Day		Kücken = Brackett	12
You Ask Me How I Gave My Heart	H.L.	C. W. Ware	16

JORDAN [v. St. John the Baptist]

JOSEPH, St.

As Joseph Was a-Walking		P. N. Miles	18
Joseph Dearest, Joseph Mild	V.	L. V. Saar	8
Joseph Tender, Joseph Mild	M.	Trad = Dickinson	9
Joseph's Carol		R. C. Maryott	13

JOSHUA [v. Biblical Passages, etc.]

JOY [v. Gladness]

Awake, Awake, Put on Thy Strength		J. Stainer	1
Blow Ye the Trumpet	(T)	R. H. Woodman	3
Deck Thyself, My Soul, With Gladness	8 a-c	F. M. Christiansen	20
Evening and Morning		M. Spicker	3
Glad that I Live Am I	a-c	G. Shaw	15
Hallelujah Chorus (Messiah)		Handel	*
Hallelujah Chorus (Saul)	TTBB	Handel	*
Ho, Every One that Thirsteth	(T)	W. C. Macfarlane	3
Ho, Every One that Thirsteth	(B)	G. C. Martin	1
Ho, Every One that Thirsteth	(S.B)	H. L. Vibbard	3
My Soul Shall Be Joyful	(A)	G. H. Federlein	3
O Be Joyful in the Lord	(T)	C. Franck	3
There Is Joy in the Presence of the			
Angels (Prodigal Son)		A. Sullivan	1
The Seven Joys of Mary (Carol)		A. Whitehead	5

JUBAL
O Had I Jubal's Lyre (Joshua)   Handel   1

JUBILATE DEO, The [*v.* Publishers' Catalogues]
Jubilate Deo   M. Andrews   9'
Jubilate Deo   T. T. Noble 9
Jubilate Deo   L. Sowerby   9
Jubilate Deo   D. M. Williams 9

JUBILEE [*v.* Festival]

JUDAH
In Judah Is God Known (St. Paul)   Mendelssohn *
O Judah, Chosen Seed (Athalia)   L.   Handel   *

JUDAS
Know'st Thou then Poor Judas   SAATB   von Bruck = Williamson 3
Judas (Friend, wherefore art thou come?)   H.   Ward-Stephens 21
Judas (Friend, wherefore art thou come?)   Ward-Stephens 21

JUDE [*v.* Biblical Passages, etc.]

JUDGES [*v.* Biblical Passages, etc.]

JUDGMENT
Behold, Judgment Will I lay to the
  Line   L. A. Coerne   2
Declare His Glory among the Heathen   (A)   G. H. Federlein 3
Enter Not into Judgment   M. Richardson 18
God's Peace Is Peace Eternal   (S)   E. Grieg   3
Great Peace Have They   (H)   J. H. Rogers 3
His Sceptre Is the Rod of Judgment
  (Judas Maccabæus)   B.   Handel   1
Judge Me, O God   8 a-c   Mendelssohn   *
Now the God of Hope   (B)   S. B. Nevin 6
The Day of Judgment   C. P. E. Bach 9
The Great Day of the Lord   Chime   G. C. Martin   1
The Last Judgment   (H)   C. P. E. Bach 9
The Lord of Heaven   H.   C. Forsyth 9
There Is No Condemnation   H. S. Irons   1
Thou Judge of the Quick and Dead   S. S. Wesley 1

JUDITH [*v.* Biblical Passages, etc.]

JUNIOR CHOIR (With Senior Choir)

Beautiful Yule-Tide		F. M. Christiansen 20
Blessed Jesus	a-c	F. M. Christiansen 20
Christ Is Risen		C. F. Mueller 26
Dawn in the Garden		W. A. Goldsworthy 4
Fairest of Roses		F. M. Christiansen 20
Hail! Festal Day	(3 Choirs—SA, SAB, SATB)	Baden-Powell 26
Hills of the North		S. Bett 8
Hosanna		Trad = Bitgood 9
O Give Thanks unto the Lord		C. F. Mueller 26
Praise Ye the Lord		Molitor = Goldsworthy 4
Resurrection	(s)	M. W. Belcher 9

JUSTICE [*v.* Righteousness]

Path of the Just	(H)	F. F. Parker 3
The Justice of God		A. Buzzi-Peccia 3

JUSTIFICATION [*v.* Atonement, Conversion, Salvation]

Greater Love Hath No Man	(s.B)	A. Rowley 18
Path of the Just	(H)	F. F. Harker 3
There Is No Condemnation		H. S. Irons 1

KEEPING

Art Thou Weary?	(B)	G. W. Chadwick 5
He that Keepeth Israel	M.	B. Treharne 3
Keep, We Beseech Thee		J. Lyon 18
Thou Wilt Keep Him in Perfect Peace	SATTB	S. S. Wesley 1
The Lord Is My Keeper		V. D. Thompson 9

KEYS [*v.* Heaven, Gate, Door, Portal, Peter]

KINDNESS [*v.* Brotherly Love]

Be Ye Kind One to Another	(B or T)	S. Liddle 14

KING

Conquering Kings Their Titles Take		J. H. Maunder 6
King All Glorious	SSATBB, SATB (T.B)	J. Barnby 1
King of Kings	H.M.L.	F. H. Brackett 31
Lead On, O King Eternal		R. H. Terry 4

KING [*continued*]

My King Rode in Through the City
  Gates   (S.A.T.B.)   L. Baumgartner 9
On the Feast of the Holy Kings   F. Erickson 9
Praise, My Soul, the King of Heaven   TTBB   M. Andrews 3
Rex Gloria, Cantata (8 Min.)   (S.A.T.B.)   S. R. Gaines 11
                         Cho, Narrator, V., P., Org.
The King of Kings   J. P. Dunn 4
The King of Love   H.M.L.   W. Dichmont 31
The King of Love   (A.B.S-B)   H. R. Shelley 3
The King's Welcome   A. Whitehead 2
The Lord Is King   R. H. Woodman 5
They Were All Looking for a King   C. Dickinson 9
Two Kings   (2 Tr. and 2 Trm.) J. W. Clokey 4
Zadok the Priest Anointed Solomon   Handel 1

KINGDOM [*v.* Holy City, Lord's Prayer]

A New Heaven and a New Earth   (B)   A. R. Gaul *
Kingdom of Light   P. Lutkin 9
The Kingdom of God   8 a-c   F. M. Christiansen 20

KINGDOM OF GOD ON EARTH [*v.* Church—Militant, Brotherhood, Missions]

I. KINGS [*v.* Biblical Passages, etc.]

KNEELING [*v.* Petition, Prayer]

Father, in Thy Mysterious Presence
  Kneeling   (S)   J. S. and H. A. Matthews 2
Father, Within Thy House We Kneel   (S)   S. D. Nevin 12

KNOCKING [*v.* Portal, Hesitancy, Decision]

Behold, I Stand at the Door   C. Whitmer 9
O Jesus, Thou Art Standing   (A)   D. Protheroe 13

KNOWING [*v.* Assurance]

If Thou Had'st Known, O Jerusalem   Ward-Stephens 22
I Know that My Redeemer Lives   S.   Handel *
Lord of the Worlds Above   (S.B.)   Mrs. H. H. A. Beach 2
My Redeemer Lives   H.L.   H. Gilbert 4

KYRIE ELEISON, The

Lord, Have Mercy		W. Rodgers	9
Kyrie Eleison	(3-fold)	T. T. Noble	9
Kyrie Eleison	(9-fold)	T. T. Noble	9

LABOR [v. Work]

Come, Labour On	a-c	F. W. Snow	5
O Son of the Carpenter		G. B. Nevin	2

LABOR DAY

Psalm to Labor (Priests' March)	Mendelssohn	11

LAKE [v. Water, Nature]

LAMB [v. Agnus Dei]

Agnus Dei (Lamb of God)	(H) v.Hrp.o.	G. Bizet	2
All in the April Evening		H. S. Roberton	14
Behold the Lamb of God (Messiah)		Handel	*
Lamb of God		V. Kallinikoff	6
Listen to the Lambs	(s) 8	R. N. Dett	3
Listen to the Lambs	TTBB(T) SSAA(S)	R. N. Dett	3
None other Lamb	(s)	H. Sanders	2
Sheep and Lambs	H.L.	S. Homer	3
Sheep and Lambs		S. Homer	3

LAMENTATION [v. Sorrow, Biblical Passages, etc.]

Lamentations (Long)	T. Tallis	1

LAMP [v. Light, Lantern]

Thy Word is a Lantern	H. Purcell	1
Thy Word is a Lantern	L. Scarmolin	8

LANTERN [v. Light, Novelties]

Like Silver Lamps (Christmas)	J. Barnby	1
Thy Word is a Lantern	L. Scarmolin	8

LAST SUPPER [v. Communion]

The Last Supper (La Cena) (20 Min.)	o.	Malipiero	11
The Tower (Cantata)	(Chorus only)	E. L. Bainton	14

LAST THINGS [*v.* Day, End, Judgment]

In the Last Days It Shall Come to Pass	(s.t)	J. H. Rogers	3
Day of Anger (Requiem)		Mozart	*

LAW [*v.* Commandments]

Great Peace Have They which Love			
Thy Law	(h)	J. H. Rogers	3
I am the Vine	(s.t)	P. James	23
If Ye Walk in My Statutes		J. Clippingdale	1
Know'st Thou the Ordinances of			
Heaven	a-c	C. Demarest	3
My Son, Forget Not My Law	m.	W. W. Adams	8
The Law of the Lord	(s)	G. H. Federlein	3

LAYING ON OF HANDS [*v.* Ordination]

And Paul Came to the Congregation		
(St. Paul)		Mendelssohn	3

LEADERSHIP [*v.* Guidance]

Christ is the Head of the Church			
(Hymn)		G. W. Stubbs	9
He Leads Us On	a-c	W. R. Voris	5
Lead Us, O Father	(a)	W. T. Timmings	8

LEGACY [*v.* Heritage, Inheritance]

In My Father's House	h.m.l.	J. G. MacDermid	37
In My Father's House	h.m.l.	Ward-Stephens	22

LEGEND

A Legend	SATB TTBB SSAA SSA	Tschaikowsky	*
Legend (Into the Woods)	(b) 6	W. Goodel	16
Legend of the Bells	SSAATBB (s)	R. V. Rhodes	13
The Blind Ploughman	h.l. (Also SATB and TTBB)	R. C. Clarke	22
The Knight of Bethlehem	8 a-c	L. Wetzel	13
The Lame Shepherd	(t)	W. R. Voris	9
The Legend of the Cross-Bill (Easter)	m.	Le Chevalier = Lemmens	19
The Miracle of St. Nicholas		Trad = Davison	35
Three Men Trudging		Provençal = Gaul	2

LENT [*v.* Ash Wednesday, Good Friday, Passion]

A Ballad of Trees and the Master	h.l. (Also SATB)	G. W. Chadwick	2
A Ballad of Trees and the Master	m.l.	L. P. Rile	9

LENT [*continued*]

Did Christ o'er Sinners Weep?		F. E. Ward	2
Jesu, Only to Think of Thee		Vittoria = Schindler	2
Legend	SATB, TTBB, SSAA, SSA	Tschaikowsky	*
Legend (Into the Woods)		W. Goodel	16
Lord, Who throughout the Forty Days		A. Fickenscher	11
Out of the Deep	(B) a-c	F. W. Snow	9
Shall We Deny Our Lord!	(A.B)	C. B. Blount	12
There Is a Green Hill Far Away		C. Gounod	*
There Is a Green Hill Far Away	(B)	C. Jenkins	4
Thy Life Was Given for Me		G. H. Knight	9
What Is My Hope?		H. B. Gaul	12

[*v.* Publishers' Announcements and Catalogues]

LEVITICUS [*v.* Biblical Passages, etc.]

LIBERTY [*v.* Freedom]

LIFE

Here Life Is Quickly Gone (Hora Novissima)	S-A-T-B	H. W. Parker	1
I Know No Life Divided	(S.B)	E. S. Barnes	2
Life, Truth, Love	M.	M. Browning	1
Lord of Our Life	(S.B)	J. T. Field	1
The Path of Life	(T)	F. L. Sealy	9
Thou Shalt Show Me the Path of Life		A. Gray	1

LIGHT

All Praise to God	(B)	Wagner = Cornell	3
Arise, Shine, for Thy Light Is Come	H.M.L.	J. G. MacDermid	37
At Eventide It Shall Be Light (*Holy City*)	S-S-A	A. R. Gaul	*
Break, Diviner Light	H-H. L-L	F. Allitsen	27
Dayspring of Eternity	(M°)	R. Wichman	9
Dayspring of Eternity	8 a-c	J. S. Matthews	9
Hail, Gladdening Light	O. or Br.	G. C. Martin	1
Hear, O Thou Shepherd of Israel	(S.B)	H. B. Gaul	9
Kingdom of Light	(H)	P. Lutkin	9
Lead, Kindly Light	TTBB	D. Buck	2
Lead, Kindly Light (Long)	(B)	C. Jenkins	4

LIGHT [*continued*]

Let there Be Light	(B)	W. R. Spence	2
Let Your Light so Shine		H. Hadley	9
Light	H.L.	F. Stevenson	2
Light at Evening-Time	(A)	S. Dalton	2
Light in Darkness	(S)	C. Jenkins	1
Light of God		Humperdinck=Shattuck	9
Light of Life (Processional)		G. F. LaJeune	9
Light of Light		J. H. Weisel	9
Light's Glittering Morn (Easter)	(B)	H. W. Parker	3
Lord, Be Our Light	(A)	G. F. Tooke	9
O Light Everlasting	SSA	A. W. Wilson	1
O Trinity of Blessed Light		J. E. West	1
O Wondrous Light		A. W. Kramer	5
Peace and Light	(T)	G. W. Chadwick	5
Rise, Crowned with Light		V. Eville	2
Round Me Falls the Light		F. W. Snow	9
Saviour, Breathe an Evening Blessing	(S)	C. Huerter	2
Send Out Thy Light	O.	C. Gounod	*
The Light at Eventide	(A)	H. B. Gaul	2
The Light of the World		J. S. Matthews	9
The Lord Is My Light	H.M.L.	F. Allitsen	27
The Lord Is My Light	(H)	F. Allitsen	27
The Lord Is My Light		H. W. Parker	3
Thou Art, O God, the Light		F. M. Christiansen	20
Thy Word Is a Lantern unto My Feet		L. Scarmolin	8
Twenty-Seventh Psalm	H.L.	C. Edwards	3
Walk in the Light	(T)	R. H. Prutting	3

LIKENESS [*v.* Image]

O God, Who Is Like unto Thee?		M. B. Foster	1
Some Morning, O Some Morning	M.	Mrs. R. R. Forman	12
To Whom then Will Ye Liken God?	(A.B)	M. Andrews	25
To Whom then Will Ye Liken God?	SATB TTBB	H. W. Parker	9

LINCOLN [*v.* Nation, Patriotism]

An Abraham Lincoln Song	(B) O.	W. Damrosch	21
Lincoln		J. W. Clokey	11

LIVING [*v.* Life]

Behold, Ye Despisers	(B)	H. W. Parker	9

LIVING [*continued*]

Glad that I Live Am I	a-c	G. Shaw	15
In Him We Live	(A.T)	H. L. Baumgartner	2

LONELINESS [*v.* Abandonment, Forsakenness]

Go Not Far from Me, O God		R. N. Dett	4
Go Not Far from Me, O God		Zingarelli=Holler	9
Jesus Walked this Lonesome Valley (Negro Spiritual)	SATBB	W. L. Dawson	13
O Was there Ever Loneliness (Olivet to Calvary)		J. H. Maunder	1
Was Ever Loneliness Like His? (Triumph of the Cross)	T.	H. A. Matthews	3

LONGING [*v.* Aspiration, Man—Search for God]

A Few More Years Shall Roll		F. Butcher	9
By the Waters of Babylon	(B)	S. Coleridge-Taylor	1
By the Waters of Babylon	(H)	C. T. Howell	2
By the Waters of Babylon		P. James	9
By the Waters of Babylon		P. Lutkin	9
By the Waters of Babylon	(S.B) O.	L. Saminsky	3
I Have Longed for Thy Salvation (Stabat Mater)	S-A-T-B	G. Rossini	1
Like as the Hart	H.M.L.	F. Allitsen	27
Like as the Hart	(S)	F. Allitsen	27
Like as the Hart	H.L.	S. Liddle	27
Like as the Hart	(S)	S. Liddle	27
Like as the Hart	(T.B)	W. C. Steere	7
Longing for Home	(M) a-c	F. M. Christiansen	20
My Eyes for Beauty Pine		H. Howells	15
My Soul Is Athirst for God (Holy City)	T.	A. R. Gaul	*
O Come to My Heart, Lord Jesus	(B)	P. Ambrose	2
O for a Closer Walk with God	(S)	M. B. Foster	*
The Roseate Hues of Early Dawn	(S)	D. D. Slater	14

LORD [*v.* Christ, God]

LORD'S DAY [*v.* Sabbath]

Send Forth Thy Spirit	SSATTBB a-c	F. J. Schuetky	11
This Is the Day		A. R. Gaul	1

LORD'S PRAYER

The Lord's Prayer		E. T. Carter 3
The Lord's Prayer		H. R. Evans 13
The Lord's Prayer		H. B. Gaul 6
The Lord's Prayer (Pastoral Symphony)		Handel 2
The Lord's Prayer		A. O. Schmutz 13
The Lord's Prayer		W. R. Voris 9
The Lord's Prayer	H.L.	A. H. Malotte 3

LORD'S SUPPER [v. Communion]

LOST [v. Bewilderment, Longing]

Lost in the Night (Missions)	a-c	F. M. Christiansen 20
The Lost Sheep	(S.B)	M. B. Foster 3
The Lost Star	SSATBB a-c	B. Gross 13
The Ninety and Nine	H.L.M.	E. Campion 3
The Ninety and Nine	(A.B)	D. Protheroe 2

LOVE [v. God—Love of]

A Song in the Night	(S.B)	R. H. Woodman 3
Behold What Manner of Love	(T)	C. A. Scholin 3
Come, O Thou Traveller Unknown		H. B. Gaul 6
Come, O Thou Traveller Unknown	(8 or 4)	T. T. Noble 3
Dwell Ye in Love		R. D. Shure 4
Eternal Love	H.L.	W. H. Pfarre 41
Faith, Hope and Love	S-S-A.	H. R. Shelley 3
God Is Love	(A)	D. Protheroe 13
God Is Love	H.L.	W. B. Olds 13
God Is Love	TTBB	H. M. Dow 3
Greater Love Hath No Man	(S.B)	J. Ireland 18
Immortal Love	H.	Handel=Milligan 9
Love Divine	S-T	J. Stainer 1
Put On, Therefore, as God's Elect		E. S. Barnes 9
The Greatest of These Is Love	(S.A.T)	R. Bitgood 9
The Greatest of These Is Love	(S.A)	M. Andrews 17
The King of Love	H.M.L.	W. Dichmont 31
The King of Love	(A.S-B)	H. R. Shelley 3
Thine Forever, God of Love	(B) Jr and Sr	H. E. Button 1
Thou Grace Divine		F. M. Christiansen 20

LOVELINESS [v. Beauty]

Lovely Appear (Redemption)		C. Gounod *

LOYALTY [v. Fidelity]

LUKE, St. [v. Biblical Passages, etc.]

Ho! Every One that Thirsteth	(T)	W. C. Macfarlane 3
Ho! Every One that Thirsteth	(B)	G. C. Martin 1
Ho! Every One that Thirsteth	(S.B)	H. L. Vibbard 3

LUKEWARMNESS [v. Hesitancy, Indecision]

LULLABY

A Cradle Hymn	SSATB	F. M. Christiansen 20
A Slumber Song of the Madonna	H.L.	M. Head 27
Christmas Eve	SAATB (A)	H. Howorth 13
Lullaby on Christmas Eve		F. M. Christiansen 20
Lullaby to the Little Christ Jesus	(S)	A. Floyd 4
Lute-Book Lullaby	SSATTB a-c	H. W. Friedell 25
Sleep, Holy Babe		F. W. Snow 53
The Chimes' Lullaby		H. R. Shelley 3
The Virgin's Lullaby	SSA	M. Reger 2
Thou Child Divine	(S.T)	French = Voris 9

LYRE

O Had I Jubal's Lyre (Joshua)	S.	Handel *

MADONNA [v. Mary, Virgin]

A Slumber Song of the Madonna	H.L.	M. Head 27
Hymn to the Madonna	(S) Hrp	E. Kremser 3
Our Lady of Sorrows	H.L.	G. O'Hara 17
Song to the Virgin		L. Woodgate 18
Unto the Birth-Giver of God		Archangelsky = Row 29
When Mary through the Garden Went		P. Judd 15

MAGI [v. Epiphany, Christmas]

The Magi Journey Far (Carol)		A. Whitehead 1

MAGNIFICAT, The

My Soul Doth Magnify the Lord		G. H. Federlein 9
My Soul Doth Magnify the Lord (Christmas Oratorio)	S-T-B Hrp	C. St.-Saens 3
My Soul Doth Magnify the Lord		D. M. Williams 9
My Soul Doth Magnify the Lord	(S.B)	L. Shenk 8

MAKER [v. God]

God of All Nature	o.	Tschaikowsky=Loomis	11
O Lord, the Maker of All Things		A. R. Gaul	9
Praise	(s.b)	A. Rowley	15

MALACHI [v. Biblical Passages, etc.]

MAN [v. Christian]

DUTY TO FELLOW MEN [v. Brotherhood, Missions, Social Service]

And All the People Saw		J. Stainer	1
Make Us Strong	8 a-c	Nagler=Dickinson	9

DUTY TO GOD [v. Consecration, Obedience]

Behold, the Master Passeth By	(a)	F. Steverson	2
My Master and My Friend	TTBB	F. H. Brackett	6
Obedience 'tis, the Lord of Hosts Demandeth	b.	F. Hiller	3

FALL OF [v. Fall]

HOPE OF IMMORTALITY [v. Immortality, Christ—Triumphant]

MORTALITY OF [v. Mortality]

NEED OF GOD [v. Aspiration]

Go Not Far from Me, O God		R. N. Dett	4
Go Not Far from Me, O God		Zingarelli=Holler	9
I Need Thee Every Hour	(s)	W. Berwald	5
Lord, We Pray, in Mercy Lead Us	(s)	Sibelius=Sammond	10
The Ninety and Nine	H.M.L.	E. Campion	3
The Ninety and Nine	(s.b)	D. Protheroe	2

PILGRIM [v. Pilgrimage]

SEARCH FOR GOD [v. Seeking]

SONSHIP UNDER GOD [v. Father]

Dear Lord and Father	(t)	J. L. Galbraith	2
Dear Lord and Father	(s.a.b)	A. B. Targett	9
Doubt Not Thy Father's Care (The Light of Life)	s-a	E. Elgar	1

MAN [*continued*]
SURRENDER TO GOD [*v.* Consecration, Conversion]

MANGER [*v.* Christmas, Lullaby]
Away in a Manger	s.	C. Dickinson	9
Away in a Manger	h.l.	E. Martin	27
Song of the Crib (Carol)		V. Williams	15
The Manger		H. Willan	9
The Virgin at the Manger	ssa(Bell)	A. Perilhou	2
The Virgin by the Manger	sa	C. Franck	3

MANNA
Dear Lord and Father	(t)	J. L. Galbraith	2
Dear Lord and Father	(s.a.b)	A. B. Targett	9
How Sweet the Name of Jesus	8	P. D. deCoster	1
The Lord Opened the Doors of Heaven		F. F. Harker	3

MANSIONS [*v.* Heaven, Man—Hope of Immortality]
Build Thee More Stately Mansions	(b)	M. Andrews	3
Build Thee More Stately Mansions		A. Farwell	11
Build Thee More Stately Mansions	a-c	C. F. Mueller	26
In My Father's House	h.m.l.	J. G. MacDermid	37
In My Father's House	h.m.l.	Ward-Stephens	22
Let Not Your Heart Be Troubled		E. Faning	1

MARCHING [*v.* Processionals]
Lead On, O King Eternal		R. H. Terry	4

MARK [*v.* Biblical Passages, etc.]

MARK, St.
Happy and Blest Are They (St. Paul)	Mendelssohn	*

MARRIAGE [*v.* Wedding]

MARTYRS
Art Thou Weary?	(s.a)	T. del Riego	2
Be Thou Faithful unto Death	t.	Mendelssohn	*
Happy and Blest Are They (St. Paul)		Mendelssohn	*
Jerusalem, Thou that Killest the Prophets			
(St. Paul)	s.	Mendelssohn	*

MARTYRS [*continued*]

Martyrs of the Arena		L. deRille	14
The Son of God Goes Forth to War		A. Sullivan	9

MARY, St. [*v.* Annunciation, Christmas, Madonna, Virgin]

Come, Marie, Elisabette	U. or 2 or SATB	C. Dickinson	9
Mary Kept All These Things	(S.A.T.B)	E. S. Barnes	6
Near the Cross Was Mary		D. W. Kennedy	9
O Jesus, Son of Mary		M. S. Smith	18
Remember Now, O Virgin Mary	SSA (S) P. and Org.	J. Massenet	3
There Stood Three Maries	(S)	H. A. Matthews	3
The Seven Joys of Mary	(S)	Trad=Whitehead	5
The Song of Mary		Fischer=Kranz	17
Thou Tiny Child of Mary		W. Wolstenholme	18

MARY MAGDALENE, St.

Come, Ye Sin-Defiled and Weary	J. Stainer	1
Mary Magdalene at the Sepulchre	Schuetz=Dickinson	9

MASONIC SERVICES

Dangers of Every Form	TTBB (T)	Wagner=Holden	2
God Is Love	TTBB	H. M. Dow	3
In the Hour when Death	TTBB	H. M. Dow	3
O Ye Who for Wisdom Here	TTBB	Wagner=Holden	2
To Him Who Rules	TTBB	H. M. Dow	3

MASTER [*v.* Christ]

Ballad of Trees and the Master		G. W. Chadwick	2
Legend (Into the Woods)	(B) 6	P. Goodel	16
Master of Men		H. A. and J. S. Matthews	2
My Master and My Friend	SATB TTBB	F. H. Brackett	6
O Master, Let Me Walk with Thee	(A)	G. W. Stebbins	2

MATTHEW, St. [*v.* Biblical Passages, etc.]

How Beautiful upon the Mountains	(S)	F. F. Harker	3
Lovely Appear (Redemption)	(S)	C. Gounod	*
v. Passion According to St. Matthew			
(Oratorio)		Bach	*

MAUNDY THURSDAY [*v.* Holy Thursday]

MEAT [v. Harvest]

Grace After Meat		Whythorne = Warlock	8
Grace Before Meat		Whythorne = Warlock	8
The Eyes of All Wait on Thee	(s)	M. B. Foster	1
The Eyes of All Wait upon Thee		A. R. Gaul	1

MEDIATOR [v. Christ—Mediator, Intercession]

God So Loved the World	H.M.L.	J. G. MacDermid	37
God So Loved the World	(s)	W. R. Voris	9
In the Hour of Trial	H.L.	Rubinstein = Milligan	5
I Will Pray the Father		F. W. Holloway	5

MEDICAL SERVICES [v. Healing, Physician]

MEEKNESS [v. Beatitudes, Humility]

Jesus, Meek and Gentle	P. Ambrose	5
Jesus, Meek and Gentle	J. Holler	9

MELCHISADECH

Thou Art a Priest Forever	S. Wesley	3

MEMORIAL SERVICES

A Dirge for Two Veterans	(s)	N. Lockwood	21
Battle-Hymn of the Republic		W. Steffe	*
Be Thou Faithful unto Death	T.	Mendelssohn	*
Greater Love Hath No Man	(s.b)	J. Ireland	18
Hush, for amidst Our Tears		R. G. Jones	13
Hymn of Peace and Good Will	(s.a.t.b)	W. A. Fisher	2
O Blest Are They	8	Tschaikowsky = Cain	13
O Rest in the Lord	A.	Mendelssohn	*
Recessional	SSATBB (T) O.	H. A. Matthews	3
Recessional	(B)	R. deKoven	7
Rest in Peace	(A)	Schubert	9
The Cross	a-c	E. S. Barnes	6
What Are These that Glow from Afar?	O.	A. Gray	18

MENTAL HEALTH [v. Healing]

Dear Lord and Father	(T)	J. L. Galbraith	2
Dear Lord and Father	(s.a.b)	A. B. Targett	9
Let This Mind Be in You	(s.b)	Mrs. H. H. A. Beach	7
Let This Mind Be in You		C. W. Cadman	26

MENTAL HEALTH [*continued*]

My Peace I Leave with You		Schubert	9
Spirit of God	(S.B)	T. A. Humason	5
The Healing Christ	H.L.	W. H. Pfarre	41
Thou Wilt Keep Him in Perfect Peace		S. S. Wesley	1

MERCY

Approach, My Soul, the Mercy-Seat	(M)	J. W. Thompson	5
Be Merciful unto Me	(B)	E. A. Sydenham	1
Blessed Jesu, Fount of Mercy		A. Dvorak	1
Father of Mercies	(B)	S. P. Waddington	1
Fifth Beatitude	TTBB	Franck = Bingham	9
God Be Merciful	(S.B)	Mrs. H. H. A. Beach	3
Lord, We Pray, in Mercy Lead Us	(S)	Sibelius = Sammond	10
Mercy and Truth		D. Bortniansky	9
My Song Shall Be Alway of Thy Mercy (Vol. 1, Sacred Duets)	(H-H)	Mendelssohn	7
Neath the Throne of Mercy	(S°)	M. Bruch	
New Every Morning Is the Love		B. Luard-Selby	1
There's a Wideness in God's Mercy	(H)	J. S. Matthews	9
To the Lord Our God Belong Mercies (*Holy City*)	T.	A. R. Gaul	*

MESSAGE [*v.* Gospel, Heralds]

Christ's Message	H.L.	C. Warford	5
The Master's Last Message	M.	C. S. Burnham	3
The Message		J. Kürsteiner	46

MESSENGER [*v.* Heralds, Ministry]

How Beautiful upon the Mountains	(S)	F. F. Harker	3
How Lovely Are the Messengers		Mendelssohn	*
Lovely Appear (Redemption)	(S)	C. Gounod	*
Now Are We Ambassadors	T-B	Mendelssohn	*
O For a Closer Walk with God	(S)	M. B. Foster	3
Prepare Ye the Way	(T.B)	G. H. Federlein	3
Prepare Ye the Way	(T.B)	L. Jewell	9
The Message		J. Kürsteiner	46
Winged Messengers of Peace	O.	H. H. Huss	3

MICAH [*v.* Biblical Passages, etc.]

MICHAEL, St.

An Italian Carol of St. Michael		H. B. Gaul 17
Then Came the Archangel (Motet)	SAATB a-c	Palestrina 1
There Was War in Heaven		W. A. C. Cruickshank 1

MIDNIGHT [v. Night]

At Midnight there Was a Cry   A. Ham 9

MIGHT [v. God—Praise to, Providence of]

O Thou in All Thy Might   (T)   C. P. Scott 2

MILITARY SERVICES [v. Armistice, Nation, Patriotism]

MILK & HONEY (A Symbol) [v. Heaven, Zion, Jerusalem]

Jerusalem the Golden	S. Thompson 13
The Lord Hath Brought Us into a Land	E. H. Thorne 1

MILLENIUM [v. Kingdom]

A New Heaven and a New Earth (Holy
City)   (B)   A. R. Gaul *

MIND [v. Mental Health]

God Be in My Mind		A. Buzzi-Peccia 26
Infinite Mind	H.L.	W. H. Pfarre 41
Let This Mind Be in You	(S.B)	Mrs. H. H. A. Beach 7
Let This Mind Be in You		C. W. Cadman 26
Let Us with a Gladsome Mind		E. P. Chapman 55

MINISTRY [v. Installation, Ordination]

Blessed Are They that Dwell in Thy House	(T)	C. Dickinson 9
Blessed Is He that Feareth the Lord		F. W. Snow 2
Breathe on Me, Breath of God		V. D. Thompson 9
Breathe on Me, Breath of God	(s°)	C. E. Wheeler 16
Breath of God	H.L.	M. T. Salter 3
Ministry of Song	8 a-c	C. F. Mueller 25
They Shall Be Named the Priests of the Lord (In Folio)	(s)	E. H. Thorne 1
We Sent unto Thee		A. Hollins 1

MIRACLES

Dear Friend, Whose Presence in the
  House. Hymn-Text (J. F. Clark)

He Went Forth Rejoicing	H.M.L.	A. H. Sovereign	42
The Blind Ploughman	H.L. also TTBB	R. C. Clark	22
The Miracle of St. Nicholas		Trad = Davison	35
Three Miracles		Marenzio = Row	29
What Have I to Do with Thee? (Elijah)	S-B	Mendelssohn	*

MIRIAM

The Song of Miriam	O.	F. Schubert	1
The Song of Miriam	O.	A. Rubinstein	3

MISERERE, The

Have Mercy upon Me, O God		J. Barnby	1
Have Mercy upon Me, O God	(S)	J. Shaw	1

      [*v.* Publishers' Catalogues]

MISSIONS [*v.* Foreign Missions, Home Missions]

God Is Working His Purpose Out		C. Harris	5
Lost in the Night	8 a-c	F. M. Christiansen	20
Send Out Thy Light	O.	C. Gounod	*
Soldiers of the Cross	SAATTB (S)	V. D. Thompson	9
Springs in the Desert	(T)	A. B. Jennings	9

      [*v.* Mendelssohn's Oratorio, "St. Paul," and Publishers' Catalogues]

MORALITY

Lord, We Pray, in Mercy Lead Us	(S)	Sibelius = Sammond	10

MORNING

Give Ear to My Words	(S-B)	J. H. Rogers	2
O Lord of Life		F. L. Sealy	9
Morning Hymn	8	G. Henschel	*
The Radiant Morn		H. H. Woodward	1

MORTALITY

Behold All Flesh Is as the Grass (Requiem)		J. Brahms	*
Man Is Mortal	8	Mendelssohn	1
O Why Should the Spirit of Mortal		J. P. Sousa	12

MOSES

And All the People Saw		J. Stainer	1
As Moses Lifted up the Serpent		E. C. Bairstow	15
As Moses Lifted up the Serpent		F. Gostelow	1
The Song of Miriam	O.	F. Schubert	1
The Song of Miriam	O.	A. Rubinstein	3

MOTHERHOOD [v. Mary, Madonna, Virgin]

John (Behold Thy Son)	H.L.	Ward-Stephens	21
John (Behold Thy Son)		Ward-Stephens	21
The Christian Virtues		F. M. Christiansen	20
The Mother at the Cross		D. W. Kennedy	9

MOTHER'S DAY

A Mother's Day Prayer	a-c	J. W. Thompson	16
Blessed Day of Motherhood		C. F. Mueller	26
Mother Mine	SSA	A. Dvorak	26
Mother, My Dear		B. Treharne	26
Noel to Honor Mary, Mother		Trad=Roques-Smith	9
Responsive Service for Mother's Day		V. R. Voris	2
The Home Light		J. M. Macy	2
Sons		R. H. Terry	32

MOUNTAINS

Come Ye to the Mountains of the Lord	H.L.	C. G. Spross	1,2
For the Mountains Shall Depart			
(*Elijah*)	(B)	Mendelssohn	*
How Beautiful upon the Mountains	(S)	F. F. Harker	3
In the Last Days It Shall Come to Pass	(S.T)	J. H. Rogers	2
Lovely Appear Over the Mountains			
(Redemption)		C. Gounod	*

MUSIC

A Chorister's Prayer	a-c	C. F. Mueller	26
Blow Ye the Trumpet	SATB (T) TTBB	R. H. Woodman	3
Come Now and Let Us Reason	(T.B)	H. Wareing	1
Let All the World in Every Corner Sing	a-c	T. T. Noble	5
Praise	(S.B)	A. Rowley	15
Praise God in His Holiness	a-c	F. W. Snow	9
Praise Ye the Lord (Long)		W. R. Voris	9

MUSIC [*continued*]

OPENING OF MUSICAL SERVICE
God of All Lovely Sounds   C. Dickinson 9
Grant Thy Grace, O Lord Jesus   C. Dickinson 9

CLOSING OF MUSICAL SERVICE
Grant, O Lord   8   T. C. Whitmer 5

MYSTERY [*v*. Communion]
Behold, I Show You a Mystery (Easter)   A. Redhead 18
Eternal Mysteries   a-c   T. T. Noble 5
Father, in Thy Mysterious Presence   (s)   H. A. and J. S. Matthews 2
The Prophecy (The Mystery of
  Bethlehem)   (s)   H. Willan 9
To the Wayfarer (Orphic Mystery)   C. Forsyth 2

NAME
How Sweet the Name of Jesus Sounds   **C. Huerter** 6
Lord, We Praise Thy Holy Name   A-T-B   G. Rossini 2
My New Name   H.L.   J. G. MacDermid 37
O Lord, Our Lord, How Excellent Thy
  Name   (S.B)   J. H. Rogers 2
O Praise the Name of the Lord   Tschaikowsky 9
Praise Ye the Name of the Lord   TTBB   A. Nikolsky 6
The Name above Every Name   H. A. Matthews 9

NATHANIEL, St. [*v*. St. Bartholomew]
*Nathaniel (Thou shalt see greater things
  than these)*   H.L. Also SATB   Ward-Stephens 21

NATION [*v*. Patriotism]
All Nations Whom Thou Hast Made   B. L. Selby 1
A Prayer for Our Country   W. R. Voris 9
A Prayer for the Nations   H.L.   J. H. Rogers 12
Behold, Thou Shalt Call a Nation   (A.B)   F. Stevenson 2
God of Our Fathers (Inflammatus)   G. Rossini 1
Land of Hope and Glory   O.   E. Elgar 27
O All Ye Nations   H. Schutz 2

NATURE
All Creatures of Our God and King   E. T. Chapman 11
A Song in Praise of the Lord   Nagler = Dickinson 9

NATURE [*continued*]

As Torrents in Summer	SATB SSA	E. Elgar	9
Behold, Thou Shalt Call a Nation	(A.B)	F. Stevenson	2
Carol of the Doves (Christmas)	a-c	Polish = Gaul	4
Christ of the Fields and Flowers		H. B. Gaul	25
Consider the Lilies	H.L.	J. P. Scott	3
Cloud, if as Thou Dost Melt		E. Elgar	1
Creation Hymn		Rachmaninoff = Bornschein	4
Dear to the Heart of God	H.	F. Vanderpool	12
Fear Not, O Land		E. Elgar	1
Gloria	H. Also SATB	A. Buzzi-Peccia	26
God in Nature	SAATTB (S)	Schubert	3
God of All Nature	(A)	Tschaikowsky	11
God of the Dew	(S.A.T)	C. Whitmer	5
Great Is Jehovah	(S)	Schubert	*
He Shall Come down Like Rain	(S°)	E. S. Barnes	3
He Shall Come down Like Rain	(H)	F. F. Harker	3
Jesu, Do Roses Grow so Red	(S)	W. Y. Webbe	9
Like as the Hart	H.M.L. Also SATB	F. Allitsen	27
Like as the Hart	H.L. Also SATB	S. Liddle	27
Like as the Hart	(T.B)	W. C. Steere	7
Like Noah's Weary Dove	(A)	H. C. Banks	2
Lo, How a Rose		M. Prætorius	*
Lo, the Winter Is Past		F. Patterson	3
Man Goeth Forth to His Work		A. Carnall	1
O For the Wings of a Dove	(S)	Mendelssohn	1
O Lovely Flowers (Song of Thanksgiving)	S.	J. H. Maunder	1
Our Master Hath a Garden		H. E. Crimp	1
Planets, Stars and Airs of Space	a-c	Bach	3
Praise	(S.B)	A. Rowley	15
Rose of Sharon (Ave Maria)		Schubert	3
Thanks Be to God		Dickson = Lucas	28
The Bird Carol		A. Whitehead	6
The Cherry-Tree Carol	(S)	Trad = Butcher	3
The Heavens Are Telling		Beethoven	*
The Lost Sheep	(S.B)	M. B. Foster	3
The Meadows of the Lord	H.	C. W. Cadman	12
The Ninety and Nine	H.M.L.	E. Campion	3
The Ninety and Nine	(A.B)	D. Protheroe	2
Trees	H.L.	O. Rasbach	3

NAZARETH

Nazareth   (L)   C. Gounod   2

NEARNESS [v. Presence]

Be Near Me, Father   H.L.   W. M. Felton 12
Be Still, Be Still   (A-B)   C. P. Scott   5
Be Still, My Soul   C. H. Kitson 15
Near the Cross Was Mary, Weeping   D. W. Kennedy   9
Saviour Divine, I Hear Thy Gentle
  Calling   M.   W. Baines 12
So Near the Cross Am I   H.M.L.   V. Eville 16

NEED [v. Man—Need of God]

I Need Thee Every Hour   (S)   W. Berwald   5
We Need Our God   (B)   W. Wild   9

NEHEMIAH [v. Biblical Passages, etc.]

NEST [v. Nature]

O For the Wings of a Dove   (S)   Mendelssohn   *

NEW JERUSALEM [v. Holy City, Zion]

NEW YEAR

A New Year Carol   a-c SATB TTBB   J. Forsyth   3
Come Let Us Anew (Carol)   F. H. Wood 18
From Glory unto Glory   E. R. Warren 26
How Burn the Stars Unchanging   (S)   C. M. Lockwood   9
I Am Alpha and Omega   (M)   A. Sullivan   1
Like Angels that Softly   J. Pache   9
New Year's Carol (12 Traditional
  Carols)   Leather=Williams 18
Now Is the Old Year Passed Away   a-c   M. Prætorius   3
Ring Out, Wild Bells   C. Gounod   *
Ring Out, Wild Bells   P. E. Fletcher   1
Ring Out, Wild Bells   L. Wetzel 13
The Carol of the Bells on New Year's Eve   A. M. Goodhart   18
The New Year   J. Pache   9

NICHOLAS, St.

The Miracle of St. Nicholas   Trad=Davison 35

NIGHT [*v*. Evening]

A Song in the Night	(s.b)	R. H. Woodman	3
In the Night Came Christ Walking	8	N. Cain	3
God Sends the Night		G. Rathbone	1
God that Madest	(s)	H. A. Matthews	2
God that Madest	a-c (a)	Trad=Lutkin	9
Morning	8	G. Henschel	*
Morning and Night		M. Spicker	3
Nightfall	(s.a.t.b)	F. L. Lawrence	9
Round Me Falls the Night		F. W. Snow	9
Saviour, When Night Involves the Skies	(b)	H. R. Shelley	3
The Day Is Past and Over	(t.t-b)	J. C. Marks	9
When Christ the Lord Was Born	(h.l)	W. Wentzell	6
What of the Night	(t)	R. G. Thompson	9

NOAH

Like Noah's Weary Dove	(a)	H. C. Banks	2

— — — — —

Le Deluge, Cantata	C. St.-Saens	3

NOVELTIES

A Christmas Folk Song	satb, sa or u.	H. Wheaton	9
(With Organ or Piano Duet)			
A Christmas Carol Cycle (4 Carols)		W. S. Nagle	3
Arioso Cantabile	o.	Bach=Lester	13
(Vocalise suitable for Choir Concert)			
Christmas in Art and Song		Thomas=Bailey	11
(Program of Songs with Lantern Slides)			
Comrades, Cantata (Long)		C. Bonner	14
(For C. E. Societies or Sunday School)			
Easter and the Forty Days, in Scripture, Art and Song (With Lantern Slides)		E. Thomas	11
Rex Gloriae, Cantata (8 min.)		S. R. Gaines	11
(Soloists, Cho., Narrator, V. P. Org.)			
The Inn at Bethlehem	(s.t.b)	Trad=Dickinson	9
(Colloquy between Mary, Joseph and Inn-Keeper)			

NUMBERS [*v*. Biblical Passages, etc.]

NUNC DIMITTIS, The

Nunc Dimittis	S. Rachmaninoff	9

NUNC DIMITTIS [*continued*]

Nunc Dimittis		L. V. Saar	9
The Song of Simeon	(T)	I. L. Strom	40

[*v.* Publishers' Catalogues]

OBADIAH [*v.* Biblical Passages, etc.]

OBBLIGATOS

SOPRANO

A Song in the Night	(S.B)	R. H. Woodman	3
Calm On the Listening Ear of Night		H. W. Parker	1
Hark, Hark, My Soul		H. R. Shelley	3
Hymn to the Saviour		E. Kremser	3
In Heavenly Love Abiding		H. W. Parker	1
Lift Up Your Heads, O Ye Gates		M. Andrews	2
List the Cherubic Host		A. R. Gaul	*
List to the Lark		C. Dickinson	9
None Other Lamb		H. Saunders	6
O Holy Night		A. Adam	*
The Omnipotence		Schubert	*
The Shepherds Had an Angel		M. Besly	14
Who Is This?		H. E. Button	1

ALTO

Come, Marie, Elisabette		Trad = Dickinson	9
Come unto Me	(TTBB)	C. W. Hawley	26
Holy, Holy, Holy		D. Emery	9
Sleep, O Sleep, Son Jesus		D. M. Williams	9

TENOR

Grieve Not the Holy Spirit		T. T. Noble	9
O Come, Let Us Worship		Mendelssohn	*
O Lord, Most Holy		C. Franck	6
Seek Ye the Lord		J. V. Roberts	2

BARITONE

Behold, Ye Despisers		H. W. Parker	9
Father of Mercies		S. P. Waddington	1
Light's Glittering Morn		H. W. Parker	3
List the Cherubic Host		A. R. Gaul	*
Thus Saith the Lord		E. S. Hosmer	9

OBBLIGATOS [continued]
INSTRUMENTAL [v. Instruments—Accompanying]

OBEDIENCE

Christ Became Obedient unto Death		J. F. Bridge	1
Let This Mind Be in You	(S.B)	Mrs. H. H. A. Beach	7
Let This Mind Be in You		C. W. Cadman	26
Obedience 'tis, the Lord of Hosts De-mandeth	B.	F. Hiller	3

OBLIGATIONS [v. Debts, Man—Duty to Men, Commandments]

O Forgive Our Debts	Thomé = Richards	26
Owe No Man Anything	F. McCollin	3

OFFENCES [v. Forgiveness]

Remember Not Our Offences	A. T. L. Ashton	18
Remember Not Our Offences	J. W. G. Hathaway	18
Remember Not Our Offences	H. Purcell	1
Surely He Hath Borne Our Griefs (Messiah)	Handel	*

OFFERINGS [v. Almsgiving, Stewardship]

Because of Thy Great Bounty	H.	E. R. Warren	9
Bringing Costly Offerings		C. St.-Saens	3
Give unto the Lord	(A)	C. W. Cadman	26
Honor the Lord with Thy Substance (Prodigal Son)	B.	A. Sullivan	1
Incense and a Pure Offering	(S.A.T.B)	Brock = Macrum	17
Let Your Light so Shine		H. Hadley	9
Lord of Spirits	a-c	F. M. Christiansen	20
Master, No Offering Costly and Sweet. Hymn-Text (E. P. Parker)			
The True Gift	M.L.	F. Frank	9
Though I Speak with the Tongues of Men	(S.T)	E. Rhode	2
Saviour, Thy Dying Love	8 a-c	W. R. Voris	9

OINTMENT [v. Anointment, Unction]

OLIVET [v. Gethsemane]

Lift High the Triumph Song	C. F. Mueller	3

PAIN

God of Righteousness	H.L.	H. Gilbert	23
The Pains of Hell		E. G. Monk	1

PALM SUNDAY [*v.* Hosanna, The]

Awake, Awake		Stainer	*
Come, Faithful People, Come	8	W. R. Voris	9
Hosanna		T. Facer	14
Hosanna	H.L.	J. Granier	3
Hosanna		J. Granier	3
Hosanna to the Son		Gibbons=Bantock	14
Jerusalem	H.L.	H. Parker	*
Jerusalem	(L)	Parker=Protheroe	13
My King Rode in Through the City Gates	(S.A.T.B)	H. L. Baumgartner	9
Oh Hark the Cry		C. A. Scholin	50
Ride on, Ride on in Majesty		L. Jewell	9
Ride on, Ride on in Majesty	(T)	J. P. Scott	26
The King's Welcome		A. Whitehead	2

PARABLES [*v.* Prodigal Son]

And the Lord Planted a Garden		E. S. Craston	1
Behold the Fig Tree	(S)	W. H. Neidlinger	7
How Many Hired Servants	T.	A. Sullivan	1
I Came not to Call the Righteous		C. Vincent	1
The Good Samaritan	H.L.	G. W. Chadwick	7
The Lost Sheep	(S.B)	M. B. Foster	3
The Ninety and Nine	H.L.	E. Campion	3
The Ninety and Nine	(A.B)	D. Protheroe	2
The Parable of the Harvest		F. J. Sawyer	1
The Penitent	H.L.	B. van de Water	2
The Prodigal's Return		T. A. Jones	1
The Publican		B. van de Water	2
The Sower	(L)	J. Jordan	3
Thou Art the Guide of our Youth		A. R. Gaul	*

PARACLETE [*v.* Holy Spirit]

PARADISE [*v.* Eden, Heaven]

O Paradise, O Paradise	(T)	M. Andrews	5
Ye Happy Souls in Paradise		P. Ladmirault	3

PARDON [*v.* Forgiveness]

PARTING [*v.* Farewell]

PASS

Behold, the Master Passeth By	(A)	F. Stevenson 2
If I Had Lived in Bethlehem	H.	W. Barickman 13

PASSION [*v.* Gethsemane, Good Friday]

The Passion Service for Good Friday (3 hrs.)	F. F. Harker 3
The Passion Trilogy	Ukranian = Koshetz 21
v. Bach Oratorios, and The Passion of Our Lord According to St. Mark, Oratorio	C. Wood 55

PASSOVER [*v.* Communion, Easter, Lent]

Christ, Our Passover		W. G. Hammond 9
Christ, Our Passover		H. W. Parker 9
Christ, Our Passover	(s)	B. Tours 9
Christ, Our Passover	(A.T)	A. Woeltge 2
Kol Nidrei		C. J. Roberts 8

PAST [*v.* Anniversaries, New Year, Retrospect]

O God our Help	(s) Chime	C. L. Williams 1
O God of All Our Glorious Past	SATB SSA U.	M. S. Daniels 11
Past and Future		H. Oakley 9

PATH [*v.* Way]

Be Near Me, Father	H.L.	W. M. Felton 12
O Thou in All Thy Might	(T)	C. P. Scott 2
Path of the Just	(H)	F. F. Harker 3
Out of Heaven		F. H. Cowen 3
The Path of Life		S. R. Gaines 6
Thou Shalt Show Me the Path of Life		A. Gray 1

PATIENCE

Let Not Your Heart Be Troubled		E. Faning 1
O Master, Let Me Walk With Thee	(A)	G. C. Stebbins ·2
O Rest in the Lord	A	Mendelssohn *
O Rest in the Lord	SATB Mendelssohn = Christiansen 20
Past and Future		H. Oakley 9
Patiently Have I Waited	M.	C. St.-Saens 1

PATRICK, St.

St. Patrick's Breastplate   a-c   C. V. Stanford 18
St. Patrick's Prayer   S. Burke 17

PATRIOTISM

America the Beautiful   H. R. Shelley 3
Anthem of Democracy   J. H. Matthews 9
Arm, Arm, Ye Brave (Judas Maccabæus) B.   Handel *
Earth's Awakening   (B)   L. J. Downing 13
God, Save America   SATB TTBB SSA   W. F. Harling 9
God Save America   M.   W. F. Harling 9
Heroes' Hymn   G. Carle 6
Land of Hope and Glory   E. Elgar 27
Let Us Now Praise Famous Men   (S.T.B)   H. B. Gaul 17
Let Us Now Praise Famous Men   U.   V. Williams 14
O God of Freedom   E. S. Barnes 5
O Lord God of Hosts, Strengthen
    and Guide this Nation   SSATBB   H. B. Gaul 3
Our United States   L. Stokowski 12
Recessional   (B)   R. deKoven 7
Recessional   SSATTBB O.   H. A. Matthews 3
Song of the World Adventurers   F. S. Converse 9

PATTERN

Blest Are the Pure in Heart   8 a-c   F. M. Christiansen 20
Consider the Lilies   H.L.   J. P. Scott 3

PAUL, St.

*Paul (Lord, What wilt Thou have me to
    do?)*   H.L.   Ward-Stephens 21
Paul (Lord, What wilt Thou have me
    to do?)   Ward-Stephens 21
— — — — — — —
St. Paul, Oratorio   Mendelssohn *

PEACE IN HEART

Be Still, Be Still   C. P. Scott 5
Fierce Was the Wild Billow   8 and 4   T. T. Noble 3
Great Peace Have They Which Love
    Thy Laws   (H)   J. H. Rogers 3
I Heard the Voice of Jesus Say "Peace" (S)   W. C. Gale 2

PEACE IN HEART [*continued*]

In Faith I Calmly Rest	(M)	Bach = Dickinson	9
In My Father's House Are Many Mansions	H.M.L.	J. G. MacDermid	37
I Will Lay Me Down in Peace		J. L. Bennett	3
Let Not Your Heart Be Troubled		E. Faning	1
O God of Love, O King of Peace		J. E. West	9
O Lord, Support Us the Whole Day Long	(A.T) Chime	H. McAmis	3
Peace Be to This House	(A)	R. H. Baldwin	3
Put on, Therefore, as God's Elect		E. S. Barnes	9
Remain with us, O Peace of God		H. A. Matthews	9
Through Peace to Light	H.M.L.	Ward-Stephens	5

PEACE IN THE WORLD

A Carol of Peace (Christmas)		G. J. Bennett	1
Give Peace in Our Time, O Lord	(S.T.B)	W. A. Fisher	2
He Maketh Wars to Cease	H.L.	J. P. Scott	26
Hymn of Peace		W. A. Fisher	2
The Plains of Peace	H.M.L.	D. Bernard	27
These Things Shall Be	(H.L)	R. Broughton	2

PEACEMAKERS [*v.* Beatitudes]

How Beautiful Upon the Mountains	(S)	F. F. Harker	3
How Lovely Are the Messengers	(A)	Mendelssohn	*
Lovely Appear	(S)	C. Gounod	*

PENITENCE [*v.* Confession]

A Penitential Prayer		Trad = Riedel	9
A Song of Penitence (in Folio)	Hrp	Beethoven	9
O Forgive Our Debts		F. Thome	26
Penitence (Busslied)	H.L.	Beethoven	8
Penitential Psalm No. 6	SATTB	di Lassus = Cain	13
The Penitent	H.M.L.	B. van de Water	2
The Penitent Thief	SSATB	A. Kastalsky	9
The Prayer of the Penitent	M.	Londonderry = Felton	12
The Prayer of the Penitent	S-A-T-B	H. A. Matthews	3

PENTECOST [*v.* Whitsuntide]

Lovely Appear	(S)	C. Gounod	*
Now When was Come the Day of Pentecost (Motet)	SAATTB	Palestrina	1

PEOPLE [*v*. Man]

All People that on Earth Do Dwell	O.	J. E. West	1
But Who Am I and What Is My People?		H. W. Richards	1
Come Now and Let Us Reason	(T.B)	H. Wareing	1
He Is Ours	(H) V.	H. Haaf	17
Onward, Ye People	SATB SSA TTBB SA	J. Sibelius	25
Praise God, Ye People		M. Vulpius	8
The People's Anthem		C. Engel	11
When Wilt Thou Save the People?		N. Coke-Jephcott	9
When Wilt Thou Save the People?	(S.M)	F. W. Snow	9

PERILS [*v*. Danger]

PERSECUTION [*v*. Martyrs, Exile]

And They All Persecuted Paul (St. Paul)			
(Recit. before Tenor Aria)	S.	Mendelssohn	*
Blest Are They Which Are Persecuted	(H)	W. Kienzl	6
Blest Are They Which Are Persecuted		Ward-Stephens	3

PETER, St.

In the Night Came Christ Walking	8	N. Cain	3
Peter (Upon This Rock)	H.L.	Ward-Stephens	21
Peter (Upon This Rock)		Ward-Stephens	21
Thou Art Peter		Palestrina	24
Thou Art Peter		Mendelssohn	1

I PETER [*v*. Biblical Passages, etc.]

PETITION [*v*. Prayer, Supplication, Pleading]

Abide With Me	(S.A.T.B)	A. Depew	6
Abide With Me	(L)	G. H. Federlein	39
Abide With Me	(H.L)	S. Liddle	27
Abide With Me	(S.A)	Liddle=Salter	27
A Petition	8 a-c	C. F. Mueller	26
Jesus, Meek and Gentle	(S)	J. Holler	9
O Jesus, Thou Art Standing	(A)	D. Protheroe	13
O Lord, Support Us	(A.T.) Chime	H. McAmis	3
So Thou Liftest Thy Divine Petition			
(Crucifixion)	T-B	J. Stainer	*

PHARAOH

Song of Miriam	Schubert	1
v. "Israel in Egypt" Oratorio	Handel	*

PHARISEE [*v.* Hypocrisy]

The Publican	H.L.M.	B. van de Water	2

PHILIP, St.

Philip (*Show us the Father*)	H.L.	Ward-Stephens	21
Philip (Show us the Father)		Ward-Stephens	21
Rejoice in the Lord, O ye Righteous		G. C. Martin	1

PHILIPPIANS [*v.* Biblical Passages, etc.]

PHYSICIAN [*v.* Healing, Mental Health]

Art Thou Weary?	(B)	G. W. Chadwick	5
Art Thou Weary?	(S.A) V.	T. del Riego	2
Blessed Be the Man		A. W. Ketelbey	1
Come, Ye Disconsolate	(S-A)	E. K. Macrum	9
Honour a Physician (Hospital Sunday)		G. Thalben=Hall	1
I Heard the Voice of Jesus Say	(S)	P. J. Mansfield	3

PILGRIMAGE [*v.* Road, Way]

A Pilgrim Prays	M.	R. Mitchell	16
Father, We Are Pilgrims	(B)	N. W. Gade	39
He Who Would Valiant Be	(B)	R. Broughton	3
Homeland, Dear Homeland		S. R. Gaines	11
Onward, Pilgrim Brothers		F. H. Holloway	5
Pilgrims' Chorus	TTBB O.	R. Wagner	*
Pilgrims' Chorus	8	R. Wagner	20
Pilgrim's Song	SATB TTBB	Tschaikowsky	*
Pilgrimage	A.	D. Buck	3
The King's Highway		D. M. Williams	9
The Pilgrim Fathers	a-c	E. J. Stringham	9
The Pilgrims	TTBB	E. MacDowell	5
The Pilgrim Pavement	(S) U.	V. Williams	8

PILLARS

The Pillars of the Earth	J. H. Rogers	2
The Pillars of the Earth	B. Tours	2

PILOT [*v.* Guidance]

Jesus, Saviour, Pilot Me   (A)   J. W. Thompson 8

PIONEERS [*v.* Pilgrims]

Pioneers   U. O.   H. Grace 8
The Sunset Trail   H.L.   C. Bennett 29
The Sunset Trail   TTBB   Bennett = Baldwin 29

PITY [*v.* Mercy]

PLAINS

Out on the Plains   Spanish = Dickinson 9
The Plains of Peace   D. Bernard 27

PLEADING [*v.* Petition]

O Saviour, I Have Naught to Plead   (A)   W. C. Gale 3

PLEASURES, EARTHLY

From Every Earthly Pleasure   (H)   S. B. Gaines 3
Jesu, Source of Purest Pleasure   C. Dickinson 9
Love Not the World   (S.A)   A. Sullivan 3
When I Survey the Wondrous Cross   (A.B)   M. Andrews 2

POOR [*v.* Charity, Almsgiving]

He That hath Pity upon the Poor   (B)   A. Whitehead 18

PORTAL [*v.* Gate, Door]

Unfold ye Portals Everlasting   O.   C. Gounod *

PORTION

The Lord is the Portion of Mine
  Inheritance   C. B. Rootham 18

POSSESSIONS [*v.* Earthly Pleasures]

Honor the Lord with Thy Substance   B.   A. Sullivan 1
Honor the Lord with Thy Substance   J. Stainer 1
Honor the Lord with Thy Substance   M. Andrews 9

POWER [*v.* God—Omnipotent]

Eternal God Whose Power Upholds   U.   R. H. Woodman 9
Hast Thou Not Known?   (H.B)   C. Pflueger 19

POWER [*continued*]

I Will Sing of Thy Power	S-A-T	P. Lutkin 9
Lord, Make me Strong		V. Eville 27
Make Us Strong		Nagler = Dickinson 9
O Thou, Whose Power Tremendous		M. Spicker 3
They That Wait Upon the Lord	(H)	F. W. Snow 9

PRAISE [*v.* God—Praise to, Christ—Praise to]

All Praise to God	(B)	Wagner = Cornell 3
A Song in Praise of the Lord		Nagler = Dickinson 9
Give Praise	(S)	F. M. Christiansen 10
Hymn of Praise	8	Tschaikowsky 3
I Love the Lord	(T)	J. L. Galbraith 2
Let All Mortal Flesh Keep Silence	(S.B)	G. Holst 18
Let All That Hath Breath	8 a-c	H. Whitford 4
My Song Shall Be Alway	S-S	Mendelssohn 7
Praise	(S.B)	A. Rowley 15
Praise the Lord		D. Protheroe 13
Praise the Lord		A. Randegger 3
Praise the Lord, O Jerusalem		J. H. Maunder 1
Praise the Lord, O My Soul	SATB	R. Jevons 9
Praise to the Lord		A. Whitehead 9
Praise ye the Lord	(S)	A. Randegger 3
Psalm of Praise		R. G. Cole 5
The God of Abraham Praise	(S)	H. R. Shelley 3

PRAYER [*v.* Petition, Lord's Prayer]

A Prayer		D. Guion 3
A Prayer for Love (Ave Maria)		Schubert = Voris 9
A Prayer for Purification		Tschaikowsky = Treharne 6
At Thy Feet	(M)	Bach 18
Be Still, Be Still	(A-B)	C. P. Scott 5
Hear My Cry, O God	7	G. Kopyloff 2
Hear My Prayer, O Lord	(B)	E. S. Hosmer 9
Hear My Prayer, O Lord	SAATB a-c	W. James 3
My Daily Prayer	H.L.	Rockwood = Lester 13
My Daily Prayer		Rockwood = Lester 13
Our Father and Our God	(A)	Arcadelt = Lockwood 9
Prayer (Cav. Rus.)	(S) o.	Mascagni = McConathy 11
Prayer for Guidance		D. H. Jones 8

PRAYER [continued]

Prayer, the Soul's Desire		F. N. Barbour	5
The Publican	H.L.M.	B. van de Water	2
The Rainbow Bridge of Prayer		F. M. Christiansen	20
The Shadow of Thy Wings	H.	M. Andrews	9
The Shadow of Thy Wings	(H)	M. Andrews	9
The Silent Hour	H.L.	C. W. Cadman	32
The World's Prayer	(S)	C. W. Cadman	12

PREACHING [v. Minister]

And Paul Came to the Congregation (St. Paul)		Mendelssohn	*
How Beautiful Upon the Mountains	(S)	F. F. Harker	3
Lovely Appear	(S)	C. Gounod	*
O Ye Priests of the Lord		F. W. Hird	1
Thou Art a Priest Forever		S. Wesley	1

PREPARATION

Prepare Ye the Way	(B.T)	G. H. Federlein	3
Prepare Ye the Way	(B.T)	L. Jewell	9

PRESENCE

Great is the Lord	(H)	M. C. Day	13
In the Secret of His Presence	M.	D. D. Wood	9
O Come Before His Presence	(T)	G. C. Martin	1
Saviour Divine, I Hear Thy Gentle Calling	M.	W. Baines	12
The Glory of His Presence	H.	E. R. Watson	9
The Presence in the Silence	a-c	T. T. Noble	5

PRIDE

Let Not the Wise Man	H.L.	J. H. MacDermid	37
Lord, My Heart Is Not Haughty		H. Nearing	38
O Why Should the Spirit of Mortal Be Proud?		J. P. Sousa	12

PRIESTHOOD OF BELIEVERS

O Ye Priests of the Lord		F. W. Hird	1
They Shall be Named the Priests of the Lord (In Folio)	(S)	E. H. Thorne	1
Thou Art a Priest Forever		S. Wesley	3

PROPHETS [v. Seers]

Awake, My Heart's Beloved	(M)	Sachs=Dickinson 9
Jerusalem, Thou that Killest the Prophets (St. Paul)	S.	Mendelssohn *
Seek Not unto False Prophets	H.L.	H. Grunn 3

PROSPERITY

O Pray for the Peace of Jerusalem	(B)	J. C. Knox 5
The God of Heaven, He Will Prosper Us		J. F. Bridge 1

PROTECTOR [v. God—Protector]

PROVERBS [v. Biblical Passages, etc.]

PRUDENCE

My Soul Be on Thy Guard	H.	H. Nearing 9
Watch and Pray		W. H. Lockett 1
Watch Ye and Pray	SA	G. R. Vicars 9

PSALM [v. Biblical Passages, etc.]

A Psalm of Deliverance	(S.A)	H. B. Gaul 17
A Psalm of Gratitude		C. W. Cadman 2
A Psalm to Labor (Priest's March)		Mendelssohn=Page 11
A Psalm of Trust		J. H. Mortimer 1
Great Is the Lord	(H)	M. C. Day 13
Penitential Psalm	SATTB	di Lassus=Cain 13
Psalm Fifty (Long)	8	F. M. Christiansen 20
Psalm of Praise		R. G. Cole 5
Psalm of Thanksgiving	(S)	F. Allitsen 6
Psalm Twenty-Three (Long)	(B)	H. G. Kinsella 4
The Psalm of Praise	(A)	C. W. Cadman 19
The Shepherd's Psalm		D. Protheroe 2
The Twenty-Third Psalm	H.L.	A. H. Malotte 3
The Twenty-Third Psalm	SATB	Malotte=Gilbert 3
Wanderer's Psalm	8	H. W. Parker 1

PSYCHO-THERAPY [v. Mental Health]

PUBLICAN

The Publican	H.M.L.	B. van de Water 2

PURIFICATION [v. Atonement, Beatitudes]

A Prayer for Purification		Tschaikowsky=Treharne	6
Create in Me a Clean Heart	(A)	F. F. Harker	26
The Lord Is in His Holy Temple		J. W. Elliott	1
The Lord Is in His Holy Temple		J. Stainer	1
Wash Me Thoroughly	8	A. Rubinstein	3

PURITY [v. Beatitudes]

Blest Are the Pure in Heart	H.L.	B. Huhn	3
Blessed Are the Pure in Heart	(A)	F. F. Harker	26
Blessed Are the Pure in Heart	(H)	D. W. Kennedy	26
Create in Me a Clean Heart	(A)	F. F. Harker	26
For Know Ye Not that Ye Are His Temple? (St. Paul)	B.	Mendelssohn	*
Greater Love Hath No Man	(S.B)	J. Ireland	18
I Beseech You, Brethren		J. Stainer	1

PURPOSE

God Is Working His Purpose Out	C. Harris	5

QUEST [v. Man—Search for God, Pilgrimage]

The Quest of the Shepherds (Christmas)	H. B. Gaul	4

QUICKENING [v. Holy Spirit]

Dayspring of Eternity	8 a-c	J. S. Matthews	9
Dayspring of Eternity	(M)	R. Wichman	9
Lord of All Power		G. W. Chadwick	5

QUIET [v. Calm]

In Quietness and in Confidence	(T)	L. Jewell	9
With Quiet Heart		F. Scherer	9

RAIN [v. Nature]

A Prayer for Dew and Rain		Trad=Gaul	21
He Shall Come Down Like Rain	(S)	E. S. Barnes	3
He Shall Come Down Like Rain	(H)	F. F. Harker	3
My Doctrine Shall Drop as the Rain		P. Armes	1
Thou Who Sendest Sun and Rain	(A)	G. W. Chadwick	5

RAINBOW

Look upon the Rainbow	H.M.L.	B. Whelpley	5

REDEMPTION [*continued*]

Daughters of Jerusalem (*Light of the World*)	B.	A. Sullivan	1
In the Night Came Christ Walking	8	N. Cain	3
Out of the Shadows	H.L.	R. H. Woodman	5
The Temple of My Heart	8	F. W. Snow	9

RED SEA [*v.* Pharaoh]

REFORMATION

Jesus, unto Thee Be Praise (A Song of the Reformation)	TTBB	Gumpeltzhaimer	9
Supplication (Huguenot Hymn of 16th Century)		A. Fuleihan	3
We Gather Together		E. Kremser	*

REFUGE [*v.* Peace, Security, Invitation]

Approach, My Soul, the Mercy-Seat		J. W. Thompson	5
Come unto Him (*Messiah*)	S.	Handel	*
Does the Road Wind Up-Hill?	(A)	W. G. Hammond	7
God Is Our Refuge and Strength	H.L.	J. G. MacDermid	37
God Is Our Refuge and Strength	8	C. F. Mueller	3
If the Lord Had Not Helped Me	(B)	E. C. Bairstow	1
Rock and Refuge	8 a-c	F. M. Christiansen	20
Rock of Ages		D. Buck	2
The Eternal God Is Thy Refuge	(B)	J. E. West	1
The Good Shepherd		A. B. Jennings	9

REFUGEE [*v.* Exile]

REIGN [*v.* God—Majesty of]

Behold, a King Shall Reign	(B)	H. C. Banks	9
Jehovah Reigns (Priests' March)		Mendelssohn = Macy	2
The Lord Reigneth	SSATBBB	N. Lockwood	25
Who Is This?	(S)	H. E. Button	1

REJOICING [*v.* Joy]

RELEASE [*v.* Deliverance]

I Wait, O Lord	L.	P. Cimara	17
O Sing unto the Lord	(S)	F. F. Harker	3

RELEASE [*continued*]

The Temple of My Heart	8	F. W. Snow	9
Worship		G. Shaw	1

REMEMBRANCE [*v.* Memorial, Past]

Call to Remembrance		Farrant = Wiseman	11
Call to Remembrance	(H)	V. Novello	1
Call to Remembrance	(T)	J. V. Roberts	1
God Remembers		C. J. Bond	6
God's Goodness Hath Been Great		O. A. Mansfield	5
Lord, Remember Not	8 a-c	Mendelssohn	8
Remember, O Thou Man	(Dbl Ch)	C. S. Lang	9
When I Remember Thee	(H)	C. P. Scott	8

RENUNCIATION [*v.* Consecration, Earthly Pleasures, Offerings]

Father, I Know that All My Life	(H)	W. M. Hawkins	3
Love Not the World	(S.A)	A. Sullivan	3

REPENTANCE [*v.* Conversion, Penitence]

A Few More Years Shall Roll	(T)	F. C. Butcher	9
If with All Your Hearts	T.	Mendelssohn	*
Love Not the World		A. Sullivan	1
Prepare Ye the Way	(T.B)	G. H. Federlein	3
Prepare Ye the Way	(T.B)	L. Jewell	9
Rend Your Heart, and Not Your Garments		J. E. West	2
Repent Ye	H.M.L.	J. P. Scott	3
We Stand in Deep Repentance	(A)	Mendelssohn	3

REPROACHES [*v.* Rebuke]

The Reproaches	(Dbl Ch) a-c	H. Willan	9
The Reproaches on Good Friday (Improperia)		Vittoria = Schindler	2
Thy Rebuke Hath Broken His Heart (*Messiah*) (T. recit. to "Behold and See")		Handel	*

REQUIEM [*v.* Death, Elegy, Funeral]

A Soldier's Requiem		R. F. McEwen	18
Requiem		G. C. Young	18

RESCUE

In the Night Came Christ Walking	8	N. Cain	3
The Lost Sheep	· (s.b)	M. B. Foster	3
The Ninety and Nine	h.l.	E. Campion	3
The Ninety and Nine	(a.b)	D. Protheroe	2

RESIGNATION [*v.* Consecration, Renunciation]

A Few More Years Shall Roll	(t)	F. C. Butcher	9
Faithful Shepherd, Feed Me	(s)	H. A. and J. S. Matthews	2
Peace and Light	(t)	G. W. Chadwick	5

RESISTANCE TO GOD [*v.* Atheism, Despising God]

REST [*v.* Peace]

Come Now and Let Us Reason	(t.b)	H. W. Wareing	1
Come unto Him (Messiah)	s.	Handel	*
Come unto Me		Beethoven = Aslanoff	3
Come unto Me	(s)	W. Coenen	2
Come unto Me	(a)	W. C. Gale	7
Come unto Me		C. B. Hawley	26
Come unto Me	(s or b)	C. Huerter	2
Come unto Me	h.m.l.	S. Liddle	18
Come unto Me	(b)	S. Liddle	18
Come unto Me	(h)	Tschaikowsky = O'Hare	26
Ye Shall Find Rest	m.	W. R. Voris	9

RESTLESSNESS [*v.* Calm, Peace]

Give to My Restless Heart	H. A. MacKinnon	9

RESURRECTION [*v.* Easter]

RETROSPECT [*v.* Anniversaries, Memorial, Past]

I Have Considered the Days of Old		P. James	2
The Old, Old Story	(a.t)	E. S. Hosmer	2

REVELATION [*v.* Incarnation, Word, Biblical Passages, etc.]

Christ the Fair Glory of the Holy Angels	E. Bullock	8
Fairest Lord Jesus	R. Diggle	9
Fairest Lord Jesus	P. Lutkin	9

REVELATION [*continued*]

I Am Alpha and Omega	(H)	A. Sullivan	1
I Am the Resurrection		C. Demarest	9
I Am the Water of Life		J. P. Dunn	4
I Declare to You the Gospel		W. A. C. Cruickshank	1
God Was Made Manifest in the Flesh			
(Two Advents)		G. M. Garrett	1
O God, Who Is Like unto Thee?		M. B. Foster	1

REVIVAL [*v.* Evangelistic Services]

Lord of All Power	G. W. Chadwick	5

REVOLT [*v.* Rebelliousness]

RICHES [*v.* Possessions]

RIGHTEOUSNESS

Behold, a King Shall Reign	(B)	H. C. Banks	9
God of Righteousness	H.L.	H. Gilbert	23
Mercy and Truth		J. Stainer	1
The Eyes of the Lord Are over the			
Righteous		J. E. West	1
The Righteous Live Forevermore	TTBB	C. E. Miller	18

RISE

Rise, My Soul	S-T	F. M. Christiansen	20
Rise Up, My Love, My Fair One			
(Easter)		H. Willan	15
Rise Up, O Men of God	a-c	T. T. Noble	5
Rise Up, Shepherd, and Follow			
(Christmas Spiritual)		R. N. Dett	4

RIVER [*v.* Nature, Water]

Deep River (Spiritual)	Trad = Burleigh	17
There Is a River	V. Novello	1

ROAD [*v.* Way]

Does the Road Wind Up-Hill	(A)	W. G. Hammond	7
O Thou in All Thy Might	(T)	C. P. Scott	2
Roads	(A)	C. Dickinson	9

ROCK

Built on a Rock	(B°) 8	F. M. Christiansen	20
Rock and Refuge	8 a-c	F. M. Christiansen	20
Rock of Ages	(s) Also TTBB	D. Buck	2
The Lord Is My Rock		R. H. Woodman	3

ROD [v. Judgment]

The Rod of Jesse Hath Blossomed	A. Bruckner	11

ROGATION DAYS

O Most Merciful		J. W. Elliott	1
On Thee Each Living Soul Awaits	S-T-B	F. J. Haydn	1
They that Sow in Tears (Holy City)		A. R. Gaul	*

ROMANS [v. Biblical Passages, etc.]

ROSE [v. Nature]

Jesu, Do Roses Grow So Red?	(s)	W. Y. Webbe	9
Lo, How a Rose		M. Prætorius	*
O Rose of Sharon (Ave Maria)		Schubert	3

RUTH [v. Biblical Passages, etc.]

Entreat Me Not to Leave Thee	H.M.L.	C. Gounod	3
Intreat Me Not to Leave Thee	A.	W. Watts	3

SABA

All They from Saba Shall Come	(T)	L. Sowerby	9

SABBATH [v. Lord's Day]

A Sabbath Prayer	M.	Reichardt=Rogers	3
The Sabbath (Vol. II of "Sacred Duets")	S-A	F. Abt	7
The Sabbath Morn (Vol. II of "Sacred Duets")	S-A	Mendelssohn	7
This Is the Day which the Lord Hath Made	(H)	W. L. Blumenschein	3

SACKCLOTH [v. Ash Wednesday]

Thou Hast Turned My Heaviness (Widow of Zarephath)	A. Gray	1

SACRAMENT [v. Baptism, Communion]

Before the Sacrament	M.	T. M. Spelman 25

SACRIFICE [v. Atonement, Victim]

And Though He Be Offered upon the Sacrifice (S. recit. to "Not only unto Him") (St. Paul)		Mendelssohn *

SAGES [v. Scholars]

SAILORS [v. Sea]

Be Still, Be Still	(A-B)	C. P. Scott 5
Eternal Father	Chimes	G. Holst 14
Requiem	H.L.	S. Homer 3
Sing to the Lord a New Song		H. Smart 1
The Haven of Rest-for-Aye	(A)	W. Lester 9
They that Go down to the Sea	(T)	G. J. Elvey 1

SAINTS [v. All Saints, Communion of Saints]

Lo, Round the Throne (Long)	O.	H. G. Ley 15
Lo, Round the Throne (Shortened Version)		H. G. Ley 15
The Saints of God	a-c	T. T. Noble 5
The Sun Shall Be No More Thy Light		H. H. Woodward 1
(For specific Saints see individual listings.)		

SALEM [v. Jerusalem, Zion]

Blessed City, Heavenly Salem		E. C. Bairstow 44

SALVATION

Behold, God Is My Salvation	(B)	L. Jewell 5
Behold, God Is My Salvation	(S)	J. H. Rogers 2
I Have Longed for Thy Salvation (Stabat Mater)	S-A-T-B	G. Rossini 1
Salvation Belongeth unto the Lord	(A)	W. Berwald 2
Save Us, O Lord		E. C. Bairstow 1
Save Us, We Pray	8	Bach = Ganschow 3

SALVATION [*continued*]

The New Song	8 a-c	F. M. Christiansen	20
The Temple of My Heart	8 a-c	F. W. Snow	9
When Wilt Thou Save the People?		N. Coke-Jephcott	9

SAMARITAN

The Good Samaritan	H.L.	G. W. Chadwick	7
v. "The Woman of Samaria," Cantata		W. S. Bennett	1

SAMSON [*v.* "Samson," Oratorio by Handel]

I SAMUEL [*v.* Biblical Passages, etc.]

II SAMUEL [*v.* Biblical Passages, etc.]

SANCTIFICATION [*v.* Church—Militant, Growth, Pilgrimage]

SANCTUARY [*v.* Altar, Refuge]

Declare His Glory	(A) 8	G. H. Federlein	3
Sanctuary	(A.T)	F. LaForge	26
Sanctuary of the Heart	H.L.	A. W. Ketelbey	27
Still, Still with Thee	(T)	S. Salter	2
Still, Still with Thee	(A.B.S-T)	A. Foote	5
This Sanctuary of My Soul		C. Wood	43
Thou Shalt Bring Them In (Israel in Egypt)	B.	Handel	3

SANCTUS, The

Holy, Holy, Holy	(M)	D. R. Emery	9
Sanctus (St. Cecilia Mass)	(T)	C. Gounod	*

SARAH

Hearken unto Me	(S)	F. Stevenson	2

SATAN

There Was War in Heaven	W. A. C. Cruickshank	1

SAUL

King Saul		Moussorgsky=Saminsky	8
	(T. or A) Org.Tr.Dr.		
Obedience 'tis, the Lord of Hosts Demandeth (Saul)	B.	F. Hiller	3

SAVIOUR [*v.* Christ]
Come, Thou Saviour of Our Race   8   F. M. Christiansen 20

SAYINGS OF JESUS [*v.* Christ—Sayings, Good Friday]

SCENT [*v.* Fragrance]
What Is this Scent so Pure and Lovely?   L. Woodgate 1

SCEPTICISM [*v.* Doubt]

SCEPTRE [*v.* King]
Give Ear, Good Christian Men (Easter
  Carol Book)   9
His Rod Is the Sceptre of Righteousness
  (Occasional Oratorio)   B.   Handel 1

SCHOOLS [*v.* Baccalaureate, Youth]
O Scholars and Sages   H. A. MacKinnon 9

SCOFFERS [*v.* Atheism, Despising God]
Who Is This?   (s)   H. E. Button 1

SCRIPTURES [*v.* Bible]

SEA [*v.* Sailors]
A Prayer for Those at Sea   H.L.   B. Hamblen 22
A Sea Prayer   D. Nyvall 16
Be Still, Be Still   (A-B)   C. P. Scott 5
Dear Lord, Who once upon the Lake   (s)   V. D. Thompson 3
He Rebuked the Red Sea (Israel in
  Egypt)   Handel *
I Saw Three Ships (*Christmas*)   M.   E. Delamarter 9
I Saw Three Ships   H. A. MacKinnon 9
Lord Christ Came Walking   (B)   H. A. MacKinnon 9
Sing to the Lord a New Song   H. Smart 1

SEARCHING [*v.* Man—Search for God, Seeking]
Search Me, O God   (A)   J. H. Rogers 3
The Searcher of Hearts   Bach 1

SEASONS [*v.* Spring, Summer, Winter]
Aspiration   8   F. M. Christiansen 20

SENNACHERIB

The Destruction of Sennacherib   TTBB   G. Bantock 51

SEPARATION [v. Farewell]

He that Spared not His Own Son   F. E. Gladstone 1
Still, Still with Thee   (A.B.S-T)   A. Foote 5
Still, Still with Thee   (S.T)   S. Salter 2
Whither Shall I go from Thy Spirit?   H.L.   J. G. MacDermid 37

SEPULCHRE [v. Grave]

SERAPHIM

A New Heaven and a New Earth   (B)   A. R. Gaul *
In Dreams I Heard the Seraphim   (A.B) 4 Hrns   J. B. Faure 3
In the Year that King Uzziah Died   D. M. Williams 9
Let All Mortal Flesh Keep Silence   (S.B) O.   G. Holst 18
    v. Saints and Seraphs (Christmas
    Cantata)   H. J. Tily 9

SERPENT

Adam Lay Ibounden (Four Ancient
    Carols)   C. K. Scott 18
As Moses Lifted up the Serpent   E. C. Bairstow 15
As Moses Lifted up the Serpent   F. Gostelow 1

SERVANT

Behold My Servant (Christmas)   J. F. Bridge 1
How Many Hired Servants   T.   A. Sullivan 1
Let This Mind Be in You   (S.B)   Mrs. H. H. A. Beach 7
Let This Mind Be in You   C. W. Cadman 26
*The Servant Is Not Greater than His
    Lord*   H.M.L.   J. G. MacDermid 37
When to the Temple Mary Went   A. B. Jennings 9

SERVICE [v. Man—Duty to God, Fellow Men, Obedience, Social Service]

Eternal Ruler of the Ceaseless Round   M. Genet 9
Eternal Ruler of the Ceaseless Round   F. L. Sealy 9
Service   C. W. Cadman 26

SHACKLES [v. Bondage, Freedom, Prison]

SHADOW

Beneath the Shadow of the Great Protection	(A)	C. Dickinson	9
I Sat Down under the Shadow		E. C. Bairstow	15
Ninety-First Psalm	H.L.	J. G. MacDermid	37
No Shadows Yonder (Holy City)	(T)	A. R. Gaul	*
Now Rest Beneath Night's Shadow		Isaac=Luvaas	11
Now the Shades of Evening Fall	S-A-T	Mendelssohn=Cornell	3
Out of the Shadows		R. H. Woodman	5
The Shadow of the Almighty	H.L.	E. S. Barnes	3
The Shadow of Thy Wings	(H)	M. Andrews	9

SHARON

By Cool Siloam's Shady Rill		E. S. Barnes	2
By Cool Siloam's Shady Rill	(s)	G. H. Federlein	12
Lo, How a Rose		M. Prætorius	*
O Rose of Sharon (Ave Maria)	(s)	Schubert	3

SHEEP

All We Like Sheep (Messiah)		Handel	*
Listen to the Lambs	(s)	R. N. Dett	3
Sheep and Lambs	H.L.	S. Homer	3

SHELTER [*v.* Refuge, Security]

SHEPHERD

A Few More Years Shall Roll	(T)	F. C. Butcher	9
Bow Down Thine Ear	(A)	E. S. Barnes	3
God Is My Refuge		Dvorak=Clokey	11
Hear, O Thou Shepherd of Israel	(T)	G. H. Federlein	9
Hear, O Thou Shepherd of Israel	(s.B)	H. B. Gaul	9
He Shall Feed His Flock	A.	Handel	*
Lo, My Shepherd Is Divine		F. J. Haydn	1
Saviour, Like a Shepherd Lead Us	(B)	W. C. Macfarlane	3
Saviour, Like a Shepherd Lead Us		C. F. Mueller	26
Shepherd, Take Me by the Hand	H.L.	Ward-Stephens	21
The Good Shepherd	H.L.	O. Barri	2
The Good Shepherd	SATB(B) also TTBB	O. Barri	*
The Good Shepherd		A. B. Jennings	9
The Good Shepherd	H.L.	B. van de Water	2
The King of Love	8	C. Gounod	3
The King of Love	(A.S-B)	H. R. Shelley	3

SHEPHERD [*continued*]

The Lord Is My Shepherd	TTBB	T. Baker	9
The Lord Is My Shepherd		J. W. Clokey	9
The Lord Is My Shepherd	(s)	S. R. Gaines	2
The Lord Is My Shepherd	H.M.L.	S. Liddle	27
The Lord Is My Shepherd	SATB	S. Liddle	27
The Lord Is My Shepherd	SSAA(S)	H. W. Parker	3
The Lord Is My Shepherd	SATB SSAA	Schubert	*
The Lost Sheep	(S.B)	M. B. Foster	3
The Ninety and Nine	H.L.	E. Campion	3
The Ninety and Nine	(A.B)	D. Protheroe	2
The Shepherd	M.	T. T. Noble	3

SHIELD [*v.* Security]

God's Peace Is Peace Eternal	(s)	E. Grieg	3
He that Dwelleth	(A)	J. L. Galbraith	2
He that Dwelleth	H.L.	J. G. MacDermid	37
He that Dwelleth		L. Meslin	27
Round Me Falls the Night		F. W. Snow	9
St. Patrick's Breastplate	a-c	C. V. Stanford	18
Salvation Belongeth unto the Lord	(A)	W. Berwald	2
The Shadow of Thy Wings	(H)	M. Andrews	9

SHINE [*v.* Light]

All Praise to God	(B)	Wagner = Cornell	3
Arise, Shine, for Thy Light Is Come	H.L.	J. G. MacDermid	37
Arise, Shine, for Thy Light Is Come	(B)	G. H. Day	3
O Love Invisible		H. A. Matthews	2
Then Shall the Righteous Shine (*Elijah*)	T.	Mendelssohn	*
Then Shall the Righteous Shine	8	F.McCollin	9

SHIPS [*v.* Sailors, Sea]

I Saw Three Ships Come Sailing In	M.	E. Delamarter	9
I Saw Three Ships Come Sailing In		H. A. MacKinnon	9

SHUT-INS

Shut in with God`		M. Attwood	23
Whither Shall I Go from Thy Spirit?	H.L.	J. G. MacDermid	37

SIGNS [*v.* Christmas]

And There Shall Be a Sign		E. W. Naylor	1

SILENCE [*v*. Stillness]

A Song in the Night	(S.B)	R. H. Woodman	3
Be Still, Be Still	(A-B)	C. P. Scott	5
Be Still, My Soul		C. H. Kitson	15
In the Silence of the Night		Norwegian = Dickinson	9
Let All Mortal Flesh Keep Silence	(S.B)	G. Holst	18
Out of the Silence	SATB TTBB	J. L. Galbraith	2
Silent and Alone	(A.T)	C. W. Henrich	2
Song of the Silent Land	a-c	P. Ambrose	5
The Heart Worships	H.L.	G. Holst	18
The Presence in the Silence	a-c	T. T. Noble	5
The Silent Hour	H.M.L.	C. W. Cadman	32

SILOAM

By Cool Siloam's Shady Rill	(S)	G. H. Federlein	12
By Cool Siloam's Shady Rill		E. S. Barnes	2

SIMEON, St. [*v*. Close of Service, Nunc Dimittis, Epiphany]

The Song of Simeon	(T)	I. L. Strom	40
When to the Temple Mary Went		A. B. Jennings	9

SIMON, St. [*v*. St. Peter]

Now Are We Ambassadors	T-B	Mendelssohn	*
Simon (*The Kingdom of Heaven is at Hand*)	H.L. (Also SATB)	Ward-Stephens	21

SIMPLICITY [*v*. Beatitudes, Humility]

The Graces of Simplicity	U. (opt. A.)	W. J. Falk	3

SIN

Come Now and Let Us Reason	(T.B)	H. W. Wareing	1
Far from Their Home		H. H. Woodward	1
Jesu, Thou Joy of Loving Hearts	(S)	E. H. Davies	1
Lead on, O King Eternal		R. H. Terry	4
O Ye that Love the Lord		H. W. Wareing	1
Surely He Hath Borne Our Griefs (Messiah)		G. F. Handel	*
The Temple of My Heart	8 a-c	F. W. Snow	9
Thy Kingdom Come	8	F. M. Christiansen	20
Turn Thy Face from My Sins	H.L.	E. Hurst	25

SLEEP [v. Lullaby]

Awake, My Soul		M. P. Ingle	9
Awake, Thou that Sleepest		J. Stainer	1
Before Sleep	TTBB	G. Holst	27
He Giveth His Beloved Sleep	M.	J. L. Roeckel	31

SMILE

In Bethlehem	M.	P. J. Clark	13
The Christ-Child Smiled		E. R. Warren	9

SOCIAL SERVICE [v. Brotherhood, Home Missions, Man—Duty to Fellow Men]

He that Hath Pity upon the Poor	(B)	A. Whitehead	18
Light in Darkness	(S)	C. Jenkins	1
Now Are We Ambassadors	T-B	Mendelssohn	*
Prayer for Service	(H) Also SSA	H. B. Gaul	26
Rise up, O Men of God	a-c	T. T. Noble	5
Serving Man Is Serving Thee		G. O'Hara	22
Soldiers of the Cross, Arise	SAATTBB (S)	V. D. Thompson	18
The Earth and Man		C. Dickinson	9
What Christ Said	(B)	P. Lutkin	9

SOLDIER [v. Armistice]

For a Soldier's Burial	(B)	L. Boulanger	17
O God of Armies, Let Me Be Thy Soldier	L.	F. T. H. Candlyn	9
	(Also SATB)		
Stainless Soldier	H.M.L.	C. Dickinson	9

SOLOMON

Consider the Lilies	H.L.	J. P. Scott	3
Consider the Lilies	S-A	R. Topliff	7
Zadok the Priest		Handel	1

SON [v. Christ]

My Son, Forget Not My Law	M.	W. W. Adams	8
O Absalom, My Son	a-c	F. M. Christiansen	20
O Son of the Carpenter		G. B. Nevin	2
The Virgin and Her Son		J. W. Clokey	4

SONG

A Song in the Night	(S.B)	R. H. Woodman	3
Be Strong, Tomorrow Comes the Song	H.L.	P. Ambrose	5

SONG [continued]

Bow Down Thine Ear	(A)	E. S. Barnes	3
Cast Down, Yet Hoping in God	(S)	F. M. Christiansen	20
Fantasia (Angel voices ever singing)	(S.A.T)	E. S. Barnes	3
God's Song	H.L.	W. Berwald	3
Jehovah, I Would Sing Thy Praise	8 a-c	Bach=Luvaas	13
Let All the World in Every Corner Sing		T. T. Noble	5
Let All the World in Every Corner Sing		E. T. Chapman	43
Now to the Lord a New Song	(S-A)	G. Borch	6
The Morning Stars Sang Together	SSATB	J. Stainer	1
The Singers		C. Harris	4
The Singers	TTBB	H. L. Vibbard	9
Tomorrow Comes the Song	H.L.	P. Ambrose	5
With a Voice of Singing		M. Shaw	14

SONG OF SOLOMON [v. Biblical Passages, etc.]

SORROW [v. Grieving, Tears, Trials, Tribulation]

God of Righteousness	H.L.	H. Gilbert	23
Nobody Knows the Trouble I've Seen (Negro Spiritual)			*
The King of Sorrow		W. A. Goldsworthy	17
The Man of Sorrows	(A)	J. H. Adams	12

SOUL

Deck Thyself, My Soul		Crüger=Whitehead	5
Go, Happy Soul	H.L. (Also SATB, TTBB)	P. Yon	25
Soul of Christ		W. Y. Webbe	9
Souls of the Righteous	4 or 8	T. T. Noble	3
The Soul at Heaven's Gate	M.	Trad=Dickinson	9
The Surrender of the Soul	8	P. Cornelius	1

SOURCE

Jesu, Source of Purest Pleasure		C. Dickinson	9

SOVEREIGN [v. Coronation]

SOVEREIGNTY OF GOD [v. King]

SOWER [v. Harvest, Seed]

The Eyes of All Wait on Thee		A. R. Gaul	1
The Sower	(L)	J. Jordan	3

SPIRIT [*v.* Holy Spirit]

God Is a Spirit	8 a-c	C. A. Scholin	26
God Is a Spirit		W. S. Bennett	1
Send Forth Thy Spirit	SSATTBB O.	F. J. Schuetky	11
Spirit of God	a-c	P. Weaver	25

SPIRITUALS [*v.* Publishers' Catalogues]

Deep River		Trad = Burleigh	3
Jedus Is Risen		Trad = Gaul	2
Listen to the Lambs	(s)	Trad = Dett	3
The Crucifixion	H.L.	Trad = Fisher	2

SPRING

Lo, the Winter Is Past		B. Farebrother	1
Rise up, My Love (Easter)		H. Willan	15
The Hallelujah of the Flowers		P. Donastia	17
The Meadows of the Lord	H.	C. W. Cadman	12

SPRINGS

He Sendeth the Springs	(s)	D. Protheroe	6
He Sendeth the Springs	(s.t)	H. W. Wareing	1
Springs in the Desert	(t)	A. B. Jennings	9
To the Wayfarer (Orphic Mystery)		C. Forsyth	2

STABLE [*v.* Manger]

In Bethlehem's Manger	v.c.Hrp	Trad = Dickinson	9

STAR [*v.* Christmas, Epiphany, Nature]

Beyond Life's Evening Star		H. A. Matthews	2
Beyond the Starry Skies	(s.b) (v.c.Hrp)	H. Gilbert	9
Lo, Star-Led Chiefs (Palestine)		W. Crotch	9
O God, Who by the Leading of a Star		T. Attwood	1
On High the Stars Are Shining		J. Rheinberger	3
O Star of Love		Ward-Stephens	22
O Thou Who Keepest the Stars Alight		F. L. Sealy	2
Over the Stars	s-a	F. Abt	3
Seek Him that Maketh the Seven Stars	(s)	J. H. Rogers	2
Stars of the Morning	(h)	C. W. Cadman	19

STATUTES [*v.* Law]

STEADFASTNESS [*v.* Confidence]

STEP [v. Way]

Step by Step   H.M.L. (Also SATB TTBB SSAA)   G. O'Hara 19

STEPHEN, St.

Be Thou Faithful unto Death   T.   Mendelssohn *
The Son of God Goes Forth to War   A. Sullivan 1

STEWARDSHIP [v. Tithes]

Giving to God   C. F. Manney 2
He that Hath Pity upon the Poor   (B)   A. Whitehead 18
Honor the Lord with Thy Substance   J. Stainer 1
The True Gift   M.L.   F. Frank 9
Though I Speak with the Tongues of
  Men and Angels   (S.T)   E. Rhode 2

          [v. Prodigal Son]

STILLNESS [v. Calm, Silence]

A Song in the Night   (S.B)   R. H. Woodman 3
Be Still, Be Still   (A-B)   C. P. Scott 5
Comes at Times a Stillness   H. W. Pierce 18
Dear Lord and Father of Mankind   (T)   J. L. Galbraith 2
Dear Lord and Father of Mankind   (S.A.B)   A. B. Targett 9
Evening and Morning   M. Spicker 3
Let All Mortal Flesh Keep Silence   (S.B)   G. Holst 18

STONE [v. Corner-stone]

Behold, I Lay in Zion a Stone   (B)   R. H. Prutting 26

STORM

Fierce Was the Wild Billow   4 or 8   T. T. Noble 3
Fierce Raged the Tempest   D. Protheroe 6
In Heavenly Love Abiding   (S)   H. W. Parker 1
The Lost Sheep   (S.B)   M. B. Foster 3
The Ninety and Nine   H.L.   E. Campion 3
The Ninety and Nine   (A.B)   D. Protheroe 2
When the Winds Are Raging   L.   A. Whiting 3

STORY [v. Gospel]

I Think when I Hear that Sweet Story U.   H. Norris 3
That Sweet Story of Old   H.L. (Also SATB, TTBB, SSA)   J. A. West 16

STORY [*continued*]

The Old, Old Story	(A.T)	E. S. Hosmer	2
The Story of the Cross		E. Turner	6

STRAYING

Great Peace Have They	(H)	J. H. Rogers	3
Sanctuary of the Heart	H.L.	A. W. Ketelbey	27
My God, My Father, While I Stray	(H)	F. Wrigley	56

STRENGTH [*v.* Power]

Make Us Strong	8 a-c	Nagler = Dickinson	9
Suddenly There Was a Sound from Heaven		Aichinger = Row	29

STRUGGLE FOR RELIGIOUS LIBERTY

The Pilgrim Fathers	E. J. Stringham	9

SUFFERING

My Father, Look upon My Anguish (The Passion)	B.	Handel	*

SUMMER

As Torrents in Summer	SATB SSA	E. Elgar	9
Come, Thou Last Summer Ray		F. M. Christiansen	20
Summer Comes Again		J. Stainer	1
Summer Ended		C. Wood	43

SUN [*v.* Nature]

All from the Sun's Uprise		P. Tomblings	15
All Praise to God	(B)	Wagner = Cornell	3
God in Nature		Schubert	1
God of the Dew, God of the Sun	(S.A.T)	T. C. Whitmer	5
Introduction and Hymn to the Sun ("Iris")		P. Mascagni	17
Sun of My Soul	(S)	V. Eville	13
Thou Who Sendest Sun and Rain	(A)	G. W. Chadwick	5
When God Paints the Sunset		F. M. Christiansen	20

SUPPLICATION [*v.* Aspiration, Petition, Prayer]

All Praise to God	(B)	Wagner = Cornell	3
A Prayer	M.	D. Guion	3

SUPPLICATION [*continued*]

A Prayer for Love (Ave Maria)	(s)	Schubert = Voris	9
A Prayer for Our Country	(s)	W. R. Voris	9
Hear My Prayer	a-c	W. James	3
I Love the Lord	(H)	J. L. Galbraith	2
I Wait, O Lord	L.	P. Cimara	17
To My Humble Supplication, Lord		G. Holst	35

SUPPORT

Hold Thou Me Up	H.L. (Also SATB)	S. R. Gaines	9
O Lord, Support Us All the Day	(A.T) Chime	H. McAmis	3
O Lord, Support Us All the Day		G. M. Cooper	18
O Lord, Support Us All the Day		G. D. Richards	25

SURRENDER [*v.* Consecration, Conversion, Man—Surrender to God]

The Surrender of the Soul	P. Cornelius	1

SURSUM CORDA, The

Lift up Your Hearts	J. H. Barnby	1

SWORD

Put on, Therefore, as God's Elect	(s)	E. S. Barnes	9
Put up the Sword	(B)	F. M. Christiansen	20
They Shall Beat Their Swords into Plow-Shares	(A.T)	M. Andrews	25
What of the Night	(T)	R. G. Thompson	9

TABERNACLE [*v.* Altar, Sanctuary, Temple]

A New Heaven and a New Earth	(B)	A. R. Gaul	*
Behold the Tabernacle of God		G. A. MacFarren	1
How Amiable Are Thy Tabernacles	(S.A.T)	E. S. Barnes	3
O How Amiable Are Thy Dwellings		O. A. King	1
O How Amiable Are Thy Dwellings		Mana-Zucca	28

TABLE [*v.* Communion]

TASTE

O Taste and See	W. G. Parkyn	18

TEACHER

Blessed Jesus	F. M. Christiansen	20

TEACHER [continued]

Teach Me, O Lord		C. F. Manney 5
Teach Me Thy Way	H.L.	H. Gilbert 23

TEARS [v. Sorrow, Weeping]

Evening and Morning		M. Spicker 3
Hush, for Amidst Our Tears		R. G. Jones 13
Jesus Saith unto Her, "Mary" (Six Carols) (Short, and suitable for Solo)		E. S. Barnes 3
Nothing Is Here for Tears		R. V. Williams 8
The Knight of Bethlehem	a-c	P. Lutkin 9

TE DEUM, The

Te Deum		Handel 1
Te Deum		T. T. Noble 3
Te Deum		A. Sullivan 1
Te Deum		H. Statham 1
Te Deum		W. Y. Webbe 9

[v. Publishers' Catalogues]

TEMPERANCE [v. Temptation]

For Know Ye Not that Ye Are His Temple? (St. Paul)	B.	Mendelssohn *
Greater Love Hath No Man	(S.B)	J. Ireland 18
I Beseech You, Brethren (St. Mary Magdalene)		J. Stainer 1
Wine Is a Mocker		H. Leslie 2

TEMPEST [v. Storm]

TEMPLE [v. Sanctuary, Tabernacle]

And Jesus Entered into the Temple		H. W. Davies 1
Blessed City, Heavenly Salem		E. C. Bairstow 44
Built on a Rock	8 a-c	F. M. Christiansen 20
For Know Ye Not that Ye Are His Temple? (St. Paul)	B.	Mendelssohn *
God Is in His Holy Temple	a-c	C. F. Mueller 3
Lord of the Worlds Above	(S.T.B)	Mrs. H. H. A. Beach 2
Open the Gates of the Temple	H.L.	Mrs. J. F. Knapp 38

(Also SATB, TTBB and SSAA)

Presentation of Christ in the Temple		J. Eccard 1

TEMPLE [*continued*]

Temples Eternal	(s)	F. M. Christiansen	20
The Living God	H.L.	G. O'Hara	23
The Temple of My Heart	8 a-c	F. W. Snow	9
When to the Temple Mary Went	v.Hrp	A. B. Jennings	9

TEMPTATION [*v.* Lord's Prayer]

Blessed Is the Man that Endureth Temptation		O. King	1
From Every Earthly Pleasure	(H)	S. R. Gaines	3
Make Us Strong	8 a-c	Nagler = Dickinson	9
My New Name	H.L.	J. G. MacDermid	37

TENDERNESS [*v.* Shepherd]

Father, Most Holy	(B°) 8	F. M. Christiansen	20
Saviour, Like a Shepherd Lead Us	(B)	W. C. Macfarlane	3
Saviour, Like a Shepherd Lead Us	(B)	C. F. Mueller	26
Saviour, Like a Shepherd Lead Us	U.	H. Norris	3

TENTS [*v.* Tabernacle]

How Goodly Are Thy Tents	(B)	W. C. Macfarlane	3
Lead On, O King Eternal		R. H. Terry	4

TERSANCTUS, The

A New Heaven and a New Earth	(B)	A. R. Gaul	*
Holy, Holy, Holy	(M)	D. R. Emery	9
Lift Up Your Hearts		J. H. Barnby	1
Tersanctus	H.	R. G. Hailing	9

[*v.* Publishers' Catalogues]

TESTIMONY [*v.* Confession]

Awake, My Heart's Beloved	(M)	Sachs = Dickinson	9
O Could I Speak	(S.A.T)	J. W. Thompson	13

THANKS [*v.* Gratitude]

Because of Thy Great Bounty	H.	E. R. Warren	9
Be Ye Kind One to Another	(B)	S. Liddle	14
O Lord, How Manifold Are Thy Works		J. H. Barnby	*
O Praise the Name of the Lord		Tschaikowsky	9
Thanks Be to God (Elijah)		Mendelssohn	*

THANKSGIVING DAY [v. Pilgrimage, Publishers' Catalogues]

A Prayer of Thanksgiving		E. Kremser	*
A Psalm of Gratitude	(s)	C. W. Cadman	2
A Thanksgiving Song		E. S. Barnes	2
Blessed Art Thou, O Israel	8 a-c	V. D. Thompson	4
Great Is Jehovah	(s) o.	Schubert	*
He Sendeth the Springs	(s.t)	H. W. Wareing	1
List to the Lark	(s) Chime	C. Dickinson	9
O Praise the Lord of Heaven	(b) o.	A. Hyde	9
O Praise the Lord of Heaven	(3 Choirs)	V. Williams	9
Praise the Lord, O Jerusalem	(m)	J. H. Maunder	1
Psalm of Thanksgiving	H.M.L. (Also SATB (s))	F. Allitsen	6
While the Earth Remaineth	(s.a.t.b)	M. Andrews	25

I THESSALONIANS [v. Biblical Passages, etc.]

THIEF [v. Good Friday]

The Penitent Thief	SSATB	A. Kastalsky	9

THIRST [v. Springs]

As Pants the Hart		H. Coleman	18
As Pants the Hart	(s)	S. Salter	9
Ho! Every One that Thirsteth	(t)	W. C. Macfarlane	3
Ho! Every One that Thirsteth	(b)	G. C. Martin	1
Ho! Every One that Thirsteth	(s.b)	H. L. Vibbard	3
My Soul Is Athirst for God (Holy City)	(t)	A. R. Gaul	*
My Soul Is Athirst for God	H.M.L.	W. Stickles	24
O Come, Every One that Thirsteth (Elijah)	S-A-T-B	Mendelssohn	*

THOMAS, St.

Thomas (Be Not Faithless, but Believing)	H.L.	Ward-Stephens	21
Thomas (Be Not Faithless, but Believing)	SATB	Ward-Stephens	21

THORNS

A Legend	a-c	Tschaikowsky	*
Who Is This?	(s)	H. E. Button	1

THOUGHT

God Be in My Mind		A. Buzzi-Peccia	26
Let This Mind Be in You	(s.b)	Mrs. H. H. A. Beach	7

TONGUES [v. Whitsuntide]

In Divers Tongues Spake the Apostles (Motet)		Palestrina	1
Now Let Every Tongue Adore Thee		Bach	35
O Taste and See	(s.a)	J. H. Rogers	3
Though I Speak with the Tongues of Men	(t.s)	E. Rhode	2
Though I Speak with the Tongues of Men		E. C. Bairstow	8

TRANSFIGURATION [v. Christ—Divinity]

O Could I Speak	(s.a.t)	J. W. Thompson	13
The Vision of Christ	8 a-c	F. M. Christiansen	20
Transfiguration (From Galilee) (Short Cantata)		M. Andrews	9

TRANSFORMING POWER [v. Conversion, Holy Spirit, Power]

Breathe on Me, Breath of God	(s)	C. E. Wheeler	16
Breathe on Me, Breath of God		V. D. Thompson	9
Breathe on Me, Breath of God		W. R. Voris	9
Breath of God	H.L.	M. T. Salter	3

TRANSGRESSION [v. Sin]

O God, Have Mercy upon Me (St. Paul)	B.	Mendelssohn	*

TRAVELLER [v. Pilgrimage]

A Prayer for Those at Sea	H.L.	B. Hamblen	22
Come, O Thou Traveller Unknown	4 or 8	T. T. Noble	*
Come, O Thou Traveller Unknown		H. B. Gaul	6
Gaelic Rune of Hospitality	8	M. W. Hill	40
Out of Heaven		F. W. Cowen	3

TREES [v. Nature]

A Ballad of Trees and the Master		G. W. Chadwick	2
A Ballad of Trees and the Master	SSAA a-c	G. D. Richards	9
A Ballad of Trees and the Master	M.	L. P. Rile	9
I Was the Tree	H.L.	G. O'Hara	23
The Christmas Tree	H.	J. W. Conant	25
Tree of the Cross	M.	L. P. Rile	9
Trees	H.L.	O. Rasbach	3

TRIALS [v. Passion, Tribulation]

All Ye who Seek	H. M. Higgs	1
In the Hour of Trial	Rubinstein = Milligan	5
In the Hour of Trial	W. Stickles	21
Trial Before Pilate	A. Koshetz	26

[v. Stainer's "Crucifixion"]

TRIBULATION [v. Abandonment, Grieving, Sorrow]

Gallia (Motet)	(s)	C. Gounod	*
Let Not Your Heart Be Troubled		E. Faning	1
Let Not Your Heart Be Troubled		A. Farwell	11
O Rest in the Lord (Elijah)	(A)	Mendelssohn	*
They that in Much Tribulation (Lauda Sion)		Mendelssohn	*
Thou Who Sendest Sun and Rain	(A)	G. W. Chadwick	5

TRINITY

Evening Hymn to the Trinity	a-c	M. Andrews	9
Glory to the Trinity	8 a-c	S. Rachmaninoff	9
Holy, Holy, Holy	(M)	D. R. Emery	9
O Gladsome Light	4 or 8	A. Kastalsky	9
O Trinity of Blessed Light		J. E. West	1
St. Patrick's Breastplate	a-c	C. V. Stanford	18
We Give Thee Thanks		G. A. MacFarren	14

TRIOS

At Eventide it Shall Be Light (Holy City)	SSA	A. R. Gaul	*
Father, Take My Hand	SAB	C. E. Scott	8
Flowery Easter	SSA	P. Donastia	17
I Will Sing of Thy Power	SAT	P. Lutkin	9
Lord, We Praise Thy Holy Name	ATB	G. Rossini	2
My Soul Doth Magnify	STB Hrp	C. St.-Saens	2
Now the Shades of Evening Fall	SAT	Mendelssohn	3
O Happy Souls that Love Thee	SAB	C. St.-Saens	2
On Thee Each Living Soul Awaits	STB	F. J. Haydn	1
Say Where Is His Star	TBB	Mendelssohn	2
Seek Ye the Lord	SAB	J. V. Roberts	26
The King of Love	STB	Mendelssohn	2

[v. Publishers' Catalogues]

TRIUMPH [v. Church—Triumphant, Victory]

A Song of Triumph	(Jr Voices or Solo)	W. Lester 13
Clap Your Hands All People	8 a-c	F. M. Christiansen 20
Lift High the Triumph Song		C. F. Mueller 3
The Hymn Triumphant	(s.b)	C. W. Cadman 12
The Soul Triumphant	(s) o.	T. T. Noble 9

TRIUMPHANT ENTRY [v. Palm Sunday]

TROUBLE [v. Peace]

Let Not Your Heart Be Troubled		E. Faning 1
Let Not Your Heart Be Troubled	h.	P. W. Reed 12
Nobody Knows the Trouble I've Seen		(Negro Spiritual) *

TRUMPET [v. Instruments]

Behold, Ye Despisers	(b)	H. W. Parker 9
Blow Ye the Trumpet in Zion	(t)	R. H. Woodman 3
Blow Ye the Trumpet in Zion	ttbb	R. H. Woodman 3
The Shofar (Trumpet) Is Sounded		Trad=Dickinson 9
The Trumpet Shall Sound (*Messiah*)	b.	Handel *
The Trumpet Shall Sound	(t)	J. P. Scott 26
The Trumpets of Christmas	(m)	R. deKoven 3

TRUST

Behold, God Is My Salvation	(s)	J. H. Rogers 2
Gracious Lord of All		Bach 1
Hymn of Trust	(l) v.	Mrs. H. H. A. Beach 5
In Faith I Calmly Rest	(m)	Bach=Dickinson 9
I Have Longed for Thy Salvation		
(Stabat Mater)	s-a-t-b	G. Rossini 1
In God We Trust		Mana-Zucca 28
In Thee O God	m. Stgs	M. Spicker 3
In that Day		F. W. Holloway 39
Lord of the Worlds Above	(s.t.b)	Mrs. H. H. A. Beach 2
They that Trust in the Lord	m.	H. P. Eames 13
They that Trust in the Lord	(s)	H. R. Spier 3
Trust in God	h.l.	B. Huhn 19
Trust in God at All Times	(s)	G. H. Knight 6

TRUTH

Be True	a-c	F. M. Christiansen	20
Heavenly Truth	c.Hrp	G. H. Knight	9
Lord of All Being	(B)	M. Andrews	9
O Eternal Truth (Commencement)		H. B. Gaul	4
(Two-Part School Ch and Mixed Ch)			
O God of Truth	TTBB	H. E. Darke	11
Mercy and Truth		Bortniansky	9
The God of Truth and Love	H.L.	B. Huhn	3
Ye Shall Find Rest	M.	W. R. Voris	9
Ye Shall Know the Truth	H.L.	W. B. Olds	13

TURNING BACK [*v.* Conversion, Retrospect]

Turn Back, O Man		G. Holst 17

TWELFTH NIGHT [*v.* Epiphany]

The Lost Star	SSATBB a-c	B. Gross 13

TWILIGHT

Twilight and Dawn	H.L.	O. Speaks 3

UNCTION

Breathe on Me, Breath of God	(S)	C. E. Wheeler	16
Breathe on Me, Breath of God		V. D. Thompson	9
Breathe on Me, Breath of God		W. R. Voris	9
Breath of God	H.L.	M. T. Salter	3
The King of Love	(A.S-B)	H. R. Shelley	3

UNDERSTANDING

Who Can Comprehend Thee?	Mozart 1
Who Is Like unto Thee	A. Sullivan 9

UNGODLINESS [*v.* Atheism, Despising God, Rebelliousness]

Blessed Is the Man	J. W. Clokey 13
Fret Not Thyself because of the Un-	
godly	F. A. G. Ouseley 1

UNITY [*v.* Church—Unity]

UNIVERSE [*v.* World]

Eternal Ruler of the Ceaseless Round		M. Genet 9
Eternal Ruler of the Ceaseless Round	(A)	F. L. Sealy 9

UNIVERSE [*continued*]

Lord of All Being	(B)	M. Andrews	9
Lord of All Being		Mrs. H. H. A. Beach	9
Planets, Stars and Airs of Space	a-c	Bach	3
Praise	(S.B)	A. Rowley	15

UNKNOWN [*v.* Understanding]

Come, O Thou Traveller Unknown	a-c (4 or 8)	T. T. Noble	3
Come, O Thou Traveller Unknown		H. B. Gaul	6
Darest Thou Now, O Soul?		D. M. Williams	9
He Who Would Valiant Be	(B)	R. Broughton	3
In Heavenly Love Abiding	(S)	H. W. Parker	1
Lost in the Night	(S) a-c	F. M. Christiansen	20
Sanctuary of the Heart	H.L.	A. W. Ketelbey	27
Two Kings		J. W. Clokey	4

UNSELFISHNESS [*v.* Brotherhood, Man—Duty to Fellow Men]

UNVEILING [*v.* Dedication, Memorial]

When First Thine Eyes Unveil		H. Howells	15

USURY

Lord, Who Shall Dwell (Ps. 15: 1–5)		W. S. Bennett	1

UZZIAH

A New Heaven and a New Earth	(B)	A. R. Gaul	*

VALLEY

Comfort Ye, My People	(T.B)	G. H. Federlein	3
Every Valley Shall Be Exalted (Messiah)	T.	Handel	*

VALOR [*v.* Courage]

He Who Would Valiant Be	(B)	R. Broughton	3
Jesus Walked this Lonesome Valley	SATBB	W. L. Dawson	13
Make Us Strong	8 a-c	Nagler = Dickinson	9

VANITY

The Lord of Heaven	M.	C. Forsyth	9
The Lord of Heaven	TTBB	C. Forsyth	9

VEIL [*v.* Unveiling]
Behold Two Blind Men Sitting   J. Stainer 1

VENERATION
Veneration of the Cross   Rachmaninoff = Douglas 9

VESPERS [*v.* Compline, Evening, Publishers' Catalogues]
Evening Hymn   (s)   Bruch = Milligan 9
Vesper Hymn   E. Delamarter 9

VICTIM
O Jesu, Victim Blest   (H)   J. B. Powell 1
O Saving Victim   N. Coke-Jephcott 9
O Saving Victim   Gounod = Tours 2
O Saving Victim   s-a-b   C. St.-Saens 2

VICTORY
Behold, Ye Despisers   (B)   H. W. Parker 9
Hallelujah Chorus (Messiah)   Handel *
On the Third Day   G. H. Federlein 3
Prepare Ye the Way   (T.B)   L. Jewell 9
Sing Alleluia Forth   (s.t.b)   D. Buck 2
Song of Victory (10 min.)   P. E. Fletcher 1
The Day Draws on with Golden Light   E. C. Bairstow 15
The Strife Is O'er   M. Vulpius 15
Whatsoever Is Born of God   H. Oakeley 1
Who Is This?   (s)   H. E. Button 1

VIGIL
Could Ye Not Watch?   b.   S. Coleridge-Taylor 1
Could Ye Not Watch? (Crucifixion)   (B)   J. Stainer *
The Vigil of the Shepherds   (s.a.b)   W. L. Blumenschein 3
Vigil   F. M. Christiansen 20
What of the Night?   (T)   R. G. Thompson 9

VINE
Bread of Heaven   F. W. Wadely 8
Except Ye Abide   (A)   C. B. Rutenber 2
I Am the Vine   (s.t)   P. James 23
O My Vineyard (Redemption)   C. Gounod *

VIRGIN MARY [v. Madonna, Mary, Manger]

At Midnight There Was a Cry		A. Ham	9
Remember Now, O Virgin Mary	SSA(S)	J. Massenet	3
The Angel Said (Suite of Five Anthems)		C. P. Waters	55
The Virgin and Her Son		J. W. Clokey	4
The Virgin's Slumber Song	SSA SATB	M. Reger	2

VIRGINS

The Ten Virgins	(Sr and Jr Ch) o.	T. Facer	14
The Ten Virgins (Cantata)		A. R. Gaul	1

VIRTUES [v. Table of Contents]

The Christian Virtues' Mother	F. M. Christiansen	20

VISION

A New Heaven and a New Earth	(B)	A. R. Gaul	*
A Prayer	M.	D. Guion	3
A Vision of Music	SSAA (A) O.	H. Gilbert	9
Be Thou My Vision		A. Baynon	18
Give Me the Vision, Lord	H.L.	C. S. Briggs	5
In the Year that King Uzziah Died		D. M. Williams	9
I Saw the Lord (The Vision)	(S-S-A)	J. W. Clokey	9
The Vision (Prayer of Thanksgiving)		Kremser=Loomis	11
The Vision of Belshazzar	TTBB	G. Bantock	51
The Vision of Christ	8 a-c	F. M. Christiansen	20

VISIT

Thou Visitest the Earth	J. H. Barnby	1

VOICE

A Voice by Jordan's Shore			
Hymn-Text by Samuel Longfellow			
I Heard a Great Voice		G. F. Cobb	1
I Heard the Voice of Christ Say			
"Peace"	(S)	W. C. Gale	2
I Heard the Voice of Jesus Say	(B)	C. Huerter	6
I Heard the Voice of Jesus Say	H.L.	F. C. Rathbun	12
My Voice Shalt Thou Hear in the			
Morning	(T)	S. Liddle	18
O Silent Hills		R. D. Shure	4
Prepare Ye the Way	(T.B)	G. H. Federlein	3

VOICE [continued]

Prepare Ye the Way	(T.B)	L. Jewell	9
The Voice that Breathed o'er Eden		Le Jeune	9
The Voice within	8 a-c	F. M. Christiansen	20
Today, if Ye Will Hear His Voice	H.L.	J. H. Rogers	5
With a Voice of Singing		M. Shaw	14
With Grateful Hearts Our Voice We Raise		V. Novello	1

WAITING [v. Patience, Advent, Delay]

I Waited for the Lord	(S-A)	Mendelssohn	*
On Thee Each Living Soul	S.T.B.	Haydn	1
Patiently Have I Waited		C. St.-Saens	*
The Son of God Goes Forth		A. Sullivan	1
They That Wait Upon the Lord		F. W. Snow	9
Waiting for the Kings	TTBB	B. Treharne	4

WAKING [v. Awakening]

Save Us, Lord, Waking		C. F. Waters	18

WALKING [v. Pilgrimage, Road, Way]

If Ye Walk in My Statutes		J. Clippingdale	1
In the Night Came Christ Walking	8	N. Cain	3
I Said: Let Me Walk	(B)	P. Lutkin	9
I Walk Alone With God	H.L.	J. B. Abbott	16
I Walked To-day Where Jesus Walked	H.L.	G. O'Hara	3
Lord Christ Came Walking	(B) a-c	H. A. MacKinnon	9
O For a Closer Walk With God	(M)	M. B. Foster	3
O For a Closer Walk With God		T. T. Noble	5
O God Who Set the Seers Aflame		H. L. Baumgartner	9
O Master Let Me Walk With Thee	L.	M. Andrews	17
O Master Let Me Walk With Thee	(A)	G. W. Stebbins	2
The Soul of the Garden	H.	W. Sektberg	17
The Walk to Emmaus		H. W. Davies	1
Walk in the Light	(T)	R. H. Prutting	3
With Quiet Heart		F. Scherer	9

WALL

And the Wall of the City		O. King	1

WANDERING

Come Unto Me, Ye Weary	(s)	C. Huerter	2
If Thou Hadst Known, O Jerusalem	(s)	Ward-Stephens	22
Patiently Have I Waited (Christmas Oratorio)	(A)	C. St.-Saens	1
Return, O Wanderer to Thy Home	(s)	W. Berwald	2
They that Wait upon the Lord	(H)	F. W. Snow	9
Turn Back, O Man		G. Holst	17

WAR

A Prayer in Time of War	(A.B)	C. Dickinson	9
A Prayer for Our Country		W. R. Voris	9
Evening Hymn in Time of War		L. Smith	18
God is Our Refuge and Strength	8	C. F. Mueller	3
Invocation (A Prayer in War-Time)		Grieg = Haeling	9
O God of Love, O King of Peace		J. E. West	9
O Lord God of Hosts		H. B. Gaul	2
Put up the Sword	8	F. M. Christiansen	20
Save Them, O Lord, Who Fight		F. Tozer	1
The Lord is a Man of War	B.B	Handel	2
The Soul Triumphant	(B) o	Noble	9
There Was War in Heaven		W. A. C. Cruickshank	1

AFTER WAR

Blessed are the Peacemakers	H.L.	Ward-Stephens	3
He Maketh Wars to Cease	H.L.	J. P. Scott	26
In Flanders' Fields		F. LaForge	26

WARNING [*v.* Rebuke]

Behold, Ye Despisers		H. W. Parker	9
Day of Anger, Day of Warning (Dies Irae)	TTBB	Mozart = James	9

WASHINGTON'S BIRTHDAY

A Prayer for Our Country		W. R. Voris	9
Homage to Washington		F. Bornschein	11

WATCHING [*v.* Christmas, Advent]

Could Ye not Watch With Me		S. Coleridge-Taylor	1
Could Ye not Watch With Me	(B)	A. R. Gaul	*
Round Me Falls the Night		F. W. Snow	9

WATCHING [*continued*]

Save Us, O Lord		E. C. Bairstow	1
The Lord His Watch is Keeping		Flemish = Dickinson	9
Wake, Awake	8	F. M. Christiansen	20
Watch and Pray		W. H. Lockett	1
What of the Night	(T)	R. G. Thompson	9
When o'er the Hills	(B)	Flemish = Dickinson	9
Ye Watchers and Ye Holy Ones		Trad = Davison	35
Ye Watchers and Ye Holy Ones	TTBB	Trad = Davison	35
Ye Watchers and Ye Holy Ones	TTBB	L. Woodgate	18

WATCH-NIGHT [*v.* New Year]

WATCHWORD

Forward, Be Our Watchword	(With Jr Ch)	L. Parker	14
Forward, Be Our Watchword	(With Jr Ch) o.	W. L. Frost	14

WATER [*v.* Billow, Waves, Sea, Thirst]

A Ballad of Christ on the Water	SSATB a-c	E. S. Barnes	3
By Babylon's Wave		C. Gounod	*
By the Waters of Babylon	(S)	S. Coleridge-Taylor	1
By the Waters of Babylon	H.L.	C. T. Howell	2
By the Waters of Babylon	(H)	C. T. Howell	2
By the Waters of Babylon	(A.T)	R. S. Stoughton	2
Dear Friend, Whose Presence in the House. Hymn-Text by J. F. Clarke			
Dear Lord Who Once Upon the Lake	(S)	V. D. Thompson	3
Fierce Was the Wild Billow	8 or 4	T. T. Noble	3
God of the Waters	SSA	G. Holst	9
I Am the Water of Life	(T)	J. P. Dunn	4
In the Night Came Christ Walking	8	N. Cain	3
Living Waters		W. Berwald	3
The Harp and the Willow		C. Loomis	13
Whosoever Drinketh of This Water	(B)	J. T. Field	1

WAY

Faith is the Way	H.L.	Ward-Stephens	21
He Knows the Way	H.M.L. V.	C. S. Briggs	31
Is This the Way to Bethlehem?	a-c	Italian = Dickinson	9
Lord, Let Thy Spirit		W. Y. Webbe	9
O Thou in All Thy Might	(T)	C. P. Scott	2

WAY [*continued*]

Prepare Ye the Way	(T.B)	L. Jewell	9
Roads	(A)	C. Dickinson	9
Show Me Thy Way, O Lord		V. D. Thompson	9
Show Me Thy Way, O Lord	H.	R. Navarro	9
The King's Highway	(S)	D. M. Williams	9
The Pilgrim Pavement	U. (S)	V. Williams	8
There is One Way	(L)	F. F. Bullard	2
The Ways	H.	O. H. Jones	9
Thou Art the Way		G. B. Nevin	4
Walk in the Light	(T)	R. H. Prutting	3

WAYFARER [*v.* Pilgrim]

Come, O Thou Traveller		H. B. Gaul	6
I Walk Alone With God	H.L.	J. B. Abbott	16
With Quiet Heart		F. Scherer	9

WEAKNESS [*v.* Strength]

Hold Thou Me Up	H.L.	S. R. Gaines	9
Hold Thou Me Up		S. R. Gaines	9
In the Hour of Trial		W. Stickles	21

WEARINESS

Art Thou Weary	(B)	G. W. Chadwick	5
Art Thou Weary	(S.A) V.	T. del Riego	2
Come Unto Him	(S)	Handel	*
They Shall Run and Not be Weary	H.L.	J. G. MacDermid	37

WEDDING

Here at Thine Altar, Lord	a-c	A. Rowley	1
Holy Ghost, to Earth Descending		A. Dvorak	1
May the Grace of God	U.	I. R. Davies	1
My God, I Thank Thee		E. H. Lemare	1
O Perfect Love	S.A. or S-A	H. T. Burleigh	12
O Perfect Love		Mendelssohn	2
O Perfect Love	H.L.	L. Sowerby	9
The Voice that Breathed o'er Eden		LeJeune	9
There Was a Marriage in Cana of Galilee		J. Stainer	1
Wedding March		Mendelssohn = Boex	12

WEEPING [v. Tears, Sorrow]

Did Christ O'er Sinners Weep?   F. E. Ward   2

WELCOME [v. Guest]

Gaelic Rune of Hospitality   8 a-c   M. W. Hill 40
There's a Wideness in God's Mercy   J. S. Matthews   9

WHITSUNTIDE [v. Holy Spirit, Pentecost, Publishers' Catalogues]

Lord, Let Thy Spirit   (B)   W. Y. Webbe   9
Thy Dove Flies Low on Whitsuntide
    (Carol)   A. Kopyloff = Gaul   2
With Other Tongues   Palestrina 27

WIDOW

Thou Hast Turned My Heaviness   A. Gray   1
What Have I to do with Thee (Elijah)   S-B   Mendelssohn   *

WILDERNESS [v. Desert]

Father of Mercies   (B)   S. P. Waddington   1
In the Wilderness (Motet)   a-c   E. L. Bainton 15
Springs in the Desert   (T)   A. B. Jennings   9
The Voice in the Wilderness   J. P. Scott 23
The Wilderness   (B)   S. S. Wesley   1

WILL

God's Will Be Done   H.   R. M. Stults 12
My Jesus, as Thou Wilt   W. R. Voris   2
Shepherd, Take Me By the Hand   H.L.   Ward-Stephens 21
Shepherd, Take Me By the Hand   Ward-Stephens 21
Thy Will Be Done   (H)   D. Protheroe 26

WINGS

Give Us the Wings of Faith   E. Bullock   8
Ninety-First Psalm   H.L.   J. G. MacDermid 37
O for the Wings   Mendelssohn   *
Take Down Thy Harp   F. M. Christiansen 20
The Shadow of Thy Wings   H.   M. Andrews   9
The Shadow of Thy Wings   (S.T.)   M. Andrews   9

WINTER

In the Bleak Mid-Winter (Christmas
    Carol)   (S.T)   H. E. Drake 18

WINTER [*continued*]

Lo, the Winter is Past		F. Paterson	3

WISDOM [*v.* Biblical Passages, etc.]

Doth Not Wisdom Cry		D. S. Smith	9
Let Not the Wise Man Glory in His Wisdom	H.L.	J. G. MacDermid	37
O God of Wisdom		F. W. Wadley	1
O Lord, How Manifold Are Thy Works		J. Barnby	1
O Wisdom, Spirit of the Holy God		T. T. Noble	9
O Wisdom which Comest		H. Willan	9
O Ye Who Seek for Wisdom Here	TTBB	Wagner = Holden	2
The Lord by Wisdom Hath Founded the Earth		G. Mead	25
Wisdom Shall Praise Herself		J. E. West	1

WISH

A Christmas Wish		G. Rich	4

WITNESSING [*v.* Missions]

And the Witnesses Had Laid down Their Clothes (St. Paul)		Mendelssohn	*
Could Ye Not Watch (*Atonement*)	B.	S. Coleridge-Taylor	1
Could Ye Not Watch (Crucifixion)	(B)	J. Stainer	*

WOES [*v.* Sorrow, Trial]

With All My Weight of Woes (Hymn to the Saviour)	(s) Hrp	E. Kremser	3

WOODS [*v.* Fields, Forest, Nature]

Into the Woods My Master Went		T. T. Noble	5
The Woods and Every Sweet-Smelling Tree		J. E. West	1

WORD [*v.* Gospel, Incarnation]

A Song in the Night	(s.B)	R. H. Woodman	3
Behold, Thou Shalt Call a Nation	(A.B)	F. Stevenson	2
He Sent His Word	H.L.	J. G. MacDermid	37
If Any Little Word of Mine	H.L.	P. Ambroise	12
In the Beginning was the Word		M. Andrews	9
O Lord, Thy Word Endureth	(A-T)	E. H. Lemare	5

WORD [*continued*]

The Enchanting Word		F. M. Christiansen	20
The Lord Gave the Word		E. Turner	6

WORK

A Song of Prayer and Work	H.L.	W. C. Macfarlane	3
Every Man's Work	(A)	G. H. Federlein	6
List to the Lark	(S) Chime	C. Dickinson	9
Man Goeth Forth to His Work		A. Carnall	1
Thy Work to Do	H.M.L.	C. S. Briggs	31

WORKERS

Jesus, Thou Divine Companion			
Hymn-Text (LeJeune)			
Psalm to Labor (Priests' March)		Mendelssohn	11

WORLD [*v.* Universe]

Bless the Lord (Long)		Franck=Sweet	25
Darkness Obscured the Earth	a-c	Haydn	3
Daughters of Jerusalem (Light of the World)	B.	A. Sullivan	3
His World is Love	H.L.	H. T. Burleigh	17
Let all the World in Every Corner Sing		G. Shaw	1
Let all the World in Every Corner Sing		T. T. Noble	5
Lord of the Worlds Above	(S.T.B)	Mrs. H. H. A. Beach	2
Love Not the World	(S.A)	A. Sullivan	3
Love Not the World	(A)	F. F. Parker	3
O How Fair, How Pure the World		A. Baas	11
O How Fair is This Thy World	H.L.	Schubert	25
The World's Desire	S.	W. B. Anderson	9
The World's Prayer		C. W. Cadman	12
Turn Back, O Man		G. Holst	17
Whenas All the World	(S.B)	M. Shaw	8
While the Earth Shook and Trembled	M.	C. P. Scott	8
World, Farewell, Thou Canst Not Hold Me		J. Rosenmuller	8

WORSHIP [*v.* Praise, Adoration]

O Come Let us Worship	(T)	Mendelssohn	*

WORSHIP [*continued*]

Worship		G. Shaw 1
Worship the Holy Babe		R. A. Dickson 25

WRATH [*v.* Anger]

Dies Irae (Requiem)		Mozart = Verdi *
The Great Day of the Lord	Chime	G. C. Martin 1
Ye Shall Find Rest	M.	W. R. Voris 9

WRITING [*v.* Gospel]

Whatsoever Things Were Written Aforetime	SSA	C. H. Lloyd 1

YEARNING [*v.* Longing]

YOKE [*v.* Invitation, Fetters]

YOUTH [*v.* School]

Comrades, a cantata (1½ hrs.)		C. Bonner 14
(For C. E. Societies, Sunday Schools, etc., Jr and Sr)		
Here, As We Come	(s)	F. M. Christiansen 20
In Thee, O God, Do I Put My Trust	M.	M. Spicker 3
Remember Now Thy Creator in the Days of Thy Youth		H. B. Gaul 9
Remember Now Thy Creator in the Days of Thy Youth	(T)	J. P. Scott 26
Remember Now Thy Creator	TTBB	F. S. Smith 21
Shepherd of Tender Youth		W. Lester 40
Take Us to Thy Care	8	Handel = Ganschow 40
Wherewithal Shall a Young Man	(T)	H. Hiles 1
Youth	SSA	P. Chesnokoff 29

ZACHARIAS [*v.* Benedictus]

Blessed Be the Lord God of Israel (Woman of Samaria)	W. S. Bennett 1

ZADOK

Zadok the Priest	Handel 1

ZAREPHATH

Thou Hast Turned My Heaviness	A. Gray 1

ZEAL [*v.* Awakening, Diligent, Church—Militant]

Awake My Soul		M. P. Ingle 9
It is Enough (*Elijah*)	B.	Mendelssohn *
Rise up, O Men of God	a-c	T. T. Noble 5

ZECHARIAH [*v.* Biblical Passages, etc.)

ZEPHANIAH [*v.* Biblical Passages, etc.]

ZION

Awake, Awake, Put on Thy Strength		J. Stainer 1
Blow Ye the Trumpet in Zion	(T)	R. H. Woodman 3
Daughter of Zion		F. C. Maker 1
Gallia	(s)	C. Gounod *
Great Is the Lord	8	H. A. Matthews 3
The Lord Will Comfort Zion	T.	P. Lutkin 16
Rise, Crowned With Light		V. Eville 2
Zion	H.L.	B. Huhn 3
Zion	H.L.	P. Rodney 8

PART II

BIBLICAL PASSAGES, PARAPHRASES AND PARALLELS

BIBLICAL PASSAGES, PARAPHRASES
AND PARALLELS

Titles only are given in the reference, and not literal quotations of specified verses.

OLD TESTAMENT

GENESIS

1 : 1–3	Let There Be Light (B)	W. R. Spence	2
1–4	In the Beginning (Creation)	Haydn	*
1–4	The Creation SATB TTBB	W. Richter	26
11	And God Said, Let the Earth Bring Forth Grass (Creation)	Haydn	*
14–16	And God Said, Let There Be Light (Creation)	Haydn	*
31	And God Saw Everything That He Had Made (Creation)	Haydn	*
2 : 8	And the Lord Planted a Garden	E. S. Craston	1
4 : 21	O Had I Jubal's Lyre (Joshua)	Handel	1
6 : 1–2, 4–9, 13–14, 18–19 7 : 5, 18–20, 22 8 : 1, 6–13, 18, 20	Le Deluge (Cantata)	C. St.-Saens	3
8–13	Like Noah's Weary Dove (A)	H. C. Banks	2
9 : 12–13, 15	Le Deluge (Cantata)	C. St.-Saens	3
28 : 15	Fear Thou Not, For I Am With Thee	J. Booth	1
16–17	Arise, O Lord, Into Thy Resting Place	G. F. Cobb	1
32 : 24, 26	Come, O Thou Traveller Unknown 4 or 8	T. T. Noble	*
24–29	And Jacob Was Left Alone	J. Stainer	1

EXODUS

3 : 14	The God of Abraham Praise (S)	H. R. Shelley	3
10 : 21	He Sent a Thick Darkness Over All the Land (Israel in Egypt)	Handel	1
13 : 5, 9	The Lord Hath Brought Us	E. H. Thorne	1
15 : 11, 13, 17–18	The Eternal Shepherd (A.B)	A. H. Ryder	2

EXODUS [*continued*]

15: 11, 13, 17–18, 21 Who Is Like Unto Thee	A. Sullivan	1
17–19 Thou Shalt Bring Them In (Israel in Egypt)	Handel	1
20–22 Song of Miriam o.	Schubert	1
20–22 Song of Miriam (s)	A. Rubinstein	3
20: 18–19 And All the People Saw	J. Stainer	1
18, 20–21 And Miriam the Prophetess (Israel in Egypt)	Handel	1

LEVITICUS

26: 3, 4 If Ye Walk in My Statutes	H. A. Chambers	1
3, 4 If Ye Walk in My Statutes	J. Clippingdale	1
1, 9, 12 My People Shall Dwell	H. W. Wareing	1

NUMBERS

6: 24, 25 The Lord Bless Thee (s)	L. Sowerby	6
24, 25 The Lord Bless Thee SATB, TTBB, SSA	P. Lutkin	16
24: 5, 6 How Goodly Are Thy Tents, O Jacob	F. A. G. Ouseley	1
24: 5, 6 How Goodly Are Thy Tents	W. C. Macfarlane	3
17 There Shall a Star From Jacob (Christus)	Mendelssohn	1

DEUTERONOMY

4: 29 *If With All Your Hearts* T.	Mendelssohn	1
7: 9, 13, 19, 21 Know Then the Lord thy God	Haydn	1
31: 6, 8 He Faileth Not (H)	H. W. Parker	9
32: 2 My Doctrine Shall Drop as the Rain	P. Armes	1
7 Blow Ye the Trumpet	R. H. Woodman	3
33: 27–29 Honor the Lord With Thy Substance	M. Andrews	9
27–29 *Honor the Lord With Thy Substance* (The Prodigal Son)	A. Sullivan	*
27–29 Honor the Lord With Thy Substance	J. Stainer	1
27 The Good Shepherd	A. B. Jennings	9
27 The Eternal God Is Thy Home	Wolf = Davies	1

JOSHUA

1: 5 He Faileth Not (H)	H. W. Parker	9
9 Make Us Strong	Nagler = Dickinson	9
24: 15 Choose Ye This Day (s.A)	C. Nordman	39

JUDGES

5: The Song of Deborah	(A.T)	P. H. Goepp	3
11: Jephtha (Oratorio)		Handel	*
13:			
14:	Samson (Oratorio)	Handel	*
15:			
16:			

RUTH

1:16–17 *Entreat Me Not to Leave Thee*	H.M.L.	C. Gounod	3
Intreat Me Not to Leave Thee	A.	Winter Watts	3
v. Ruth (Oratorio)		Georg Schumann	3

I SAMUEL

2:8 The Pillars of the Earth		J. H. Rogers	2
The Pillars of the Earth		B. Tours	1

II SAMUEL

18:33 Oh Absalom, My Son		F. M. Christiansen	20
19:4 Oh Absalom, My Son		F. M. Christiansen	20
22:3 Lord, Thou Hast Been Our Refuge		E. C. Bairstow	1

I KINGS

1:39, 40 Zadok the Priest		Handel	1
6:17, 18, 21 What Have I To Do With Thee? (Elijah)		Mendelssohn	*
8:13, 27, 30, 37, 39 **9:1–3** I Have Surely Built Thee an House	(A.T.B)	W. Boyce	1
18:30, 36, 37 Lord God of Abraham (Elijah)		Mendelssohn	*
19:10 It Is Enough (Elijah)		Mendelssohn	*

I CHRONICLES

28:20 He Faileth Not	(H)	H. W. Parker	9
29:10, 11, 13, 14 Blessed Be Thou, Lord God of Israel		A. M. Greenfield	9
Blessed Be Thou, Lord God of Israel	M.	A. M. Greenfield	9

II CHRONICLES
32 : 21 The Destruction of Sennacherib   TTBB   G. Bantock 51

NEHEMIAH
2 : 20 The God of Heaven   J. F. Bridge 1

JOB
5 : 17 Behold, Happy Is the Man
 Whom the Lord Correcteth
 (Job)   E. T. Chipp 1
7 : 16 It Is Enough (Elijah)   Mendelssohn *
10 : 15 What Have I To Do With Thee
 (Elijah)   Mendelssohn *
17 : 7 Now Are Mine Eyes Grown Dim   M.   Haydn 3
19 : 25–26 I Know That My Redeemer
 Liveth (Messiah)   Handel *
23 : 3 *Hope Thou in God*   H.L.   G. B. Nevin 5
33 : 3 If With All Your Hearts (Elijah)   Mendelssohn *
35 : 10 A Song in the Night   R. H. Woodman 3
38 : 7 The Morning Stars Sang Together
 Before the Heavens Were Spread
 Abroad   H. W. Parker 6
 33 Knowest Thou the Ordinances
 of Heaven?   C. Demarest 3
42 : 3 My God, How Wonderful Thou
 Art   8 a-c   F. M. Christiansen 20

PSALMS
1 : 1–6 First Psalm   SATB TTBB   F. LaForge 3
 1–6 Blessed Is the Man   J. W. Clokey 13
2 : 1 Why Do the Heathen Rage?   R. H. Woodman 3
 1–2 *Why Do the Nations*   B.   Handel *
 9 There Shall a Star From Jacob
 (Christus)   Mendelssohn 1
3 : 8 Salvation Belongeth Unto the
 Lord   (A)   W. Berwald 2
4 : 1 *God of Righteousness*   H.L.   H. Gilbert 23
 1, 2, 4 Give Ear Unto My Prayer   J. Arcadelt 1
 5 Trust in God   (H)   G. H. Knight 6
 9 I Will Lay Me Down in Peace   J. L. Bennett 3
5 : 1–3, 11 Give Ear to My Words   (S.B)   J. H. Rogers 2
6 : 7 *What Have I To Do With Thee,
 O Man of God?* (Elijah)   S-B.   Mendelssohn *

PSALMS [*continued*]

7 : 10 My Defence Is of God		B. Huhn	3
8 : 1, 3–5 O Lord, Our Lord	(s.b)	J. H. Rogers	2
1 Jehovah, Lord God of Hosts	8 a-c	J. Stainer	1
Eighth Psalm	8	L. Spohr	1
10 : 14 *What Have I To Do With Thee,* *O Man of God?* (Elijah)	s-b	Mendelssohn	*
11 : 4 The Eyes of the Lord		H. B. Gaul	6
13 : 1, 2 How Long Wilt Thou Forget Me?	(l) v.	Tschaikowsky = Peery	12
1, 2 *How Long Wilt Thou Forget Me?*	m.	W. Oetting	9
1, 2 *How Long Wilt Thou Forget Me?*	l.	L. Sowerby	5
1–5 How Long Wilt Thou Forget Me?		A. D. Schmutz	13
14 : 1 *The Fool Hath Said*	h.l.	G. O'Hara	8
15 : Psalm Fifteen		J. W. Clokey	13
1–5 Lord, who shall dwell		W. S. Bennett	1
16 : 5 The Lord Is the Portion of Mine Inheritance		C. B. Rootham	18
8 Cast Thy Burden (Elijah)		Mendelssohn	*
17 : 6, 8, 9 The Shadow of Thy Wings	(h)	M. Andrews	9
18 : 2 I Will Call Upon the Lord (Woman of Samaria)		W. S. Bennett	1
4, 5 *God of Righteousness*	h.l.	H. Gilbert	23
4, 5 The Pains of Hell		E. G. Monk	1
19 : 1 The Heavens Declare		W. H. Harris	15
1 The Heavens Declare (Long)		C. St.-Saens	1
1–4 The Heavens Are Telling		Haydn	*
8 If Ye Walk in My Statutes		J. Clippingdale	1
14 Let the Words of My Mouth		H. Blair	1
14 Let the Words of My Mouth		Beethoven = Ward	9
20 : 6–8 Send Out Thy Light		C. Gounod	*
6–8 Gallia	(s)	C. Gounod	*
9 Rejoice Greatly		H. H. Woodward	1
21 : 1, 3, 5 The King Shall Rejoice		Handel	1
13 *Be Thou Exalted*	h-h, l-l	B. Huhn	3
22 : 1 My God, Why Hast Thou Forsaken Me?	(Dbl Ch)	Mendelssohn	1

PSALMS [*continued*]

Psalm 22	M. O.	E. Bloch	3
19 *Be Thou Exalted*	H-H, L-L	B. Huhn	3
19 Go Not Far From Me	SSATBB	Zingarelli=Holler	9
23 Praise Him, Ye That Fear Him		Mendelssohn=Whitehead	9
23: 1–6 The Lord Is My Shepherd		J. W. Clokey	4
1–6 The Lord Is My Shepherd	(S)	S. R. Gaines	2
1–6 The Lord Is My Shepherd	O.	Schubert	1
1–6 *The Twenty-Third Psalm*	H.L.	A. H. Malotte	3
1–6 The Twenty-Third Psalm	(M)	Malotte=Gilbert	3
2 *Beside the Still Waters*	H.L.	B. Hamblen	54
The King of Love	(A.S-B)	H. R. Shelley	3
Lo, My Shepherd Is Divine		Haydn	1
24: 7–10 Lift Up Your Heads		B. Klein	8
7–10 Lift Up Your Heads		H. Norris	12
Fling Wide the Gates		J. Stainer	*
Open the Gates of the Temple	H.L.	Mrs. J. F. Knapp	38
Open Wide the Gates	8 a-c	W. Howorth	13
25: 3 *Show Me Thy Ways, O Lord*		R. Navarro	9
3 Cast Thy Burden Upon the Lord (Elijah)		Mendelssohn	*
5 *God of Righteousness*	H.L.	H. Gilbert	23
7 Lord, Remember Not	8 a-c	Mendelssohn	8
Gracious and Righteous Is the Lord		H. Hiles	1
14 The Secret of the Lord		J. E. West	1
17 *My Soul Is Athirst for God* (The Holy City)	T.	A. R. Gaul	*
26: 6 I Will Wash My Hands in Innocency		E. C. Bairstow	15
6 I Will Wash My Hands in Innocency	(S)	J. H. Rogers	3
27: 1, 2, 3, 5 The Lord Is My Light	(S.A.B)	V. H. Percy	23
1, 3, 5 *The Lord Is My Light*	H.M.L.	F. Allitsen	27
1, 3, 5 The Lord Is My Light	(H)	F. Allitsen	27
1, 3, 5 The Lord Is My Light		H. W. Parker	3
4, 6, 11 One Thing Have I Asked	a-c	V. D. Thompson	4
11 Show Me Thy Way, O Lord		V. D. Thompson	9
The 27th Psalm	H.L.	C. Edwards	3
28: 2 The Lord Is My Light		R. H. Woodman	3
2, 9 The Lord Is My Light	(S.A.B)	V. H. Percy	23

PSALMS [*continued*]

30: 11, 12	Thou Hast Turned My Heaviness (The Widow of Zarephath)		A. Gray 1
31: 1	*In Thee, O God, Do I Put My Trust*	M.	M. Spicker 3
2, 5	Bow Down Thine Ear	(A)	E. S. Barnes 3
32:	Blessed Are They	(S.T.B)	E. Marzo 2
33:	My Soul Shall Be Joyful		G. H. Federlein 3
	The King of Love	(A.S-B)	H. R. Shelley 3
	The King of Love	H.M.L.	W. Dichmont 31
34: 4	I Sought the Lord	(A)	B. Levenson 3
4	I Sought the Lord		F. Stevenson 2
15–16	The Eyes of the Lord		H. B. Gaul 6
	The Eyes of the Lord		J. E. West 1
35: 1	Like as the Hart	(T.B)	W. C. Steere 7
	My Soul Shall Be Joyful		G. H. Federlein 3
37: 1, 7	*O Rest In the Lord*		Mendelssohn *
4	O Ye That Love the Lord		H. W. Wareing 1
	My Soul Shall Be Joyful		G. H. Federlein 3
38: 6	What Have I To Do With Thee	S.B.	Mendelssohn *
21	Go Not Far From Me	SSATBB	R. N. Dett 4
	Go Not Far From Me		Zingarelli=Holler 9
39: 1	Give Unto the Lord	(A)	C. W. Cadman 26
4	Lord, Make Me To Know Mine End		C. Lucas 17
5	Lord, Let Me Know Mine End	a-c	J. C. Marks 12
12	When Thou With Rebukes		E. Bullock 18
40: 1	Patiently Have I Waited	M.	C. St.-Saens *
1, 4	I Waited for the Lord		Mendelssohn *
5	My God, How Wonderful Thou Art	8 a-c	F. M. Christiansen 20
41: 2, 3	*My Soul Is Athirst* (Holy City)		A. R. Gaul *
42: 1	As Pants the Hart		S. Salter 9
1, 3, 5	Like as the Hart	H.M.L.	F. Allitsen 27
1, 3, 5	Like as the Hart	(S)	F. Allitsen 27
1, 3, 5	Like as the Hart	(T.B)	W. C. Steere 7
1, 6	Like as the Hart	M.L.	S. Liddle 27
5	Hope Thou In God	TTBB	F. C. Mayer 3
	42nd Psalm	(S) TTBB and Ch.	Mendelssohn *
43: 1–5	Judge Me, O God	8	Mendelssohn *

PSALMS [*continued*]

43 : 3–5	Send Out Thy Light		C. Gounod *
4	I Will Go Unto the Altar of God		H. Gadsby 1
4	I Will Go Unto the Altar of God		C. Harris 1
5	Why Art Thou So Full of Heavi ness	(H)	P. D. deCoster 9
	Just Judge of Heaven	(A)	G. M. Garrett 1
	The Fool Hath Said	H.L.	G. O'Hara 8
46 : 1	God is My Refuge		Dvorak = Clokey 11
	God is Our Hope and Strength	H.L.	J. E. West 5
	God is Our Refuge	H.L.	J. G. MacDermid 37
	God is Our Refuge and Strength	(S)	Mueller 3
	God is Our Refuge and Strength	(O)	F. H. Wood 18
4	There Is a River		V. Novello 1
9	He Maketh Wars to Cease		J. P. Scott 26
47 : 1–9	O Clap Your Hands	U.	C. Thomas 5
48 : 1	Great Is Jehovah	(S) O	Schubert *
1	Great Is the Lord	8	H. L. Thomas 16
8, 13	Behold, I Send the Promise of My Father		J. V. Roberts 1
12, 13	Blow Ye the Trumpet		R. H. Woodman 3
50 :	Psalm 50 (Long)	8 a-c	F. M. Christiansen 20
51 : 1, 11, 13, 15, 17	*O God Have Mercy* (St. Paul)	B	Mendelssohn *
2–3	Wash Me Thoroughly		A. Rubinstein 3
9	*Turn Thy Face From My Sins*	H.L.	E. Hirst 25
9	Blot Out My Transgressions	(4 Trms)	Beethoven 1
9–11	Turn Thy Face From My Sins	(H)	T. Attwood 3
10	Create in Me a Clean Heart	(A)	F. F. Harker 26
53 : 1	The Fool Hath Said		G. O'Hara 8
54 : 1	*Save Me, O God*		A. Randegger 3
55 : 1, 2, 4	Give Ear Unto My Prayer		Arcadelt 1
6	O for the Wings		Mendelssohn *
22	O Cast Thy Burdens Upon the Lord (Penitence, Pardon and Peace—Cantata)	B.	J. H. Maunder 1
22	Cast Thy Burdens Upon the Lord (Elijah)		Mendelssohn *
57 : 1	Be Merciful Unto Me	(B)	E. A. Sydenham 1
8–11	Awake Up My Glory		W. G. Wood 1
9–10	Awake Up My Glory		G. W. Chadwick 5

PSALMS [*continued*]

61: Lord, Hear My Cry		Bohm = Davenport 19
Psalm 61	H.M.	H. V. Milligan 3
62:**8** Trust in God at All Times	(H)	G. H. Knight 6
63:**4** I Will Go Unto the Altar of God		C. Harris 1
65:**9** Enrich Us With Thy Bounty		Bach = Besly 27
9, 12, 13 O God, Who Is Like Unto Thee		M. B. Foster 1
13 O Lord, How Manifold		J. Barnby 1
13 Praise the Lord, O Jerusalem		J. H. Maunder 1
66:**8** I Sought the Lord	(A)	B. Levenson 3
13 Kol Nidrei		Trad = Roberts 8
67: Be Merciful, O Lord	(H)	B. Godard 8
God Be Merciful		Mrs. H. H. A. Beach 3
68:**1** Let God Arise		T. W. Surette 9
1-3, 32, 34, 35 Let God Arise		T. T. Trimnell 1
11 The Lord Gave the Word		E. Turner 6
18 Thou Art Gone Up On High (Messiah)		Handel *
19 Behold, I Send the Promise of My Father		J. V. Roberts 1
Look Upon the Rainbow	H.M.L.	B. Whelpley 5
69:**1** *Save Me, O God*		A. Randegger 3
21 *Thy Rebuke Hath Broken His Heart* (Messiah) (T. Recit. to "Beholu ana See")		Handel *
70: Haste Thee, O Lord, To Deliver Me	(S)	P. W. Smale 18
71:**1** A Prayer for Love (Ave Maria)	(S)	Schubert = Voris 9
12 Go Not Far From Me		R. N. Dett 4
12 Go Not Far From Me		Zingarelli = Holler 9
17 O God, Who Is Like Unto Thee		M. B. Foster 1
72:**6** He Shall Come Down Like Rain	(S)	E. S. Barnes 3
18 And Blessed Be the Lord God		W. S. Bennett 1
18, 19 Sing to the Lord a New Song		H. Smart 1
76:**1-3, 11, 12** In Jewry Is God Known		F. A. G. Ouseley 1
In Jewry Is God Known		J. C. Whitfield 14
In Judah Is God Known (St. Paul)		Mendelssohn *
77:**5** I Have Considered		P. James 23
19 Sing to the Lord a New Song		H. Smart 1
78:**23-25** The Lord Opened the Doors of Heaven		F. F. Harker 3

PSALMS [*continued*]

78 : 53 He Sent a Thick Darkness (Israel in Egypt)		Handel 1
80 : 1 Hear, O Thou Shepherd of Israel		G. H. Federlein 9
1 Hear, O Thou Shepherd of Israel		H. Gaul 9
1, 3, 4, 5, 7 Give Ear, O Shepherd of Israel	(T)	R. S. Stoughton 2
10 A Day in Thy Courts		G. A. MacFarren 1
81 : 1–3 Sing We Merrily		O. King 1
2, 3 Blow Ye the Trumpet	(T)	R. H. Woodman 3
84 : 1 *How Lovely Are Thy Dwellings*	H.L.	S. Liddle 27
1 How Lovely Are Thy Dwellings		J. Brahms *
1–3 O How Amiable Are Thy Dwellings		Mana-Zucca 28
1–4 How Amiable Are Thy Tabernacles	(S.A.T)	E. S. Barnes 3
1–6 O How Amiable Are Thy Dwellings		O. A. King 1
4 Blessed Are They That Dwell in Thy House	SSAA	J. Brahms 9
4 Blessed Are They That Dwell in Thy House	(T)	C. Dickinson 9
10 A Day in Thy Courts		W. C. Macfarlane 3
85 : 1, 2, 8, 10 Lord, Thou Hast Been Favorable		V. C. Thomas 5
10, 11 Mercy and Truth		J. Stainer 1
86 : 10 *What Have I To Do With Thee*	S-B	Mendelssohn *
11 Teach Me Thy Way	(S)	L. Spohr 1
To My Humble Supplication, Lord		G. Holst 35
87 : 3 Glorious Things of Thee Are Spoken	(B)	W. Merrill 9
89 : 20 I Have Found David, My Servant	SSAATB	C. C. Palmer 15
90 : 1 Lord, Thou Hast Been Our Refuge		E. C. Bairstow 1
1 *Lord, Thou Hast Been Our Dwelling Place*	H.L.	L. B. Phillips 27
2 Great and Marvelous (Holy City)		A. R. Gaul *
91 : 1, 2, 4 Whoso Dwelleth Under the Defence		G. C. Martin 1
7 *Hear Ye, Israel*	S.	Mendelssohn *

PSALMS [*continued*]

91 : 1, 5, 6, 9–12	91*st Psalm*	H.L.	J. G. MacDermid 37
	He That Dwelleth		L. Meslin 27
	He That Dwelleth	(A)	J. L. Galbraith 2
	The Shadow of the Almighty	H.L.	E. S. Barnes 3
	The Shadow of Thy Wings	(S.T)	M. Andrews 9
92 :	Good It Is to Thank the Almighty	(B)	Schubert 1
93 : 1–5	The Lord Is King		R. H. Woodman 5
94 : 1	O Sing Unto the Lord	(T)	F. W. Snow 9
14–16	Declare His Glory	(A)	G. H. Federlein 3
17–19, 22	If the Lord Had Not	(B)	E. C. Bairstow 1
95 : 1–3	Come, Let Us Sing To the Lord	(O.)	Mendelssohn *
4, 6	In His Hands	H–H	Mendelssohn *
5–7	O Come Let Us Worship	(T) (O)	Mendelssohn *
7	*Today If Ye Will Hear His Voice*	H.L.	J. H. Rogers 5
96 : 3–6, 10	Declare His Glory	(A)	G. H. Federlein 3
6, 9	I Have Surely Built Thee an House	(ATT.B)	W. Boyce 1
7–9	Ascribe Unto the Lord		H. Blair 1
9	Beauty in Holiness	a–c	F. M. Christiansen 20
9	*The Beauty of Holiness*	H.L.	M. VanDyke 27
9	Worship the Lord in the Beauty of Holiness		T. Smith 2
11	Let the Heavens Rejoice (Holy City) Cho.		A. R. Gaul *
97 : 2	Clouds and Darkness		A. Dvorak 36
10–11	O Ye, That Love the Lord		H. W. Wareing 1
12	Rejoice in the Lord, Ye Righteous		G. C. Martin 1
98 : 1–10	Sing to the Lord		Mendelssohn *
100 : 4	O Come Before His Presence	(T)	G. C. Martin 1
	All People That on Earth Do Dwell	O.	J. E. West 1
	Jubilate in B Minor		H. Gaul 25
	The 100th Psalm	(S.A.T.B) O.	V. Williams 18
	All From the Sun's Uprise		P. Tomblings 8
	O Be Joyful in the Lord	(T)	C. Franck 3
	I Make a Joyful Noise		C. F. Mueller 26
102 : 1, 2, 8, 10–13	Hear My Prayer, O Lord	(B)	W. Berwald 9
	Hear My Prayer	(A)	L. Saminsky 8
103 : 1, 2	The Lord Opened the Doors of Heaven		F. F. Harker 3

PSALMS [*continued*]

PSALMS [continued]

114:	Psalm 114	H.O.	E. Bloch	3
115: 1	Not Unto Us, O Lord (Long)		Mendelssohn	1
	6–7 O Come, Let Us Worship		Mendelssohn	*
	12 But the Lord Is Mindful	A.	Mendelssohn	1
	But the Lord Is Mindful	SATB	Mendelssohn	20
	13 Blessed Is He That Feareth the Lord		F. W. Snow	2
116: 15	I Love the Lord	(S or T)	J. L. Galbraith	2
	I Will Go Unto the Altar of God		C. Harris	1
117: 1	Praise the Lord		A. Randegger	3
118: 19–22	Open Me the Gates of Righteousness	(B)	M. B. Foster	1
	24 This Is the Day Which the Lord Hath Made	(H)	W. L. Blumenschein	3
119: 9–11	Wherewithal Shall a Young Man		H. Hiles	1
	33 If Ye Walk in My Statutes		J. Clippingdale	1
	33–40 Teach Me, O Lord		T. Attwood	1
	89 O Lord, Thy Word Endureth		E. Lemare	5
	105 Thy Word Is a Lantern Unto My Feet		H. Purcell	1
	105 Thy Word Is a Lantern Unto My Feet		L. Scarmolin	8
	165–6 Great Peace Have They		J. H. Rogers	3
	174 I Have Longed for Thy Salvation (Stabat Mater)	S-A-T-B	G. Rossini	1
	175 Thou Wilt Keep Him		S. S. Wesley	2
121: 1–3	Lift Thine Eyes (Elijah)	SSA	F. F. Harker	26
	1–6 I Will Lift Up Mine Eyes		J. Barnby	1
	4 He Watching Over Israel (Elijah)		F. Stevenson	2
	5 The Lord Is My Keeper		V. D. Thompson	9
	8 I Sought the Lord		J. W. Clokey	13
	121st Psalm		F. La Forge	12
	I Will Lift Up	H.M.	J. G. MacDermid	37
	I Will Lift Up Mine Eyes	T	L. Jewell	3
	I Will Lift Up Mine Eyes	(A)	L. Sowerby	
	11, 12 For He Shall Give His Angels		Mendelssohn	*
122:	I Was Glad When They Said	(B)	J. L. Galbraith	2
	1, 2, 6–9 O Pray for the Peace		J. C. Knox	5
124: 8	The God of Heaven		J. F. Bridge	1
125: 1, 2	They That Trust in the Lord	M.	H. P. Eames	13

PSALMS [*continued*]

125 : 1–3 They That Trust in the Lord	(s)	H. Spier 3
126 : A Psalm of Deliverance	(s.a)	H. Gaul 17
5, 6 They That Sow in Tears (Holy City)		H. Gaul 17
127 : 1 The God of Heaven		J. F. Bridge 1
2 *He Giveth His Beloved Sleep*	m.	J. L. Roeckel 31
Except the Lord Build		Handel *
128 : 1 Blessed Is He That Feareth the Lord		F. W. Snow 2
1 Then Shall the Righteous (Elijah)		Mendelssohn *
1 *What Have I To Do With Thee*	s.b.	Mendelssohn *
128th Psalm		L. V. Saar 3
130 : In Deep Distress	(t)	Mendelssohn 1
From the Deep I Called	8 a–c	J. Stainer 1
Out of the Depths	l.	J. H. Rogers 5
Out of the Depths (De Profundis)	aatbb	L. Saminsky 11
132 : 8, 9, 15 Arise, O Lord, Into Thy Resting Place		G. F. Cobb 1
134 : Behold Now, Praise Ye the Lord	(b)	G. H. Federlein 3
Psalm 134		17
135 : 9, 12 His Salvation Is Nigh Them (Woman of Samaria)		W. S. Bennett 1
Behold Now, Praise Ye		G. H. Federlein 3
136 : 1 Ye Shall Dwell in the Land	(s.b)	J. Stainer 1
1 The Lord Hath Brought Us		E. N. Thorne 1
9 All Nations Whom Thou Hast Named		B. L. Selby 1
137 : 1–8 By the Waters (Alter last verse)		Coleridge-Taylor 1
1–8 By the Waters		P. James 9
1–8 By the Waters		P. Lutkin 9
By the Rivers of Babylon	(c.Tr.h)	L. Saminsky 8
By Babylon's Wave		C. Gounod 11
Psalm 137	h.o.	E. Bloch 3
138 : 7 He Watching Over Israel (Elijah)		Mendelssohn *
7 Search Me, O God	(a)	J. H. Rogers 3
139 : 1, 3 O Lord, Thou Hast Searched Me (Woman of Samaria)	(a)	W. S. Bennett 1

PSALMS [*continued*]

139 : 7-12 *Whither Shall I Go From Thy Spirit*	H.C	J. G. MacDermid 37
11 Thou Wilt Keep Him		S. S. Wesley 1
18 Still, Still With Thee	(A.S.S-T)	A. Foote 5
23 Search Me, O God	(A)	J. H. Rogers 3
The Wings of the Morning	H.L.	M. Rigby 5
141 : 2 Incense and a Pure Offering	(S.A.T.B)	Brock = Macrum 17
143 : 9-11 Deliver Me, O Lord		J. Stainer 1
145 : 8-10 Praise the Lord, O Jerusalem		J. H. Maunder 1
9-12 *The Lord Is Loving Unto Every Man*	H.L.	J. E. West 5
13 One Generation Shall Praise Thy Name	TTBB (T)	J. N. Ashton 4
15-16 The Eyes of All		M. B. Foster 1
15-16 The Eyes of All		A. R. Gaul 1
16 O God, Who Is Like Unto Thee		M. B. Foster 1
146 : God, My King, Thy Might Confessing		M. E. Schwartz 17
147 : 8, 12, 14 Man Goeth Forth to His Work		A. Carnall 1
12, 13 Praise the Lord, O Jerusalem	(S)	J. H. Maunder 1
O All Ye Nations	a-c	H. Schutz 2
148 : 7-9, 13 He Sendeth the Springs	(S.T)	H. W. Wareing 1
12-13 Sing We Merrily		O. King 1
149 : Praise Jehovah		A. Dvorak 2
150 : 6 Let All That Hath Breath	8 a-c	H. Whitford 4
150th Psalm		F. LaForge 26
150th Psalm		C. Franck 4
Praise the Lord	(S)	A. Randegger 3
O Praise the Lord of Heaven	(B) O.	A. Hyde 9
Praise Ye the Lord	(Dbl Ch)	C. St.-Saens 3

PROVERBS

3 : 5, 6, 24, 26 The Lord Shall Be Thy Confidence		J. V. Roberts 1
3 : 9-10, 19, 20 Honour the Lord With Thy Substance	(B)	J. Stainer 1
Honour the Lord	B.	A. Sullivan 1
3 : 19 The Lord by Wisdom Hath Founded the Earth		G. Mead 25

PROVERBS [continued]

8 : The Lord by Wisdom Hath
Founded the Earth   G. Mead 25
17 : 3 The Fining Pot Is for Silver
(Holy City)   S-A-T-B   A. R. Gaul *
19 : 17 He That Hath Pity Upon the
Poor   (B)   A. Whitehead 18

ECCLESIASTES

1 : 4 One Generation Passeth Away
(Motet)   a-c   E. Walker 15
12 : 1 Remember Now Thy Creator   (T)   J. P. Scott 26
1 Remember Now Thy Creator   H. B. Gaul 9
6 Face to Face   H.M.L.   H. Johnson 47

SONG OF SOLOMON (Canticles)

2 : 1 By Cool Siloam's Shady Rill   E. S. Banks 2
3, 4 The Woods and Every Sweet-
Smelling Tree   (S.T)   J. E. West 1
10 Rise Up, My Love, My Fair One   H. Willan 15
8 : 6, 7 Greater Love Hath No Man   (S.B)   J. Ireland 18
O Rose of Sharon (Ave Maria)   (S)   Schubert 3

ISAIAH

1 : 18-20 Come Now and Let Us Reason   H. W. Wareing 1
2 : 2-4 *Come Ye to the Mountains of*
the Lord   H.L.   C. G. Spross 12
4 What of the Night?   (T)   R. G. Thompson 9
4 They Shall Beat Their Swords (A.T)   M. Andrews 25
5 : 17 Behold the Days   H. H. Woodward 1
6 : 1 In the Year That King Uzziah
Died   D. M. Williams 9
1-3 A New Heaven (Holy City)   (B)   A. R. Gaul *
14 And There Shall Be a Sign   E. W. Naylor 1
7 : 17 O Thou that Tellest (Messiah) (A)   Handel *
8 : 1, 3, 4, 5 O Lord, Our Lord, How
Excellent   J. H. Rogers 2
9 : 2 *The People That Walked*
(Messiah)   B.   Handel *
6 For Unto Us a Child Is Born
(Messiah)   Handel *

ISAIAH [*continued*]

10: **1** The Rod of Jesse Hath Blossomed		A. Bruckner	11
11: **6, 7, 9** Behold the Days Come	(T)	H. H. Woodward	1
12: **2–6** Behold, God Is My Salvation	(S)	J. H. Rogers	2
Behold, God Is My Salvation		L. Jewell	5
3 Therefore With Joy (Woman of Samaria)		W. S. Bennett	1
19: *Arise, Shine for Thy Light*	H.M.L.	J. G. MacDermid	37
21: **11–12** What of the Night, O Watchman?	(T)	R. C. Thompson	9
24: **13** He Sendeth the Springs		H. W. Wareing	1
25: **1, 4, 9** O Lord, My God	(B)	J. Nares	1
8–9 I Declare to You the Gospel		W. A. C. Cruickshank	1
26: Thou Hast Turned My Heaviness (Widow of Zarephath)		A. Gray	3
3, 4 Thou Wilt Keep Him	(S)	J. A. West	2
Thou Wilt Keep Him	H.L.	R. Cox	5
4 Praise the Lord		A. Randegger	3
6, 7 I Will Wash My Hands in Innocency		E. C. Bairstow	15
28: **16** Behold, I Lay in Zion a Stone	(B)	R. H. Prutting	26
30: **13–19** In Quietness and in Confidence	(T)	L. Jewell	9
21 Therefore With Joy (Widow of Samaria)		W. S. Bennett	1
29 A Song in the Night	(S.B)	R. H. Woodman	3
31: **2** Beneath the Shadow	(A)	C. Dickinson	9
32: **1–2** Arise, Shine	(B.H)	A. Foote	5
1, 2, 13, 15–17 Behold a King Shall Reign	(B)	H. C. Banks	9
33: **2** Thou Wilt Keep Him	(S)	J. A. West	2
17 The Sun Shall Be No More		H. H. Woodward	1
35: **1, 6, 8, 10** The Wilderness		S. S. Wesley	1
1–6, 8–10 The Wilderness		J. Goss	1
1, 4, 8, 10 Springs in the Deserts	(T)	A. B. Jennings	9
5–6 *He Shall Feed His Flock* (Messiah)	A.	Handel	*
9–10 Then Shall the Righteous (Elijah)		Mendelssohn	*
10 It Shall Come to Pass (Holy City)	S-S-A	A. R. Gaul	*

ISAIAH [*continued*]

35 : 10 Praise the Lord		A. Randegger	3
10 *The Ransomed of the Lord*	H.L.	J. G. MacDermid	37
36 : 3 Thou Wilt Keep Him		S. S. Wesley	1
40 : 1–3 Comfort Ye (Messiah)		Handel	*
1–5 Comfort Ye	(T.B)	G. H. Federlein	3
3–5 Prepare Ye the Way	(T.B)	L. Jewell	9
4 Every Valley (Messiah)		Handel	*
6, 7 Seek Ye the Lord	(A)	F. W. Perry	2
6, 8, 28–31 *They Shall Run and Not Be Weary*	H.L.	J. G. MacDermid	37
9 Glad Tidings to Zion		F. M. Christiansen	20
9 O Thou That Tellest (Messiah)		Handel	*
11 *He Shall Feed His Flock* (Messiah)	A.	Handel	*
18 To Whom then Will Ye Liken God		H. W. Parker	9
18 To Whom then Will Ye Liken God	TTBB	H. W. Parker	9
18 Who Is Like Unto Thee, O Lord		A. Sullivan	1
28–31 They That Wait Upon the Lord	(H)	F. W. Snow	9
41 : 1, 11 Behold, My Servant	(B)	J. F. Bridge	1
10 Fear Thou Not		J. Booth	1
10 Hear Ye, Israel (Elijah)		Mendelssohn	*
42 : 5–8 Thus Saith the Lord	(B.S)	E. C. Hosmer	9
10 Sing to the Lord a New Song		H. Smart	1
43 : 1–3 Fear Thou Not		J. Booth	1
5 The Ninety and Nine	H.M.L.	E. Campion	3
18 Lord, Remember Not	8 a-c	Mendelssohn	8
44 : 23 Look on the Fields		C. MacPherson	1
45 : 17, 18 A New Heaven and a New Earth		A. R. Gaul	*
47 : 17 Prepare Ye the Way of the Lord	(T.B)	G. H. Federlein	3
Prepare Ye the Way of the Lord	(T.B)	L. Jewell	9
48 : 1, 18 Hear Ye, Israel		Mendelssohn	*
49 : 8–13 Sing, O Heavens	(B)	G. H. Federlein	5
50 : 1 The Lord Will Comfort Zion		V. Eville	2
51 : 1–5 Harken Unto Me		F. Stevenson	2
4–6 Harken Unto Me		A. Sullivan	2
Harken Unto Me		C. F. Manney	2

ISAIAH [*continued*]

51 : 9, 17 Behold, a King Shall Reign (Festival)	(B)	H. C. Banks 9
10, 12–13 *Hear Ye, Israel*	S.	Mendelssohn *
52 : 1, 2, 7–10 Awake, Awake, Put on Thy Strength		J. Stainer 1
7 Lovely Appear	(S)	C. Gounod 3
7 How Beautiful	(S) (Also Solo)	F. F. Harker 3
7–8 How Beautiful	a-c	J. W. Work 25
7 Good Tidings to Zion		F. M. Christiansen 20
53 : 1 *Hear Ye, Israel* (Elijah)	S.	Mendelssohn *
3 He Was Despised (Messiah)		Handel *
4, 5 Surely, He Hath Borne (Messiah)		Handel *
5 *Is It Nothing to You*	S-A	M. B. Foster 7
6 All We Like Sheep (Messiah)		Handel *
54 : 1, 8, 10, 11 *As the Rain Cometh Down*	H.L.	J. G. MacDermid 37
10 *For the Mountains Shall Depart* (Elijah)	B.	Mendelssohn *
13 Behold the Days Come		H. H. Woodward 1
55 : 1–3 *Come Ye to the Waters*	H.L.	J. E. Roberts 5
1–3 Ho, Everyone	(T)	W. C. Macfarlane 3
1–3 Ho, Everyone	(S.B)	H. L. Vibbard 3
1–3 O Come Everyone (Elijah)	(S-A-T-B)	Mendelssohn *
1–3, 7–12 Ho, Everyone that Thirsteth	(B)	G. C. Martin 1
5, 8–13 Behold Thou Shalt Call a Nation		F. Stevenson 2
6–7 Seek Ye the Lord	(A.S.T)	F. W. Perry 2, 9
60 : 1 *Arise, Shine for Thy Light Has Come*	H.M.L.	J. G. MacDermid 37
1 O Thou That Tellest (Messiah)		Handel *
1–2 For Behold Darkness (Messiah)		Handel *
1–3 Arise, Shine	(B.H)	A. Foote 5
1–3 O Come Redeemer of Mankind	(S)	A. W. Merchant 1
18 Behold, the Days Come		H. H. Woodward 1
19 The Sun Shall Be No More		H. H. Woodward 1
61 : 6–8 And When They Had Ordained Them Elders		E. H. Thorne 1
63 : Hosanna in the Highest	(S.B)	J. Stainer 1

ISAIAH [*continued*]

65: 17, 18 A New Heaven and a New
Earth   (B)   A. R. Gaul   *

JEREMIAH

1: 8 *Be Thou Faithful Unto Death*   T.   Mendelssohn   *
3: 4 Thou Art the Guide of Our Youth   A. R. Gaul   *
4: 1 Oh Israel Return   F. Sealy   9
9: 23 *Let Not the Wise Man Glory in*
His Wisdom   H.L.   J. G. MacDermid 37
10: 10 The Lord Is the True God   J. Barnby   1
The Lord Is the True God   O. A. Mansfield 6
23: 5, 6 Behold the Days   H. H. Woodward 1
5, 6 O Come Redeemer of Mankind   (S)   A. W. Marchant 1
32 *Seek Not After False Prophets*   H.L.   H. Grunn   3
31: 6, 7, 13 Fear Not, O Israel   (S.A.B)   M. Spicker   3
6, 7, 13 Fear Not, O Israel   D. Buck   3
12 Therefore They Shall Come and
Sing (Woman of Samaria)   W. S. Bennett 1
50: 2 Declare His Glory   (A)   G. H. Federlein 3

LAMENTATIONS

1: 12 *Is It Nothing to You?*   S-A   M. B. Foster   7
3: 23 New Every Morning Is the Love   B. L. Selby   1

EZEKIEL

34: 20–28 The Good Shepherd   A. B. Jennings 9
36: 28, 30, 34, 35 Ye Shall Dwell in the
Land   (S.B)   J. Stainer   1

DANIEL

9: 9 *To the Lord Our God Belong Mercies*
(Holy City)   T.   A. R. Gaul   *
12: 3 *These Are They (Holy City)*   S.   A. R. Gaul   *

JOEL

2: 1 Blow Ye the Trumpet   (T)   R. H. Woodman 3
12, 13 *If with All Your Hearts*   T.   Mendelssohn   *
21, 24, 26 Fear Not, O Land   E. Elgar   1
Fear Not, O Land   G. Bantock   14
Zion   H.L.   B. Huhn   3

JOEL [*continued*]

2 : 12, 13 Turn Ye to Me		W. A. Barrett 1
3 : 18 In That Day		F. W. Holloway 39
14 The Day of the Lord		A. S. Warrell 15
14 The Great Day of the Lord		G. C. Martin 1

AMOS

5 : 7, 8 Seek Him That Maketh	(s)	J. H. Rogers 2

OBADIAH

1 : 15 The Day of the Lord		A. S. Warrell 15

MICAH

4 : 1, 3, 6, 8, 9 In the Last Days	(s.t.b)	J. H. Rogers 2

HABAKKUK

2 : 20 The Lord Is in His Holy Temple		J. W. Elliott 1
20 God Is in His Holy Temple	TTBB	C. F. Mueller 3

ZEPHANIAH

1 : 14 The Great Day of the Lord		G. C. Martin 1
2 : 3 The Great Day of the Lord		G. C. Martin 1

HAGGAI

2 : 6, 7 *But Who May Abide* (Messiah)	B.	Handel *

ZECHARIAH

1 : 4 The Great Day of the Lord	Chime	G. C. Martin 1
2 : 3 The Great Day of the Lord		G. C. Martin 1
3 : 9 Behold, I Lay in Zion a Stone	(B)	R. H. Prutting 26
9 : 9 Rejoice Greatly		H. H. Woodward 1
9–10 *Rejoice Greatly* (*Messiah*)	S.	Mendelssohn *
17 How Great, O God, Is Thy Goodness	(s)	R. F. Donovan 6
14 : 7 *It Shall Come to Pass* (Holy City)	S-S-A	A. R. Gaul *

APOCRYPHA

MALACHI

1 : 11 In Every Place Incense		J. E. West 1
10 *Bring Ye All Tithes*	H.L.	J. G. MacDermid 37

MALACHI [*continued*]

3:2 Rejoice Greatly		H. H. Woodward 1
1, 3 *But Who May Abide* (*Messiah*)	B.	Handel *

WISDOM

3:1, 2, 3 *Souls of the Righteous*	H.L.	T. T. Noble 3
Souls of the Righteous		T. T. Noble 3
18:14, 15 A Song in the Night		R. H. Woodman 3

ECCLESIASTICUS

43:11 *Look Upon the Rainbow*	H.M.L.	B. Whelpley 5
44:1 Let Us Now Praise Famous Men		V. Williams 14
1 Let Us Now Praise Famous Men		H. Gaul 17

BARUCH

4:22, 23 *My Hope Is in the Everlasting*	T.	J. Stainer 1
5:8, 9 The Woods and Every Sweet-Smelling Tree	(S.T)	J. E. West 2

JUDITH

16:15 Sing to the Lord a New Song		H. Smart 1
The Lord Is Long-suffering (Judith)	L.	C. H. H. Parry 3

NEW TESTAMENT
MATTHEW

2:1 In the Days of Herod	(T.B)	S. Salter 3
13–15 The Flight into Egypt	SSA (S) O.	M. Bruch 3
3:3 Prepare Ye the Way	(T.B)	G. H. Federlein 3
Prepare Ye the Way	(T.B)	L. Jewell 9
5:3 *Blessed Are the Poor in Spirit*	H.L.	F. F. Harker 3
3–10 The Beatitudes		H. R. Shelley 3
3–12 The Beatitudes		A. B. Jennings 9
8 Blest Are the Pure in Heart		F. M. Christiansen 20
Blest Are the Pure in Heart	H.L.	B. Huhn 3
Blest Are the Pure in Heart	(A)	F. F. Harker 26
Blest Are the Pure in Heart	(H)	D. W. Kennedy 26
Blest Are the Pure in Heart	a-c	Bourke=Holler 9
10, 11 Blest Are They Which Are Persecuted	(H)	W. Kienzl 6
12 O Forgive Our Debts		Thome=Richards 26
16 Let Your Light So Shine		H. Hadley 9

MATTHEW [*continued*]

6 : 9–13 *v.* Lord's Prayer
    13 Thine Is the Kingdom (Holy
       City)   A. R. Gaul *
    28–34 *Consider the Lilies*   H.L.   J. P. Scott 3
    Consider the Lilies   S-A   R. Topliff 7
8 : 23 Fierce Was the Wild Billow   8 or 4   T. T. Noble 3
9 : 9 Matthew   Ward-Stephens 21
    13 I Came Not to Call the Righteous   C. Vincent 1
    30 Open Our Eyes   a-c   W. C. Macfarlane 3
    37–38 The Parable of the Harvest   F. J. Sawyer 1
    9 Follow Me   (T)   H. R. Shelley 39
    O, Our Father   N. Lockwood 25
11 : 11 Among Those That Are Born
      of Women   C. T. Powell 1
    28–30 Come Unto Me   S. Liddle 18
        v. Invitation
    Come Unto Him (Messiah)   S.   Handel *
        v. Invitation
    Come, Ye Disconsolate   (S-A)   E. K. Macrum 9
    Come, Ye Sin-Defiled and Weary   J. Stainer 1
    Jesus Is Calling   V.   A. P. Risher 5
13 : 27 Sing to the Lord a New Song   H. Smart 1
    33, 35–37 Watch and Pray   W. H. Lockett 1
    43 Then Shall the Righteous (Elijah) Mendelssohn *
14 : 1–3 Let Not Your Heart Be
      Troubled   E. Faning 1
    18, 19 Thou Art Peter   Palestrina 24
    18, 19 *Peter* (*Upon This Rock*)   SATB H.L. Ward-Stephens 21
    18, 19 Thou Art Peter   Mendelssohn *
    22–27 Fierce Was the Wild Billow 8 or 4 T. T. Noble 3
18 : The Ninety and Nine   (A.B)   D. Protheroe 2
19 : 13–15 *Suffer Little Children*   H.   C. Heinroth 9
    Suffer Little Children   B. Lambord 9
    Christ and the Children   F. Nagler 9
    Christ and the Children   L. Norden 9
    21 Follow Me   (T)   H. R. Shelley 39
20 : 12 And Jesus Entered into the
      Temple (Olivet to Calvary)   J. H. Maunder *
    Whene'er the Steep of Olivet
      (Olivet to Calvary)   J. H. Maunder *

MATTHEW [*continued*]

MARK

MARK [*continued*]

Suffer Little Children	(T)	S. Salter 3
10:21 Follow Me	(T)	H. R. Shelley 39
11: *v.* Hosanna, The		
14:3–9 Master, No Offering Costly		
(Hymn)		E. B. Parker —
37 Could Ye Then Not Watch (12		
Passion Motets)	a-c	M. Haydn 3
37 Could Ye Not Watch		
(Crucifixion)	(T.B)	J. Stainer *
48 Are Ye Come With Swords (12		
Passion Motets)	a-c	M. Haydn 3
50 All My Friends Forsake Me (12		
Passion Motets)	a-c	M. Haydn 3
15:38 Then the Veil Was Rent (12		
Passion Motets)	a-c	M. Haydn 3
16:1–8 Mary Magdalene at the		
Sepulchre		Schuetz=Dickinson 9
At the Sepulchre	(B)	G. B. Nevin 2
At the Sepulchre	TTBB	G. B. Nevin 2

LUKE

1: My Soul Doth Magnify	S-T-B	C. St.-Saens 2
v. Magnificat (The)		
When Cæsar Augustus (Carol)	SATBB	A. Whitehead 8
The Annunciation	(A.T.B)	R. H. Woodman 3
5 In the Days of Herod	(T.B)	S. Salter 3
26, 27, 30–33 The Angel Gabriel		H. Smart 1
26–28 And the Angel Gabriel		W. H. Monk 1
28 *Ave Maria*	H.L. V.	J. Raff 5
32–33 Arise, Shine	(B.H)	A. Foote 5
46–55 *v.* Magnificat (The)		
68 Arise, Shine	(B.H)	A. Foote 5
68 Behold My Servant	(B)	J. F. Bridge 1
68, 69 Blessed Be the Lord God of		
Israel (Woman of Samaria)		W. S. Bennett 1
78 Dayspring of Eternity		J. S. Matthews 9
2:8 While Shepherds Watched	SATB TTBB SSAA	H. Jüngst 9
8–14 There Were Shepherds		
(Messiah)		Handel *
10 To Us a Child of Hope	(S)	W. Berwald 3

LUKE [*continued*]

2: 14 Gloria in Excelsis		G. Borch 8
19 Mary Kept All These Things	(S.A.T.B)	E. S. Barnes 6
22 When to the Temple		A. B. Jennings 9
22 While By My Sheep		H. Jüngst 9
29–32 The Song of Simeon	(T)	I. L. Strom 40
29–32 Nunc Dimittis	U.	D. M. Williams 9
5: 27 Follow Me	(T)	H. R. Shelley 39
7: 36–50 Master, No Offering Costly (Hymn)		E. B. Parker —
8: 4–15 The Sower	(L)	J. Jordan 3
9: 23 Follow Me	(T)	H. R. Shelley 39
59 Follow Me		H. R. Shelley 39
11: The Lord's Prayer	V.	
2 O, Our Father		N. Lockwood 25
9–10 Ask, and It Shall Be Given		T. Adams 1
12: 27 Consider the Lilies [*v.* Matthew 6 : 28–34]		
32 *Come Ye Blessed (Holy City)*	A.	A. R. Gaul *
32 Be Not Dismayed		M. Prætorius 8
14: 11 *The Humble Shall Be Exalted*	H.L.	J. E. Roberts 5
15: 3–7 The Ninety and Nine	(A.B)	D. Protheroe 2
10 There Is Joy in the Presence (Prodigal Son)		A. Sullivan 1
10–32 The Prodigal Son		A. Sullivan 1
v. The Prodigal Son		
11 The Prodigal's Return		T. A. Jones 1
11–25 *The Penitent*		B. van de Water 2
17 *How Many Hired Servants* (Prodigal Son)	T.	A. Sullivan 1
22 Bring Forth the Best Robe (Prodigal Son)		A. Sullivan 1
18: 10–14 *The Publican*	H.M.L.	B. van de Water 2
15–77 *Suffer Little Children*	H.	C. Heinroth 9
Suffer Little Children		B. Lambord 9
Christ and the Children		L. Norden 9
Christ and the Children		F. Nagler 9
44 Darkness Was Over All		M. Haydn 3
19: 42–43 O Jerusalem (Olivet to Calvary)		J. H. Maunder 1
If Thou Hadst Known		Ward-Stephens 21

LUKE [*continued*]

22:52 Are Ye Come With Swords		M. Haydn	3
23:28, 33, 34, 46 Daughters of Jerusalem (Light of the World)		A. Sullivan	1
39–43 And One of the Malefactors (Crucifixion)		J. Stainer	*
39–45 The Penitent Thief	SSATB	A. Kastalsky	9
44 Darkness Obscured the Earth		M. Haydn	3
45 Then the Veil Was Rent		M. Haydn	3
And When They Came to the Place (Olivet to Calvary)		J. H. Maunder	1
24:1–10 Mary Magdalene at the Sepulchre		Schuetz=Dickinson	9
At the Sepulchre	(B)	G. B. Nevin	2
At the Sepulchre	TTBB	G. B. Nevin	2
6 Eye Hath Not Seen		M. B. Foster	1
13–35 The Walk to Emmaus		H. W. Davies	1
The Walk to Emmaus	(B.H)	G. B. Nevin	2
15, 16 Come, O Thou Traveller Unknown	a-c	T. T. Noble	3
Come, O Thou Traveller Unknown		H. B. Gaul	6
38 Watch Ye and Pray	S-A	G. R. Vicars	9

JOHN

1: In the Beginning Was the Word		E. C. Austin	9
1 *He Sent His Word*	H.L.	J. G. MacDermid	37
1–5, 14 In the Beginning	(A)	E. C. Hosmer	2
In the Beginning		M. Andrews	9
7 And All the People Saw		J. Stainer	1
16, 17 God So Loved the World (Crucifixion)		J. Stainer	*
16, 17 They That Sow in Tears (Holy City)		A. R. Gaul	*
29 Agnus Dei	(s)v.h. and o.	G. Bizet	2
29 Behold the Lamb of God		Handel	*
29 *Lamb of God*		B. S. Kallinikoff	6
29 Behold the Master Passeth By	(A)	F. Stevenson	2
32 This is the Record of John		O. Gibbons	1
38 Andrew (Come and See)		Ward-Stephens	21

JOHN [*continued*]

1: 45–50	Nathaniel		Ward-Stephens 21
2: 1, 2	There was a Marriage in Cana		J. Stainer 1
3: 1	*Behold What Manner of Love*	H.L.	J. G. MacDermid 37
5–7, 16	*God So Loved*	H.M.L.	J. G. MacDermid 37
7, 12	And All the People Saw		J. Stainer 1
14–16	As Moses Lifted Up the Serpent		E. C. Bairstow 15
16	*Is It Nothing to You?*	S-A	M. B. Foster 7
4: 5, 6	Then Cometh Jesus (Woman of Samaria)	(A)	W. S. Bennett *
7, 9, 10	For With Thee Is the Well of Life (Woman of Samaria)	(S.A.B)	W. S. Bennett 1
11	Beloved, If God So Loved Us		J. Barnby 1
13	I Am the Water of Life		J. P. Dunn 4
13–14	Whosoever Drinketh of This Water	(B)	J. T. Field 1
13, 14	Jesus Answered and Said Unto Her (Woman of Samaria)		W. S. Bennett 1
18	O Love That Casts Out Fear		W. Berwald 3
	O Love That Casts Out Fear		Coke-Jephcott 9
19–23	The Woman Said Unto Him (Woman of Samaria)	(S)	W. S. Bennett 1
23–24	God Is a Spirit		C. A. Scholin 26
	God Is a Spirit (Woman of Samaria)		W. S. Bennett 1
25, 26	Who Is the Image of the Invisible God (Woman of Samaria)	(A.B.)	W. S. Bennett 1
27–29	The Woman Then Left Her Water-pot (Woman of Samaria)	(A)	W. S. Bennett 1
35	Look on the Fields		C. Macpherson 1
39, 40	And Many of the Samaritans (Woman of Samaria)		W. S. Bennett 1
41	And Many More Believed	(A)	W. S. Bennett 1
42	Now We Believe		W. S. Bennett 1
6: 32–35	Jesus Said Unto the People		J. Stainer 1
33–58	O, Bread of Life	(B)	F. M. Christiansen 20
41, 48	I Am the Bread of Life		J. S. Matthews 2

JOHN [*continued*]

6: 43 *Murmur Not, O My Soul*		Bach	14
50, 51, 58 O Living Bread Who Once Did Die		P. W. Whitlock	5
8: 12 *Arise, Shine for Thy Light*	H.M.L.	J. G. MacDermid	37
12 The Light of the World		J. S. Matthews	9
9: 30 Open Our Eyes	a-c	W. C. Macfarlane	3
10: 11 *The Good Shepherd*	H.L.	O. Barri	2
The Good Shepherd	(T) TTBB	O. Barri	*
The Good Shepherd		A. B. Jennings	9
30–37 *The Good Samaritan*	H.L.	G. W. Chadwick	7
11: 13 *v.* Hosanna (The)			
25 I Am the Resurrection		C. Demarest	9
12: *v.* "Palm Sunday"			
3–8 Master, No Offering Costly (Hymn)		E. B. Parker	—
26 Follow Me	(T)	H. R. Shelley	39
32 As Moses Lifted Up the Serpent		E. C. Bairstow	15
35 Walk in the Light	(T)	R. H. Prutting	3
13: And Jesus, Knowing That His Hour (Olivet to Calvary)		J. H. Maunder	1
6 *God So Loved*	H.M.L.	J. G. MacDermid	37
The Servant Is Not Greater Than His Lord	H.M.L.	J. G. MacDermid	37
21 One of My Disciples		M. Haydn	3
34 *A New Commandment Give I Unto You* (Olivet to Calvary)	B.	J. H. Maunder	1
14: 1–3 *In My Father's House*	H.L.	R. G. Cole	5
2–4, 27 *In My Father's House Are Many Mansions*	H.M.L.	J. G. MacDermid	37
In My Father's House Are Many Mansions		Ward-Stephens	22
11, 21 Beloved, If God So Loved Us		J. Barnby	1
15 If Ye Love Me, Keep My Commandments		G. George	1
If Ye Love Me, Keep My Commandments	(H)	F. F. Harker	26
15–17 If Ye Love Me (Short)		G. George	1
16 I Will Pray the Father	(T)	F. W. Holloway	5
18 Eye Hath Not Seen		M. B. Foster	1
18–19 *My Redeemer Lives*	H.L.	H. Gilbert	4

JOHN [*continued*]

14 : 23, 27 Let Not Your Heart		E. Faning 1
27 Peace I Leave With You		J. V. Roberts 1
My Peace I Leave With You		Schubert 9
15 : 4, 5, 7, 12 I Am the Vine		P. James 23
10–17 Thaddeus		Ward-Stephens 21
12 *This Is My Commandment*	H.L.	P. J. Clark 13
13 Greater Love Hath No Man	(S.B)	J. Ireland 18
16 : 6, 33 Peace I Leave With You		J. V. Roberts 1
22 Let Not Your Heart		E. Faning 1
17 : 5 Yonder Behold Him		M. Haydn 3
25 Near the Cross Was Mary Weeping		D. W. Kennedy 9
19 : 25 There Stood Three Maries	(S)	H. A. Matthews 3
25–27 *John (Behold Thy Son)*		Ward-Stephens 21
John (Behold Thy Son)	SATB	Ward-Stephens 21
20 : 1–16 Mary Magdalene at the Sepulchre		Schuetz=Dickinson 9
At the Sepulchre	(B)	G. B. Nevin 2
At the Sepulchre	TTB	G. B. Nevin 2
13 They Have Taken Away My Lord	(S)	A. L. Scarmolin 39
27 Thomas (Be Not Faithless, But Believing)		Ward-Stephens 21
21 : 22 Follow Me	(T)	H. R. Shelley 39

ACTS

2 : 1 Now When Was Come the Day of Pentecost (Motet)	SAATTB	Palestrina 1
4 With Other Tongues Spake the Apostles		Palestrina 1
4 : 12 None Other Lamb	(S)	H. Saunders 6
7 : 58 And the Witnesses Had Laid (St. Paul)		Mendelssohn *
8 : 1 And the Witnesses Had Laid (St. Paul)		Mendelssohn *
9 : 6 *Paul (Lord, What Wilt Thou Have Me To Do?)*	H.L.	Ward-Stephens 21
Paul (Lord, What Wilt Thou Have Me To Do?)	(SATB)	Ward-Stephens 21

ACTS [*continued*]

9 : 29 And Paul Came to the Con-
gregation (St. Paul)   Mendelssohn *
13 : 2, 3 And Paul Came to the Con-
gregation   · Mendelssohn *
41 Behold, Ye Despisers   (B)   H. W. Parker 9
14 : 23 And When They Had Ordained
Them Elders   E. H. Thorne 1
17 : 28 In Him We Live   (A.T)   H. L. Baumgartner 2

ROMANS

6 : 9–11 Christ Our Passover   (S)   B. Tours 9
11, 12 *My Hope Is in the Everlasting* T.   J. Stainer *
8 : 1, 9, 14 There Is, Therefore, No
Condemnation   H. S. Irons 1
26, 27 The Searcher of Hearts   Bach 1
32, 34, 38, 39 He That Spared Not
His Own Son   F. E. Gladstone 1

I CORINTHIANS

2 : 9, 10 Eye Hath Not Seen   M. B. Foster 7
3 : 13–15 Every Man's Work   G. H. Federlein 6
16, 17 I Beseech You, Brethren
(St. Mary Magdalene)   J. Stainer 1
For Know Ye Not That Ye Are His
Temple? (St. Paul)   B.   Mendelssohn *
5 : 7–8 Christ, Our Passover   W. G. Hammond 9
Christ, Our Passover   H. W. Parker 9
Christ, Our Passover   (S)   ·B. Tours 9
Christ, Our Passover   (S.T)   A. Woeltge 2

II CORINTHIANS

3 : 18 From Glory Unto Glory   E. R. Warren 26
5 : 20 *Now Are We Ambassadors* (St.
Paul)   (T.B)   Mendelssohn *
13 : 11 Put on, Therefore, As God's
Elect   E. S. Barnes 9

GALATIANS

1 : 4, 5 Who Gave Himself for Our Sins
(The Light of the World)   A. Sullivan 1

GALATIANS [*continued*]
6 : 9 Let Us Not Be Weary in Well
    Doing   G. A. Macfarren   1

EPHESIANS
2 : 4, 5 God, Who Is Rich in Mercy   G. M. Garrett   1
5 : 14 Awake, Thou That Sleepest   J. Stainer   1

PHILIPPIANS
2 : 9–11 For It Became Him   O. King   1
4 : 6, 7 The Night Is Far Spent   B. Steane   1

COLOSSIANS
3 : 12–15 Put on, Therefore, As God's
    Elect   (s)   E. S. Barnes   9
   15–17 Let the Peace of God Rule   (h)   J. Stainer   1
4 : 8 We Sent Unto Thee   A. Hollins   1

I THESSALONIANS
4 : 14 Behold, Ye Despisers   (b)   H. W. Parker   9
   18 Eye Hath Not Seen   M. B. Foster   1
5 : 5, 16–23 *Awake Thou That Sleepest*   h.l.   Ward-Stephens   22

I TIMOTHY
3 : 16 God Was Made Manifest in the
    Flesh (Two Advents)   G. M. Garrett   1

II TIMOTHY
4 : 17 *And They All Persecuted Paul*
    (St. Paul)   s.   Mendelssohn   *

HEBREWS
1 : 3 O Brightness of Thy Immortal
    Father's Face   W. R. Voris   9
   8 His Sceptre Is a Rod of Righteous-
    ness (Occasional Oratorio)   Handel   1
4 : 9 Eye Hath Not Seen   M. B. Foster   1
   12 *He Sent His Word*   h.l.   J. G. MacDermid   37
   16 Let Us Come Boldly Unto the
    Throne   C. A. Lloyd   1
11 : 3 *He Sent His Word*   h.l.   J. G. MacDermid   37

HEBREWS [*continued*]
  11 : 10 *Eye Hath Not Seen*   A.   A. R. Gaul *
  13 : 8 Yesterday, Today and Forever (H)   J. S. Matthews 9

I PETER
  1 : 24–25 Behold, All Flesh Is as the
        Grass (Requiem)   J. Brahms *
  2 : 9, 24 Greater Love Hath No Man   J. Ireland 18
  24 *He Sent His Word and Healed*
      Them   W. B. Olds 13
  3 : 8–12 Be Ye All of One Mind (H)   A. E. Godfrey 1

ST. JOHN
  1 : 5 Thou Wilt Keep Him   S. S. Wesley 1
  13–19 This Is the Record of
      John   SAATB (T) a-c O. Gibbons 1
  2 : 15, 17 *Love Not the World* H.L. Ward-Stephens 22
  3 : 1 Behold What Manner of Love H.L. J. G. MacDermid 37
    Behold What Manner of Love (T) C. A. Scholin 3
  4 : 8 God Is Love TTBB H. M. Dow 3
    God Is Love H.L. W. B. Olds 13
    God Is Love (A) D. Protheroe 13
    Dwell Ye in Love B. F. Johnston 4
    Dwell Ye in Love R. D. Shure 4
  11 Beloved, If God So Loved Us J. Barnby 1
  18 O, Love That Casts Out Fear W. Berwald 3
    O, Love That Casts Out Fear N. Coke-Jephcott 9

JUDE
  1 : 16 *Murmur Not, O My Soul* A.   Bach 15

REVELATION
  1 : 5–6 Open to Me the Gates of
      Righteousness (B) M. B. Foster 1
  6 They Shall Be Named the Priests
    of God   E. H. Thorne 1
  8 I Am Alpha and Omega J. Stainer 3
  10 I Heard a Great Voice (A) E. F. Johnston 4
  10–12 *My New Name* H.L. J. G. MacDermid 37
  2 : 10 *Be Thou Faithful* T. Mendelssohn *

REVELATION [*continued*]

3:20 *Arise, Shine for Thy Light*		J. G. MacDermid	37
20 Christ Knocking at My Sad Heart		P. Otis	16
Behold, I Stand at the Door (Long)	(M)	C. Whitmer	9
Behold, I Stand at the Door	(S.B)	J. Bach	*
O Jesus, Thou Art Standing	(A)	D. Protheroe	13
4:1–8 Last Judgment		L. Spohr	1
5:6–13 Last Judgment		L. Spohr	1
7:2, 3, 9, 10, 12 And I Saw Another Angel		C. V. Stanford	3
7–9 I Beheld, and Lo!	(S)	W. C. Gale	9
9, 13, 16, 17 Lo! A Great Multitude	(S)	C. S. Norris	2
(Echo Choir and Congr.)			
9, 14–17 Last Judgment		L. Spohr	1
9–15 I Beheld, and Lo! (Long)		H. J. Stewart	9
13 Who Are These?		R. Redhead	1
14–15 *These Are They*	S	A. R. Gaul	*
15–16 *They Shall Hunger No More* (Holy City)	S-M	A. R. Gaul	*
17 And God Shall Wipe Away All Tears	(A)	A. W. Coombs	3
17 Evening and Morning		M. Spicker	3
11:15 Hallelujah Chorus (Messiah)		Handel	*
12:7, 8, 10, 12 There Was War in Heaven		W. A. C. Cruickshank	1
14:7, 8, 13 Last Judgment		L. Spohr	1
13 Blest Are the Departed	TTBB a-c	H. Parker	3
Blest Are the Dead	8	L. Spohr	1
Blest Are the Dead	TTBB	L. Spohr	1
Forever Blest Are the Dead		Mendelssohn	*
O Blest Are They	8 a-c	Tschaikowsky=Cain	13
19:6, 16 Hallelujah Chorus (Messiah)		G. Handel	*
20:1–4 A New Heaven (Holy City)		A. R. Gaul	*
4 I Saw the Souls		F. A. G. Ouseley	1
4 I Sought the Lord		F. Stevenson	2
6 *They Shall Be Named the Priests of God*		E. H. Thorne	1
21:3 Behold the Tabernacle of God		G. A. Macfarren	1
3 Behold the Tabernacle of God		D. M. Williams	9
3 Behold the Tabernacle of God	(S.A)	J. H. Rogers	3

REVELATION [*continued*]

21 : 4 And God Shall Wipe Away All Tears	(A)	A. W. Coombs 3
4 Evening and Morning		M. Spicker 3
4 *They That Trust in the Lord*	M.	H. P. Eames 13
14, 23–**25** And the Wall of the City		O. King 1
It Shall Come to Pass (Holy City)	SSA	A. R. Gaul *
22 : 1–**5** I Am the Water of Life		J. P. Dunn 4
5 And the Wall of the City		O. King 1

MEMORANDA

MEMORANDA

MEMORANDA

MEMORANDA